Japan and East Asia in Transition

Japan and East Asia in Transition

Trade Policy, Crisis and Evolution, and Regionalism

Hidetaka Yoshimatsu
The Graduate School of East Asian Studies, Yamaguchi University

First published 2003 by
PALGRAVE MACMILLAN
Houndmills, Basingstoke, Hampshire RG21 6XS and
175 Fifth Avenue, New York, N.Y. 10010
Companies and representatives throughout the world

PALGRAVE MACMILLAN is the global academic imprint of the Palgrave Macmillan division of St. Martin's Press, LLC and of Palgrave Macmillan Ltd. Macmillan® is a registered trademark in the United States, United Kingdom and other countries. Palgrave is a registered trademark in the European Union and other countries.

ISBN 1–4039–1160–6

This book is printed on paper suitable for recycling and made from fully managed and sustained forest sources.

A catalogue record for this book is available from the British Library.

Library of Congress Cataloging in Publication Data
Yoshimatsu, Hidetaka.
    Japan and East Asia in transition : trade policy, crisis and evolution, and regionalism / Hidetaka Yoshimatsu.
        p.   cm.
    Includes bibliographical references and index.
    ISBN 1–4039–1160–6
    1. Japan—Foreign economic relations—East Asia.   2. East Asia—Foreign economic relations—Japan.   I. Title.

HF1602.15.E2Y67 2003
337.5205—dc21
                                                              2003041427

10   9   8   7   6   5   4   3   2   1
12   11   10   09   08   07   06   05   04   03

Printed and bound in Great Britain by
Antony Rowe Ltd, Chippenham and Eastbourne

Contents

List of Tables and Figure

Tables

Figure

Preface

In the 1990s, Japan was at an historical turning point. Not only did Japan need to shift from the catching-up political economic system to the matured one but it also had to reformulate external policy and relations in response to changes caused by the end of the Cold War. However, political gridlock after party realignments in summer 1993 prevented Japan from tackling these issues effectively through in-depth policy debates. Moreover, a decade-long economic slump has gradually robbed the vitality of the Japanese people and industry. In the new millennium, Japan is facing new challenges represented by the advent of China.

Under these circumstances, how to develop mutually beneficial economic relationship with the East Asian countries has become increasingly crucial for Japan's external relations as well as domestic economic performance. Although the importance of alliances with the United States does not change, sincere efforts to show independent initiatives towards East Asia are required.

This book seeks to draw a picture of the evolving economic relationship between Japan and East Asia after the mid-1990s by analysing Japan's commitments in the three sets of policy areas: trade remedy measures, the regional financial and industrial transformations, and regional economic integration and cooperation. Theoretically, it highlights the issues of Japan's regional leadership role, bilateral relationship with China, and the influence of domestic politics on Japan's external policy and relations. Different versions of several chapters in this book have appeared in academic journals: 'Trade policy in transition? The political economy of antidumping in Japan', *Journal of the Asia Pacific Economy*, 6(1), 2001; 'Social demand, state capability and globalization: Japan–China trade friction over safeguard', *The Pacific Review*, 15(3), 2002; and 'Japanese policy in the Asian economic crises and the developmental state concept', *Journal of the Asia Pacific Economy*, 8(1), 2003. Permission to use these materials is gratefully acknowledged.

It is a pleasure to acknowledge my debt to those who have provided assistance to the completion of this study. Through the preparation of this book, many scholars have offered valuable comments and suggestions. I am particularly thankful to Shinichi Ichimura, William James, Makoto Sakurai, Eric Ramstetter, Noriatsu Matsui, and Dai Erbiao. I am also grateful to officials at the Ministry of Economy, Trade and Industry, and Ministry of Foreign Affairs as well as organisations such as the Federation of Japan Towel Industry Associations and Thai Automotive Institute for their spending valuable time for an interview. This book is based on my academic expertises in International Political Economy, International Relations, East Asian Studies and Japanese Politics. I am indebted to Professors Peter Drysdale, John Ravenhill, Barry Buzan, Geoffrey Underhill, Wyn Grant and Aurelia George Mulgan for their intellectual guidance and encouragement.

I also wish to express my deep gratitude to three organisations. The first is the International Centre for the Study of East Asian Development (ICSEAD). My interests in East Asia were fostered and developed when I was a researcher at this institute, and talks and discussions with other colleagues helped me develop and sharpen my ideas about the relationship between Japan and East Asia. The second is my current affiliation, the Graduate School of East Asian Studies, Yamaguchi University. The school, founded in 2001 for the doctoral course, provided me with excellent research environments. The third is the Heiwa Nakajima Foundation. The financial assistance from the foundation constituted a base of my career as a researcher.

Finally, my gratitude goes to my wife, Mutsumi, and my son, Satoshi. Without their understanding and cooperation, this publication could not have been possible.

Hidetaka Yoshimatsu

List of Abbreviations

ADB	Asian Development Bank
AEM	ASEAN Economic Ministers
AFTA	ASEAN Free Trade Area
AIA	ASEAN Investment Area
AID plan	Asian Industries Development plan
AJCEP	ASEAN–Japan Closer Economic Partnership
AMEICC	AEM–METI Economic and Industrial Cooperation Committee
AMF	Asian Monetary Fund
AOTS	Association for Overseas Technical Scholarship
APEC	Asia-Pacific Economic Cooperation
APT	ASEAN Plus Three
ARF	ASEAN Regional Forum
ASEAN	Association of Southeast Asian Nations
ASEM	Asia–Europe Meeting
ATC	Agreement on Textile and Clothing
BOI	Board of Investment
CFEOT	Council on Foreign Exchange and Other Transactions
CLM-WG	Working Group on Economic Cooperation in Cambodia, Laos and Myanmar
DIP	Department of Industrial Promotion
DRAM	dynamic random access memory
EAEC	East Asian Economic Caucus
EAEG	East Asian Economic Group
EC	European Community
EU	European Union
EVSL	Early Voluntary Sectoral Liberalisation
FDI	foreign direct investment
FJKIA	Federation of Japan Knitting Industry Associations
FJTIA	Federation of Japan Towel Industry Associations
FTA	free trade agreement
GATT	General Agreement on Tariffs and Trade
GDP	gross domestic product
IIMA	Institute for International Monetary Affairs
IMF	International Monetary Fund
IPRs	intellectual property rights

IRP	Industrial Restructuring Plan
IT	information technology
JAMA	Japan Automobile Manufacturers Association
JCFA	Japan Chemical Fibres Association
JCSFWA	Japan Cotton and Staple Fibre Weavers' Association
JETRO	Japan External Trade Organisation
JFA	Japan Ferroalloy Association
JICA	Japan International Cooperation Agency
JODC	Japan Overseas Development Corporation
JSA	Japan Spinners' Association
JSEPA	Japan–Singapore Economic Partnership Agreement
JTIA	Japan Textiles Importers Association
JTIF	Japan Textile Industry Federation
KIEP	Korea Institute for International Economic Policy
LDP	Liberal Democratic Party
MAFF	Ministry of Agriculture, Forestry and Fisheries
METI	Ministry of Economy, Trade and Industry
MFA	Multi-Fibre Arrangement
MFPRI	Ministry of Finance, Policy Research Institute
MOF	Ministry of Finance
MOFA	Ministry of Foreign Affairs
MOI	Ministry of Industry
NAFTA	North American Free Trade Agreement
NATO	North Atlantic Treaty Organisation
NEDO	New Energy and Industrial Technology Development Organisation
NIEs	newly industrialised economies
ODA	official development assistance
PCs	personal computers
PDPs	plasma display panels
R&D	research and development
SICGC	Small Industry Credit Guarantee Corporation
SIFC	Small Industrial Finance Corporation
SMEs	small- and medium-sized enterprises
TAI	Thai Automobile Institute
TFT-LCDs	thin film transistor-liquid crystal displays
TVs	televisions
VER	voluntary export restraint
WTO	World Trade Organisation

1
Introduction

Japan has stood at a unique position in East Asia.[1] It has long been the sole developed nation in the region. In particular, its economic power has been preponderant, accounting for roughly two-thirds of total gross domestic product (GDP) in East Asia. Japanese trade, investment and official loans have sustained economic growth in major East Asian countries and 'virtual' economic integration in East Asia.

Japan seems to be at a turning point in its relations with East Asia. After more than one decade from the end of the Cold War, Japan is required to reconsider its diplomatic posture, which has been characterised by close relations with the United States and restrictive involvements in regional affairs. Given the growing economic, political and even cultural linkages with East Asia, Japan is in a position to assume more responsibility and role in the region. Moreover, regional forces towards cooperation and competition have intensified as a consequence of the Asian financial crisis in 1997–98 and the rise of China as an economic power. Equally important are the stronger moves towards regional integration in other parts of the world, which encouraged Northeast Asian countries and the Association of Southeast Asian Nations (ASEAN) members to develop their own regional cooperative frameworks.

Although Japan has been in the midst between the West and Asia for a long time, its policy stance has been rather stable. As the primary ally of the United States in East Asia as well as the regional economic superpower, Japan could pursue national interest not feeling economic blackmail or threat from any nation in East Asia under the solid framework of the US–Japan alliance. However, under the rapidly evolving environments, Japan is forced to redefine its relations with East Asia including a more decisive political role in regional affairs. This study seeks to explore how Japan has changed its economic policy towards and economic relationship with East Asia since the mid-1990s in the rapidly changing regional environments.

Japan in evolving domestic, regional and international environments

Since the mid-1990s, domestic, regional and international environments surrounding Japan have gradually changed its relations with East Asia. In the domestic front, Japan has faced various changes, most of which had unfavourable influences on its economic performance. In the political domain, the single-party reign of the Liberal Democratic Party (LDP) ended in August 1993 after it enjoyed thirty-eight years of conservative dominance. Although the party returned to power in June 1994, it has been obliged to form a coalition government with, or to require extra-cabinet cooperation from, other small parties. Compared with the stable years of the LDP's single dominance, political gridlock after 1993 made it difficult for Japanese policy-makers to formulate persistent and far-reaching public policies.

In 1994, Japan scrapped the multi-member district system for elections to the Lower House of the Diet. Under the new election system, the previous arrangement of 511 seats divided into 130 districts was replaced with a combination of 300 single-seat districts and 200 seats down from eleven regional lists. The Japanese bureaucracy also experienced vital changes in the 1990s. In 1998, the Ministry of Finance (MOF) suffered from public criticisms due to a series of corruption scandals, which undermined the prestige of the bureaucracy. In 1999, Japan decided on the most drastic structural reforms for the government in the post-war era, and the reorganised administrative system began to work in January 2001.

More serious changes occurred in the economic domain. The Japanese economy has plunged into a deep recession since the bursting of the asset bubble in 1992. Japan's average GDP growth rate declined from 2.1 per cent in 1990–94 to 1.3 per cent in 1995–99. The national government debt increased from 50 per cent of GDP in 1990 to 63 per cent in 1995 to 102 per cent in 2000 as a consequence of attempts to stimulate the economy with fiscal policy (ICSEAD 2002: 19–20). The large non-performing loans, which plagued the Japanese economy in the 1990s, is still a serious problem in the new century. The official estimates based on the self-assessments by financial institutions amounted to 63 trillion yen in March 2000 (ICSEAD 2001: 12). Although all these changes occurred in the domestic front, they are likely to have critical influences on Japan's external economic policy and relations.

In the late 1990s, some East Asian countries have raised their industrial competitiveness in sectors where Japan once held preponderant strength. South Korea and Taiwan have caught up with Japan in producing several technology-intensive goods such as synthetic fibres, semiconductors and liquid crystal displays. China is emerging as an economic rival to Japan, rapidly improving international competitiveness in the relatively technology-intensive machinery sectors as well as in the labour-intensive sectors such as textiles. In 2000, China was the world's primary producer of crude steel, chemical fibres, air-conditioners, colour televisions, and so on.

The economic prominence of Northeast Asian countries has caused serious influences on regional balances of economic power. The East Asian region, which achieved impressive economic growth through the 1980s and mid-1990s, plunged into a serious economic depression due to the Asian financial crisis that was sparked by the devaluation of the Thai baht in July 1997. While the Northeast Asian economies have maintained or recovered to growth trends rather smoothly, Southeast Asian countries slowed down their economic performance after the crisis. In addition, China's continuous economic rise has gradually had great impacts on the economic activities of Southeast Asian countries. China surpassed ASEAN as a recipient of foreign direct investment (FDI) in 1992, and their gap has expanded afterwards. China's exports have gradually driven out products from Southeast Asian countries in the US and European markets. For instance, China's share in total imports in the United States rose from 6.1 per cent in 1995 to 8.2 per cent in 2000, while that of ASEAN declined from 5.7 per cent to 5.4 per cent in the same period (Maruya and Ishikawa 2001: 4). Thus, the economic rise of Northeast Asian countries and the resultant changes in relative position of economic power in East Asia are likely to force Japan to redefine its interest in East Asia and reformulate its basic regional policies.

In the international scene, the end of the Cold War provided Japan with challenges. While the Japanese government needed to redefine its security alliance with the United States, it was forced to respond to changes in US economic diplomacy, which intensified partially unilateral orientation. In the economic domain, the establishment of the World Trade Organisation (WTO) in January 1995 provided the member countries with more incentives to utilise international rules and systems in order to defend their economic interests. Moves towards stronger regionalism in North America and Europe have intensified the perception of the need among policy-makers in East Asia to promote their own regional cooperation frameworks. In fact, the East Asian countries held the first summit meeting under the ASEAN Plus Three (APT) framework in December 1997, and agreed in May 2000 to build a network of bilateral swap and repurchase agreement facilities between the ASEAN countries, China, Japan and South Korea (the Chiang Mai Initiative).

Given these drastic changes at the domestic, regional and international levels after the mid-1990s, the Japanese government has been likely to redefine its strategies and interests in its relations with East Asia. In fact, the government has taken new initiatives in external economic policy. A representative of such initiatives is a shift in trade policy from a multilateral-centred to a multi-layered approach in which bilateral and regional arrangements are considered in addition to multilateral frameworks. Based on the new strategies, the Japanese government signed the Japan–Singapore Economic Partnership Agreement, the first free trade agreement for Japan in January 2002. The Japanese government has shown increasing interest in the APT frameworks, taking the lead in launching the Chiang Mai Initiative.

In addition to these positive and cooperative initiatives, Japan is likely to adopt policies and measures designed to preserve its economic interest. This is both because the position of Japanese industry has gradually declined in East Asia inviting rising competitive pressure from the neighbouring countries, and because the maintenance of the operations of Japanese firms in the Asian markets has become increasingly crucial.

The main argument of this study is that the recent regional evolutions have produced proactive and strategic reactions in Japan's economic policy towards East Asia. The Japanese government has taken proactive initiatives in response to the regional evolutions by committing substantially to the sound development of the regional economies. At the same time, it has become more strategic in preserving its national interests in the rapid economic and industrial transformation in East Asia. While the government has changed the basic stance on regional trade arrangements and trade remedy measures, it has strengthened initiatives to maintain distribution of economic power in the region. This book examines this argument in three sets of policy areas: trade remedy measures, the regional financial and industrial transformations, and regional integration and cooperation.

The first area is trade policy for import relief. Japan's trade policy and trade relations have attracted interests from scholars, business leaders and government officials. For a long time, the main issues regarding Japan's trade concerned disputes with developed countries over Japan's exports and the opening of the Japanese market (Mikanagi 1996; Schoppa 1997; Lincoln 1999). The Japanese government tended to settle trade disputes on the basis of the bilateral, reconciliatory approach. It launched bilateral negotiations and resolved the disputes by concluding bilateral agreements represented by voluntary export restraint agreements.

Since the mid-1990s, several Japanese industries have suffered from rising import pressure, and demanded that the government introduce import relief measures. Japan's trade issues have gradually shifted from disputes with developed countries to friction over imports from developing countries, those from East Asian countries in particular. Changes in the pattern of trade friction pose several questions. How have the Japanese government and industries responded to rising import pressure? How has the government regarded import remedy measures such as antidumping and safeguard as devices to settle trade friction? Has the government changed its basic approach to trade disputes? Various factors including relative decline in the competitiveness of Japanese industry and the development of the international trading system are likely to affect policy preferences and policy prescriptions of the Japanese government.

The second area is relevant to particular economic phenomena in the region. The most critical incident for the East Asian economies in the 1990s was the Asian financial and economic crisis in 1997–98. The crisis had serious negative impacts on the Japanese economy, since Japanese firms had been deeply involved in the crisis-hit economies through trade, investment and financial loans. While the economic turmoil in major East Asian countries exacerbated Japan's domestic recession by reducing its exports, Japanese firms' operations in these countries shrank due to the depressed demand in the local markets.

Another economic phenomenon that had a critical influence on Japan's economic relationship with East Asia is regional industrial transformation. Japan's status as the techno-economic giant in East Asia has gradually eroded since the mid-1990s. The newly industrialised economies (NIEs) have caught up with Japan in some technology-intensive sectors. Potentially more important is that the sense of the China threat has rapidly permeated in Japan since the late 1990s. Indeed, China's economic rise provides Japanese industry with new business opportunities by fostering the huge consumer market and production bases with relatively cheap labour costs. At the same time, China's economic prominence has had unfavourable effects on the Japanese economy. Some Japanese industries have suffered from serious influences through increased imports from China and the relocation of manufacturing operations to the country. Chinese products have gradually penetrated Southeast Asia, crowding out those exported from Japan or manufactured locally by Japanese affiliated firms. It is of great interest to explore how Japan has reacted to the Asian financial crisis and regional industrial transformation in order to protect its own national interests.

The third area is regional economic cooperation and integration. Moves towards regionalism have gained momentum in East Asia since the late 1990s. The East Asian countries, which recognised the need to protect their interest through regional frameworks, developed the APT summit meetings as a comprehensive forum covering political, security and economic affairs in the region. In addition, the East Asian countries have broadened the institutional frameworks of the APT to finance, economic cooperation, agriculture, and so on. Japan, the regional economic superpower, should have been deeply involved in the recent development of regional economic cooperation and integration.

In considering Japan's involvement in regional cooperation, two issues seem to be particularly important. The first is how the leading political actors have committed themselves to regional integration and cooperation. Indeed, the Ministry of Foreign Affairs (MOFA) and the Ministry of Economy, Trade and Industry (METI) have been engaged in regional cooperation policies.[2] However, they are not the major political players in Japanese politics. As economic interdependence between Japan and East Asia has deepened, the East Asian affairs have increasingly influenced interests and behaviour of Japan's main political actors. In other words, when the main political players represented by the LDP and MOF found vital interest in promoting integration and cooperation with East Asia, we might expect that Japan's regional policies changed from the inside.

The second is how Japan can develop the sound and trustworthy relationship with China for regional cooperation. The development of regional cooperation in East Asia has been initiated by ASEAN for the ASEAN Regional Forum (ARF) and Asia–Europe Meeting (ASEM), or Australia for the Asia-Pacific Economic Cooperation (APEC) forum. However, the development of regional integration after the mid-1990s has been led by Northeast Asian countries. Collaboration between Japan and China, the two major regional powers, has become increasingly important for fuelling East Asian regionalism in keeping pace with moves in other parts of the world.

There are quite a few studies that have examined Japan–East Asian economic relationship (Katzenstein and Shiraishi 1997; Miyashita and Sato 2001; Wan 2001; Inoguchi 2002; Sudo 2002). Compared with these studies, this work has two distinctive characteristics. First, it seeks to explore Japan–East Asian economic relationship mainly focusing on variables at the regional and domestic levels. In the previous studies, international politics – the relationship with the United States in particular – has often been given primary interest in explaining Japan's external policy. However, this study examines Japan–East Asian relationship by highlighting domestic policy development caused by changes in Japan's position in East Asia. Second, this book highlights recent developments in the Japanese and East Asian political economy. It focuses on Japan–China economic friction after the late 1990s, analysing Japan's initiatives directed at China such as safeguard policy and intellectual property policy. This book also explores the development of the APT frameworks and its implications for regional integration in East Asia. Accordingly, this study does not include in-depth historical analysis, but contains valuable information about the recent development of Japan's regional economic policies and economic cooperation in East Asia.

Three analytical focuses

This study seeks to explore the changing nature of Japan's economic policy towards East Asia. An analytical framework will be presented in each chapter, but this study has three sets of overarching analytical frameworks at the regional, bilateral and domestic levels.

The first and regional level focus is Japan's position in East Asia in terms of leadership role and influence. There is a contrasting view on Japan's leadership role. One perspective posits that Japan did not show an independent leadership role largely due to its position in international politics. Japan long had a weak desire to take a high-profile foreign policy stance because the existing international order based on the US hegemony offered favourable environments for Japan (Hellmann 1988; Blaker 1993; Miyashita 1999). For instance, Hellmann (1988: 356) argues that 'Japan was and is a passive actor, responding to the shifting configurations of international political power, adjusting to the changing distribution of economic activity and wealth, and adopting the prevailing international political mores'. According to this view, Japan's foreign policy has been formulated in accordance with US policy preferences, being highly responsive to explicit and tacit pressures from the country.

The opposite perspective posits that Japan has played an assertive and independent leadership role, pursuing its own national interests. Some scholars stress Japan's willingness to form a Japan-centred economic bloc in East Asia. The scholars in this school hold that Japan has sought to become the centre of a potentially self-sustaining Asian economic bloc through careful manoeuvring of its foreign policy (Fallows 1994; Johnson 1995: 314–16; Taylor 1995). Others have highlighted signs of changes towards a more independent posture. They argue that Japanese political elite willingly adopts a more regional perspective, shifting from reactive manners to a more activist foreign policy stance (Hughes 2000; Maswood 2001). One of the main interests of this book is whether and how the evolving regional environments have affected Japan's posture on an independent leadership in regional economic affairs.

The second analytical focus is bilateral relationship between Japan and China. The Chinese economy has become increasingly important for Japan since the early 1990s. Not only has bilateral trade between the two countries grown rapidly after the mid-1990s, but China also became a major recipient of Japanese FDI. The continuous growth of the Chinese economy expands business chances for Japanese firms by yielding the huge market and manufacturing bases. At the same time, China's economic prominence has had unfavourable effects on the Japanese economy. As a direct threat, the expansion of imports from China has put some Japanese firms and industries at a defensive position, and Chinese firms and products are crowding out Japanese rivals from the markets in third countries including Southeast Asia. As an indirect threat, China's economic rise is likely to change regional distribution of economic power by reducing the relative position of Southeast Asia.

Compared with the drastic evolutions in economic linkages, Japan and China have not shown outstanding developments in political relations. The historical legacy of Japan's wartime behaviour still impedes the two countries from developing trustworthy relationship. The Chinese authorities have been apprehensive about the potential for Japan's return to militarism exemplified by the textbook issues, Prime Minister's visit to the Yasukuni Shrine and the expansion of operations of the Self-Defence Forces. The Japanese government has been concerned about China's growing military might and activities of Chinese research ships in Japanese waters after the late 1990s.

Several scholars have conducted in-depth analysis on the Sino–Japan relationship, providing valuable insights for the prospect on their future (Taylor 1996; Drysdale and Zhang 2000; Austin and Harris 2001). However, there have occurred significant regional economic evolutions – China's economic prominence itself is a major element – which have affected the overall Sino–Japan relationship. It is important to recast the Sino–Japan relationship by taking into account the recent economic evolutions.

Some observers argue that China and Japan will be unable to develop cooperative relationship in the near future (Webber 2001: 362–3). They consider that historical problems will impede the two countries from developing cooperative and trustworthy relationship. Others present a more optimistic view. For instance, Xide (2002) argues that the Sino–Japan relationship will be relatively stable because the two countries have vested interests in realising the friendly and cooperative partnership. Increased economic interdependence has the potential to mitigate political tension by increasing mutual exchange of people and information, and creating vested interests in each country. Moreover, recent moves towards regionalism in East Asia might intensify rivalry for leadership between Japan and China, on the one hand, and urge their collaboration for making regional development more viable, on the other. This study seeks to consider how regional economic evolutions including China's economic advent have influenced the overall Sino–Japanese relationship.

The third analytical focus is domestic politics. The focus at the domestic level is particularly important in explaining variations and inconsistencies in a state's foreign economic policy. It is common that there are variations in a state's external policies under the seemingly similar international and regional circumstances. The variables in domestic politics often provide a key to explain such variations.

This study, which highlights domestic politics as a main factor shaping Japan's external economic policy towards East Asia, takes into account two sets of variables. The first set of variables is policy preferences of domestic actors, which consist of political actors and societal actors. Some scholars have argued that preferences or ideas of policymakers are the key to determine the government policy (Krasner 1978; Nordlinger 1981; Skocpol 1985). They stress the autonomy of public officials to pursue their own policy goals by adopting a particular government policy. Others have focused on policy preferences of societal actors (Ray 1981; Milner 1988; Frieden 1990). This pressure group model posits that a state's policy is a function of interests and capabilities of societal interest groups that compete with each other for higher benefits or incomes and form political coalitions to attain this objective.

The focus on preferences of political actors is important in the studies of Japanese politics and political economy because Japanese policy-making has long been seen as being dominated by central bureaucrats, and thereby major policy initiatives spring from them (Johnson 1982, 1995; Pempel 1982: ch. 2). At the same time, a growing number of scholars have paid attention to policy preferences of major societal actors as a critical variable influencing Japanese policy-making (Rosenbluth 1989; Mason 1992; Calder 1993). Indeed, compared with domestic public policies, external relations and foreign policies are more insulated from the influence of societal actors. The central bureaucrats are capable of formulating foreign policies rather autonomously on the basis of their own policy preferences. However, as economic activities of Japanese firms have permeated in the world markets, the Japanese government has been forced to consider the interests of private actors and get their collaboration even in foreign economic policies.

The second set of variables that formulate domestic politics regarding Japan's regional economic policy is political institutions. An institution is an elusive concept, defined broadly as 'the rules of the game in a society or, more formally, the humanely devised constraints that shape human interaction' (North 1990: 3), or narrowly as 'a set of rules that structure social interactions in particular ways' and whose knowledge 'must be shared by the members of the relevant community or society' (Knight 1992: 2–3). The intuitions aggregate preferences of societal actors and political actors, and their differentiations have vital influences on the government's policy by conditioning the political access of the actors to the policy-making process, and characterising the relative influence of major political apparatuses such as the administrative branch, legislative branch, political parties, central bank, and so on.

A group of scholars have attributed Japan's passive posture in foreign affairs to factors regarding domestic institutions and institutional characteristics. Calder, a representative of this school, holds that Japan has failed to show international initiatives because of particular domestic political structures including strong sectionalism in the bureaucracy, the absence of powerful central executives and the unique electoral system (Calder 1988). Van Wolferen (1989) also argues that Japan is incapable of assuming the leadership role because it lacks a strong political power centre.

Garrett and Lange (1996: 50) identify two types of institutions: 'socioeconomic institutions' that organise interests in the private sector, and 'formal institutions' that aggregate these interests in the public arena and determine the responsiveness of governments to them. This study has interests in formal institutions through which societal and political actors' preferences and demands pass through before becoming policy outcomes. These institutions also influence particular characteristics of the policy-making process and eventual policy choices. They include domestic political systems such as the electoral system and the parliamentary cabinet system as well as virtual practices among government agencies and between the government and ruling parties.

The main interests of this study regarding domestic politics are how the evolving regional environments surrounding the Japanese economy and industry have changed the policy preferences of political and societal actors for regional policy and relations with the East Asian countries, and how particular political institutions have defined the development of policy changes.

Outline of the book

The aim of this study is to investigate how Japan has changed its economic policy towards, and economic relationship with, East Asia since the mid-1990s in the rapidly changing regional and international environments. This book seeks to address this question in three policy areas: trade remedy measures, policies towards the regional financial crisis and industrial evolutions, and commitments to regional cooperation in East Asia.

Chapter 2 examines Japan's evolving antidumping policy and its background. For a long time, Japan maintained trade policy on the basis of the bilateral, reconciliatory approach. However, trade policy preferences of Japanese economic bureaucrats are likely to change in response to the development of the international trading system and increasing trade conflicts with Asian developing countries. Chapter 3 focuses on Japan's safeguard policy. Like the antidumping policy, the Japanese government was reluctant to use this import restrictive measure. However, as several Japanese industries have stood in a defensive position against rising import pressure, the government is likely to rely on this policy tool in order to protect the domestic market. This chapter examines policy preferences of Japanese policy-makers and societal actors in the trends of growing economic interdependence.

In Chapter 4, Japan's responses to the Asian financial and economic crisis are considered. The main interests of this chapter are how the Japanese government reacted to the crisis and what philosophies and ideas sustained such reactions. I address these questions by examining changes in policies and institutions regarding industrial cooperation and detailed industrial cooperation policies towards Thailand. Another regional phenomenon that had a critical influence on Japan's economic relationship with East Asia after the mid-1990s is regional economic transformation exemplified by China's industrial prominence. Chapter 5 confirms the relative positional changes of Japanese industry in East Asia, and explores Japan's strategic responses to such changes. The focus of Chapters 6 and 7 is Japan's position on regionalism and regional cooperation in East Asia. Chapter 6 highlights two political power centres – the LDP and MOF – and examines their commitments to regional cooperation after the mid-1990s. In particular, this chapter explores how regional economic evolutions have affected basic preferences of these two actors for regional cooperation. Chapter 7 examines the development of regionalism in East Asia from a broader perspective. In achieving the sound development of regional cooperation in East Asia, Sino–Japan collaboration becomes a critical issue. This chapter identifies demand and supply conditions for Japan–China co-leadership and constraints on them.

Chapter 8 evaluates the evidence on Japan's evolving external economic policy in the detailed cases, and asks what kinds of regional policies and measures Japan have adopted under the evolving regional environments. It takes a close look at Japan's aspiration for a regional leadership role, bilateral relationship with China, and the characteristics of domestic politics as factors creating variations in Japan's East Asian policy. The limitations of the study are discussed, and suggestions are made regarding areas for further research.

2
Evolving Policy Preferences in Antidumping Policy

Over the last two decades, Japan's trade policy and trade relations have been the subject of controversy. The major controversies have concerned disputes with developed countries over Japan's exports and the opening of the Japanese market (Kusano 1983; NIRA 1989; Mikanagi 1996; Schoppa 1997; Lincoln 1999). After the late 1980s, several basic industries suffered from increased imports from developing countries, enhancing the likelihood that these industries will call on the government to introduce protectionist measures. This raises an additional trade issue. How do the import competing industries and government react to rising import pressure? This chapter seeks to address this question by focusing on the antidumping policy in Japan.

Dumping refers to an exporting firm's selling in a foreign market at a price lower than it charges in other markets, usually in its home country. An importing country is allowed to impose an antidumping duty to offset the dumping margin of a dumped product, provided that it can be shown that such dumping is causing or threatens to cause 'material injury' to domestic industries in the importing country. The General Agreement on Tariffs and Trade (GATT)/World Trade Organisation (WTO) regime provides antidumping measures under GATT Article VI and the Agreement on Implementation of Article VI of the General Agreement on Tariffs and Trade 1994 (the Antidumping Agreement).[1]

Developed countries, mainly the United States, Canada and Australia, and the European Community (EC), have resorted to antidumping suits to restrain imports from developing countries (Table 2.1). Since the mid-1990s, antidumping investigations have been increasingly used by developing countries including India, Mexico and Brazil. Japan has

Table 2.1 Number of antidumping initiations in major countries, 1995–2001

	1995	1996	1997	1998	1999	2000	2001	Total
US	14	22	15	36	47	47	74	255
India	6	21	13	27	65	41	75	248
EC	33	25	41	22	65	32	28	246
Argentina	27	22	15	8	24	45	26	167
South Africa	16	33	23	41	16	21	6	156
Australia	5	17	42	13	24	15	23	139
Canada	11	5	14	8	18	21	25	102
Brazil	5	18	11	18	16	11	16	95
Mexico	4	4	6	12	11	7	5	49
South Korea	4	13	15	3	6	2	4	47
World Total	157	224	243	254	356	281	330	1,845

Source: The author compiled from data on the WTO homepage.

been one of the major defenders, with dumping duties imposed on 77 products by December 1996. Cases where Japan is a complainant have been rare. Japanese industry has filed six antidumping cases to date: four from the textile industry and two from the ferroalloy industry (Table 2.2).[2] In the three cases filed in the 1980s, the petitions were withdrawn before initiating an investigation mainly because of the introduction of a voluntary export restraint (VER). In contrast, the government imposed dumping charges in the three cases filed after the 1990s.

Table 2.2 Antidumping suits in Japan

Date	Complainant	Defender	Filed item	Result
27/12/1982	JSA	South Korea	Cotton yarn	VER, withdrawal
6/3/1984	JFA	Norway, France	Ferrosilicon	Withdrawal
21/10/1988	FJKIA	South Korea	Knit sweater	VER, withdrawal
8/10/1991	JFA	China, Norway, South Africa	Ferrosilicon manganese	Dumping duties on Chinese imports
20/12/1993	JSA	Pakistan	Cotton yarn	Dumping duties
28/2/2001	Five firms	South Korea, Taiwan	Polyester staple fibre	Dumping duties

Note: JSA, FJKIA, and JFA denote the Japan Spinners' Association, Federation of Japan Knitting Industry Associations and Japan Ferroalloy Association, respectively.
Source: The author compiled from newspaper reports.

In this chapter, I examine antidumping policy formation and antidumping politics in Japan. Drawing on detailed analysis of the institutional framework regarding antidumping and the filed dumping cases, I explore how evolving trade policy preferences of the Ministry of Economy, Trade and Industry (METI) have changed antidumping policy and politics in Japan, and what has altered METI's policy preferences. I argue that while METI's bureaucrats sought to settle dumping cases by swiftly inducing the industries concerned to hold inter-industry meetings and utilising bilateral VERs in the 1980s, they have over time pursued strict application of the antidumping legislation on the basis of the rule-governed principles embedded in the GATT/WTO system.

In the following section, I take a brief look at the literature on the determinants of trade policy to provide a theoretical framework for this chapter. I then investigate the institutional framework for activating antidumping files in Japan. The following two sections delve into the process of the filed cases. By comparing three cases in the 1980s and three cases after the 1990s, I explore whether and why trade policy preferences of METI bureaucrats have evolved.

Theoretical perspectives on antidumping policy and politics in Japan

A major issue with respect to trade policy and trade politics is what determines the formation of trade policy. An extensive literature that has addressed this question is classified into two groups: the supply side and the demand side explanations. The supply side approach stresses the effects of the national interest and domestic political institutions in the formation of trade policy. Some political scientists have high-lighted the behaviour of policy-makers towards realising the national interest through public policy (Krasner 1978; Nordlinger 1981). This view postulates that public officials are not mere intermediaries for societal interest groups, but maintain autonomy to pursue their own policy goals by withstanding societal pressure. The ability of policy-makers to advance the national interest relies on the extent to which domestic political institutions render them susceptible to demands from societal groups. The political institutions constitute the filter through which demands from domestic actors are transformed into policies, and their political behaviour responds to the opportunities and constraints created by these institutions (Goldstein 1988; Garrett and Lange 1996). Thus, domestic political institutions and institutional changes are the key variables in determining the patterns and shifts of trade policy.

The demand side approach links general economic conditions and pressure group demands to trade policy formation. This approach regards trade policy as the product of competition among societal interest groups that react to changes in market conditions. Macroeconomic factors are often cited as important variables. Employment is the most important macroeconomic factor in generating the demand for protection (Takacs 1981; Bergsten and Cline 1983: 77–82). Widespread unemployment resulting from rising imports imposes severe adjustment costs on domestic workers, and an increase in imports tends to lead to demands for protection. Dornbusch and Frankel (1987) raise variations in the exchange rate as the most important macroeconomic determinant of protection. They argue that appreciation of the dollar leads to demand for protection because the overvalued currency undermines the competitiveness of exports and import competing sectors by raising the price of domestically produced goods.

Some scholars who adopt the demand side approach have focused on policy preferences of particular interest groups as a critical determinant of trade policy. Theoretical and empirical interests have been directed towards clarifying conditions under which particular groups develop particular preferences for trade policy. Some observers have focused on factors of production such as labour and capital as central factors in creating different policy preferences (Rogowski 1989). Others have highlighted sectoral or firm-based factors as keys to develop particular policy preferences (Ray 1981; Milner 1988; Frieden 1990). The characteristics of sectors including the number of firms or workers in an industry, an industry's size or geographic concentration have been regarded as critical factors in affecting concrete policy preferences and outcomes of trade politics.

This chapter explores trade policy and politics of antidumping in Japan with particular attention to supply side factors. Indeed, various demand side factors can explain some aspects of antidumping policy and practices in Japan, especially the issue of why so few antidumping cases have been petitioned. In general, the antidumping system is unfamiliar in Japanese society, a non-litigious society, in which the people prefer to settle conflict 'out of court' (Miyazaki 1998). In addition, few Japanese industries suffered from import pressure until the mid-1980s due to low imports of manufactured products. The ratio of manufactured goods in total imports remained less than 40 per cent until 1987. It grew from 39.8 per cent to 56.9 per cent between 1987 and 1996, and the import volumes of several final products have increased greatly during this period. However, some of these imports were conducted by Japanese firms themselves as intra-firm trade. For instance, imports of consumer electric products grew 17 times from 24 billion yen in 1985 to 410 billion yen in 1996.[3] However, Japanese electronics firms imported most of them through intra-firm transactions. According to METI's survey data on overseas operations of Japanese companies, the share of exports to Japan by affiliates of Japanese electronics firms in Asia in total sales increased steadily from 22.2 per cent in 1986, to 28.7 per cent in 1995, to 31.8 per cent in 1999 (METI 1989: 228–9; 1998: 188; 2002: 130). In 1995, the share of intra-firm trade in total exports to Japan by affiliates of Japanese electronics firms in Asia was 88.9 per cent (METI 1998: 213).

The above explanations give credence to the argument that demand side factors are directly relevant to antidumping practices in Japan. However, supply side factors have particular implications in accounting for antidumping trade policy and politics in Japan. As is widely known, the Japanese government has intervened in the market to sustain the sound and steady development of particular industrial sectors. In particular, METI has utilised various industrial policy measures including fiscal, tax and trade policies, subsidies and 'visions' (Komiya *et al.* 1988). METI has also used administrative guidance as a way of achieving particular policy objectives or coordinating industrial interests (Shindo 1992; Oyama 1996).[4] An equally important fact is that METI and industrial sectors have forged close relationships through various consultation channels. They are linked through formal channels such as sector-specific advisory councils and the submission of position papers regarding sectoral policy issues and *amakudari* practices.[5] The industrial sectors have also developed continuous give-and-take relationships with METI's bureaus and sections through various informal channels and actions. These patterns of connection are likely to yield the possibility that policy preferences of bureaucrats not only influence overall trade policy but also impinge on detailed actions of Japanese industries.

This prediction is strengthened by some evidence regarding preparation for petitioning an antidumping complaint in several industries. Although only six cases became lawsuits, several material industries including steel and petrochemicals prepared for an antidumping suit. Steel manufacturers have been interested in antidumping against imports of steel materials from developing countries since the Japan Iron and Steel Federation set up a special committee on the prevention of unfair trade in December 1982. The petrochemical industry also conducted an antidumping investigation of ethylene glycol and acrylonitrile in 1983. The textile producers' associations other than the Japan Spinners' Association (JSA) and the Federation of Japan Knitting

Industry Associations (FJKIA), which petitioned a suit, also conducted a preliminary investigation for an antidumping suit. In September 1988, the Japan Chemical Fibres Association (JCFA) conducted an antidumping investigation of Korean acrylic filament by organising a special working group to investigate import routes. In early 1994, the Japan Cotton and Staple Fibre Weavers' Association also prepared for an antidumping suit against imports of Chinese cotton spun fabric.

Despite moves to prepare for a suit, the above industries did not resort to a real suit. Although the industries' decisions not to petition a suit sprang from various factors including overall market trends and comparison between costs for filing a suit and likely benefits from a petition, government intervention also seems to be a critical element. Kodama (1989: 35) explains this point as follows:

> A ministry that had jurisdiction over an industry which hoped to lodge a complaint always showed attitudes that it neither encouraged nor rejected filing preparations under the principle of "the administration of the law". However, the Ministry informally encouraged the industry to conduct "prior consultation" about application documents, and repeated traditional "administrative guidance". The Ministry pointed out that evidence collected by the industry was insufficient, hinting that a complaint would end in vain unless more evidence was collected.

Accordingly, examination of policy preferences of METI, which has jurisdiction over manufacturing industries, is a useful way of understanding antidumping policy formation in Japan.

In addition, unlike in other industrialised countries, adopting antidumping restrictions has been a difficult policy option for Japanese bureaucrats. Opening the domestic market has been one of the major trade policy objectives since the early 1980s when Japan began to incur huge trade surpluses. Quite a few market-opening measures were adopted as a way of rectifying trade imbalances or responding to pressure from foreign countries.[6] Given these overall policy trends, preferences of government officials are likely to impinge on the treatment of antidumping petitions that lead to restrain imports.

The institutional systems for antidumping in Japan

The legal bases for antidumping in Japan are Article VIII of the Customs Tariff Law and the Cabinet Order Relating to Antidumping Duty. The antidumping system was legally adopted in 1920, and an antidumping petition by an industry was introduced in the 1951 amendment of the law. The order was enacted in 1967 in accordance with the establishment of the Antidumping Code at the GATT Kennedy Round.

Japan's antidumping legislation has been amended several times to keep it consistent with international norms. It has several notable features. First, the provisions of the law and cabinet order regarding antidumping are rather simple compared with those of other developed countries. Before being amended in December 1994, the antidumping legislation was extremely vague and simple.[7] While Article VII of the law consisted of 13 sections, the cabinet order had 14 articles. After the amendment, the amount of description doubled in the law and increased roughly 2.5 times in the cabinet order. Article VIII (changed from VII) of the law comprises 37 sections and the cabinet order has 20 articles. These provisions are still rather sparse compared with the US antidumping legislation, which includes detailed enforcement regulations.

While antidumping suits are accompanied by complicated procedures, the provisions of the law describe basic matters regarding the filing procedures (Sections 1 to 12), the modification and abolition of antidumping duties (Sections 12 to 24), and the extension of the imposition period (Sections 25 to 29). Accordingly, technical matters including documents for petitions, formation of an investigation body and the determination of dumping and material injury needed to be supplemented by an order for procedure or guidelines. However, the government was for a long time reluctant to formulate them. The private sector required the government to outline the details of interpretations and applications of the law and order. The Japan Textile Industry Federation (JTIF), in cooperation with *Nippon Keidanren* (Japan Business Federation), prepared a draft of the guidelines, and this came into force as the Guidelines for Procedures Relating to Countervailing Duty and Antidumping Duty in December 1986. In drafting the guidelines, the textile federation consulted with officials at the Ministry of Finance (MOF), not with METI officials. This was because METI was reluctant to draft such guidelines.

Although the guidelines do not have legal enforcement effects, they serve to clarify the procedural rules by stipulating that the reception office for application was MOF's Planning and Legal Division and that the period for determining whether to initiate an investigation was approximately two months after receiving a written application. They also contained a detailed form for application. The specification of the reception office and the attachment of an application form were important for facilitating a suit because these enabled an industry to avoid 'prior consultation' with the ministry that has jurisdiction over the industry (Kodama 1989: 37). Several provisions of the guidelines also reflected the private sector's hope to facilitate the procedure for a suit. Article I, Section 4 (2) stipulates that a complainant is not required to submit evidence that is not reasonably available. This clause, adopted from a relevant provision in the US law, aimed to avoid a case when an industry abandons a suit because the government requires that the complainant submit sufficient evidence. Article II, Section 2 (2) also stipulates that 'when there is sufficient evidence to initiate an investigation, the government shall, in principle, initiate the investigation'. This clause aims to restrict the government's discretion to determine whether or not an investigation is to be initiated. As explained below, the law basically admits the broad discretion of the administrative authorities, and the private sector-initiated guidelines tried to restrict this discretion.

Second, the administrative institution for antidumping has been weak and insufficient compared with counterpart institutions in developed countries. In the United States, 'dumping' determinations are made by the International Trade Administration of the Department of Commerce, and 'material injury' determinations by the International Trade Commission. In the EC, the Directorate-General in Charge of External Relations of the EC Commission is involved in all stages of the investigation including the decision to initiate a proceeding (Trebilcock and Howse 1995: 101–2). There is no such permanent organisation that has the responsibility for enforcing antidumping procedure in Japan. Furthermore, an investigation is not conducted by a sole agency but by a body comprising officials from plural agencies in Japan. Thus, when an investigation is to be initiated, an investigation body is formed by several officials from METI, MOF, and the Ministry that has jurisdiction over the industry concerned (the guidelines Article VI, Section 3). So it is unlike the US system in which the Department of Commerce and International Trade Commission have jurisdiction over the separate procedural parts, since MOF and METI have overlapping jurisdiction on the antidumping proceedings.

MOF has a section that is responsible for administering antidumping and countervailing duties: the Planning and Legal Division. However, METI did not have a section to handle trade dispute issues. The dumping issue was handled by the Tariff Division at the International Trade Policy Bureau whose major business was to administer general matters regarding tariffs. In October 1995, METI set up the Trade Policy

Planning and Investigation Division at the International Trade Administration Bureau. The division's two operations are analysis of trends in exports and imports for drawing up forecasts and handling antidumping, countervailing and emergency duties, and safeguard measures. The deficiency in the administrative system reflects the fact that appeals for rectifying unfair trade practices have been rare in Japan. At the same time, the insufficiency might constitute a factor in discouraging METI bureaucrats from accepting a petition, preferring a negotiated settlement.

Third, administrative authorities have broad discretion in antidumping procedure in Japan. This stems partly from the inadequacy of the articles in the law and cabinet order. At the same time, the legislation itself provides the government with broad discretion. Dumping duties are normally imposed when a fact of dumping exists and a dumped product causes or threatens to cause material injury to a domestic industry. In addition to these two conditions, the Japanese law (Section 1) stipulates a third condition: 'if it is found necessary to protect such domestic industry'. This opens the possibility that the government may not impose duties even if there is a proven case of dumping and a finding of material injury.[8] The law (Section 5) also states that the government shall initiate an investigation, 'if it is found to be necessary'. This clause provides the government with discretion not to initiate an investigation even when there is sufficient evidence with respect to the fact of dumping and the fact of material injury.

Three antidumping cases in the 1980s

The cotton yarn case in 1982

The first antidumping and countervailing files in Japan were lodged in 1982. On 27 December 1982, JSA petitioned MOF to institute an antidumping suit against South Korea and a countervailing duty suit against Pakistan. The association claimed that massive imports of cheap cotton yarn from the two countries had caused serious damage to domestic cotton spinners. The import volume of cotton yarn in 1982 totalled 596,700 bales, 51 per cent more than that in the previous year, and imports from South Korea and Pakistan grew by 37.5 and 72.9 per cent per year, respectively.[9] On 18 April 1983, Korean spinners announced that they would accept a VER at the meeting with their Japanese counterparts. They agreed to hold cotton yarn exports to an annual maximum of 270,000 bales for three years. JSA dropped the case against South Korea immediately. As for the countervailing suit, the government decided in February 1983 to investigate charges that cotton yarn exports from Pakistan had been subsidised by the government because the Pakistani government refused to withdraw export subsidies. In August 1983, the Pakistani government agreed to withdraw export subsidies. JSA dropped the case against Pakistan in February 1984 after the completion of Pakistani loans to cotton producers in January.

Through the preparation and petition process, METI sought to settle the trade disputes swiftly, not making them political conflicts. Before filing the complaints, JSA called on METI to engage in bilateral negotiations to restrain disorderly imports with South Korea and Pakistan, but METI refused.[10] When JSA filed the cases, there were no detailed rules regarding the procedures for a petition and an investigation. Although MOF showed a clear-cut view on this matter, considering that the absence of rules would not impede a suit, METI was prudent in the investigation procedure, being anxious about foreign criticism of the less transparent administrative procedure.[11]

JSA had an inter-industry meeting with its South Korean counterpart on 17 and 18 January 1983 and with its Pakistani counterpart on 22 February. Japanese spinners were reluctant to engage in inter-industry negotiations with less successful prospects, hoping that the government would initiate an investigation.[12] Accordingly, JSA was likely to have the meetings, accepting METI's administrative guidance. When the dumping issue was resolved at the inter-industry meeting in April 1983, METI commented that 'we welcome the settlement of the trade dispute by negotiations that our spinning industry dropped the case after evaluating a voluntary export restraint by the Korean industry'.[13] Several observers who examined this case argue that METI tacitly approved the first non-unilateral quantitative restraints on textile imports, not objecting to inter-industry agreements (Friman 1990: 135; Uriu 1996: 86). In fact, METI orchestrated such agreements behind the scenes.

The ferrosilicon case in 1984

The ferroalloy industry is another representative industrial sector that suffered from rising import pressure in Japan. In March 1984, the Japan Ferroalloy Association (JFA) petitioned MOF to institute an antidumping suit against France and Norway and a countervailing duty suit against Brazil to curb a sharp rise in imports of ferrosilicon.[14] Domestic demand for ferrosilicon was some 400,000 tons annually for the previous five years, but imports rose sharply from 120,105 tons in 1979 to

243,141 tons in 1982, increasing its share in Japan's total domestic demand to 60 per cent. In particular, imports from the three countries increased from 87,000 tons in 1982 to 149,000 tons in 1983, pushing up their shares in total imports from 37 to 53 per cent. In addition, import prices between 1982 and early 1983 were cheaper than domestic prices by 60,000 yen per ton. JFA claimed that France and Norway exported ferrosilicon at a price 10 to 20 per cent cheaper than domestic prices, and Brazil exported it with subsidies of 11 per cent f.o.b. prices. Because of steep import rises, domestic production decreased from 343,989 tons in 1979 to 186,597 tons in 1982, a 46 per cent drop over three years. Three domestic manufacturers retreated from production in 1981, and five plants run by four manufacturers out of twelve plants run by ten manufacturers suspended production in 1983.[15]

Three months after the petition, the government decided to suspend the preliminary investigation and JFA dropped the cases. Two factors explained this quick termination. First, import prices of ferrosilicon rose sharply as the worldwide production of crude steel recovered. The prices increased from US$570 per ton in early 1983 to US$650 in February–March 1984 to US$750 in July–September. Second, the three governments concerned, notified their Japanese counterpart of their intentions to take responsibility for arresting unfair exports. The Brazilian government proposed that it strive to maintain fair exports at official policy talks. France and Norway sent a message that the governments would guide companies to maintain proper exports. This case ended in a 'grey' solution: guidance by exporting countries.

JFA began preparations for a suit in November 1982 by setting up a working group. In March 1983, JFA finished surveys of imports from seven countries, and planned to lodge a complaint with MOF the following month. However, when the association consulted with METI about a suit, METI was extremely cautious about it on the grounds that since import expansion for rectifying trade imbalances was Japan's major policy issue, an antidumping file that would lead to import restrictions was problematic.[16] METI's position was weak in the ferrosilicon trade issue. A major cause of the declining competitiveness of Japanese ferrosilicon was the high price of domestic electricity, which accounted for some 60 per cent of total production costs. A suit by the ferroalloy industry was likely to lead to criticism of METI's energy policy, which had failed to resolve the problem of high electricity costs.[17] JFA increased pressure on the government by gaining support from steel manufacturers, who are the users of ferrosilicon, and obtained METI's accord to accept a suit. However, when JFA got this accord one and a half years after it began preparations, import prices of ferrosilicon had already climbed to unproblematic levels.

The knitted sweater case in 1988

The third antidumping file was petitioned against Korean knitted sweaters in 1988. The Japanese knitting industry suffered from rising imports of knitted sweaters after 1985. The appreciation of the yen increased the attractiveness of the Japanese market to overseas suppliers, encouraging the entry of knitted sweaters from producers in South Korea, Taiwan and China. South Korea, in particular, accelerated an export drive. Imports of Korean sweaters increased 41.8 per cent in 1986, 25.9 per cent in 1987, and 77.2 per cent from January to July 1988.[18] Responding to the Japanese request, the Korean government announced in June 1988 that it would adopt a monitoring measure on price and volume of exports. However, the measure had almost no effect. The import volume of Korean knitted sweaters in July 1988 was 14 million units, 29 per cent up from the previous year and 0.68 million units up from the previous month.[19] On 21 October 1988, the association eventually lodged an antidumping complaint with MOF, claiming that the export prices of Korean knitted sweaters were 30 per cent lower than normal market prices. After five days of negotiations between the Japanese and Korean industries, on 2 February 1989 South Korea announced a VER. This limited the annual growth rate to less than 1 per cent for the next three years under a price monitoring system. FJKIA withdrew the petition in March 1989.

Compared with the previous two cases, this case became more politicised, involving the conflicting interests of various actors. The major textile industrial associations such as JTIF and JCFA helped FJKIA collect data, and provided financial and personnel assistance.[20] The ruling Liberal Democratic Party (LDP) was also involved in the case. In late December 1988, Kabun Muto, Chairman of the LDP's Special Committee on Textile Measures, visited South Korea seeking to coordinate relations between the governments and industries of both countries. The Japan Federation of Textile Workers' Unions (*Zensen Domei*), and the Democratic Socialist Party that supported it, also openly supported the suit. In contrast, the Japan Textiles Importers Association (JTIA) was strongly opposed to the suit. In January 1988, FJKIA and the Knit Products Committee of JTIA organised meetings where they discussed measures to restore ordered imports of knit products. However, FJKIA decided on the suit without prior consultation in the middle of ongoing negotiations. Some members of the Knit Products Committee hinted at the possibility that JTIA would secede from JTIF.[21]

METI formally took a positive stance on activating antidumping measures. The joint advisory committee of the Textile Committee of the Industrial Structure Council and the Textile Industry Council had deliberated and drawn up the textile industry report every five years. The 1988 report recommended that 'appropriate measures such as antidumping and countervailing duties based on GATT rules should be introduced, when a sharp increase in imports was caused by unfair trade practices'.[22] However, since imports of knitted sweaters became a trade dispute, METI had been reluctant to resolve the issue in the form of a lawsuit and searched for a negotiated settlement. In April 1988, METI sent Eiichi Tamori, Deputy Director-General of the Consumer Goods and Service Industries Bureau, to South Korea to ask for the Korean government to restrain exports of knit products. Even after FJKIA passed a resolution to file a suit the following month, METI made efforts to persuade the association to postpone it. METI sought to extract from the Korean government a promise to restrain exports, and successfully drew an announcement that Korea would adopt export-monitoring measures in June 1988. However, when METI's Eiichi Tamori visited South Korea one month later to confirm details of the measures, the Korean government could not show him how their proposal would work, on the grounds that the effectiveness of the measures would depend on the private sector.[23] Accepting encouragement from both governments, FJKIA and JTIF held an inter-industry meeting with the Korean industry in August and October, but no substantial progress was achieved.

In October 1988, FJKIA finally filed a suit with MOF after it confirmed that the monitoring measure had almost no effect. The association reportedly informed the then Prime Minister Noboru Takeshita of its intention to lodge a suit, without informing METI. FJKIA feared that METI would use administrative guidance to dissuade it from filing a suit, arguing that evidence was insufficient.[24] In fact, the Japanese government claimed that the submitted evidence was insufficient. FJKIA provided additional evidence in November and December, carefully avoiding its submissions being used as a pretext to postpone the date when the government would determine whether to initiate an investigation (Kodama 1989).

In January 1989, the government informally notified that it would initiate an investigation after confirming that the petition was sustained by sufficient evidence. On 25 January, the Korean Textile Products Exporters Association proposed to hold an inter-industry meeting, and the meeting was held for five days from 28 January. On 2 February, the Korean association announced that it would accept a VER. Indeed, the

Korean industry proposed an inter-industry meeting, but METI had moved behind the scenes. Shigeo Tanahashi, a director of the Consumer Goods and Service Industries Bureau, visited South Korea in late December 1988 and proposed that the Korean Ministry of Commerce and Industry search for a voluntary settlement between the industries. The Korean ministry persuaded the executives of the Korean Textile Products Exporters Association to hold an inter-industry meeting.[25]

Thus, METI's basic stance on the knit trade dispute was to avoid resolving it by a suit and to search for a negotiated settlement. This stance was shown clearly in the statement of METI's Eiichi Tamori at the press conference in May 1988: 'in the resolution of knitted sweater dumping, it was desirable that the relevant industrial associations pursue the matter independently in order to prevent the politicisation of the issue in South Korea'.[26] METI feared that a suit would lead to the deterioration of Japan–Korea relations and would provoke international criticism that such an action runs counter to Japan's commitment to increase imports and reduce its trade surplus. Furthermore, the Japanese government hoped to sustain the steady economic development of newly industrialised economies (NIEs) in Asia given that the US government intensified a protectionist stance against imports from the NIEs because of growing trade deficits.[27] For instance, the Japanese government took the lead in including the phrase 'talks and collaboration between advanced industrialised countries and the NIEs' in the Economic Declaration at the Group of Seven Summit in Toronto, Canada in June 1988. With this policy orientation, Japan needed to increase imports from the Asian NIEs.

The above three cases had several characteristics in common. METI, which was unwilling to resolve the dumping disputes by a suit, made serious efforts to discourage the industries from filing a petition, encouraging them to search for a negotiated settlement at the inter-industry meetings. After the industrial associations petitioned a suit, METI informally induced the parties to accept a VER before it had to initiate an investigation. In all the cases, the industries withdrew the petition before the government initiated an investigation.

Three antidumping cases after the 1990s

The ferrosilicon manganese case in 1991

On 8 October 1991, JFA lodged the second antidumping suit against imports of ferrosilicon manganese from China, South Africa and Norway. When JFA brought the charges, four domestic companies manufactured some 110,000 tons of ferrosilicon manganese and 190,000 tons were imported.[28] Imports from China were particularly salient, with a rise in share of the total domestic demand from 17.4 per cent in 1989 to 39.1 per cent in 1991. Average import prices fell from US$761 per ton in July 1989 to US$522 in July 1990, down 30 per cent. The import surge allegedly reduced sales of Japanese manufacturers by 9 per cent and their market share by 7 per cent.[29] JFA required the Chinese government and the ferroalloy association to restore orderly exports at the Japan–China ferroalloy meetings in August 1990 and June 1991. The Chinese government and the ferroalloy association promised to make efforts to restore orderly exports, but export prices declined further.

JFA considered that an antidumping suit was indispensable for the sustenance of the ferroalloy industry in Japan. Although JFA petitioned a suit against imports of ferrosilicon in 1984, the government did not initiate an investigation. Eventually, the domestic production of ferrosilicon shrank sharply from 197,000 tons in 1982 to 41,000 tons in 1992. As a consequence, the number of ferroalloy companies and their employees fell respectively from 38 and some 7000 in 1980 to 22 and some 3100 in 1990.[30] Ferrosilicon manganese, whose production required relatively low electricity costs, was almost the last product in which Japanese ferroalloy manufacturers could retain a competitive edge against imported products.

In late November 1991, MOF and METI decided to initiate an investigation. In June 1992, the government announced an interim determination of dumping margins for three countries: from 5.7 to 26.6 per cent for China, 18.9 per cent for Norway, and from 1.2 to 1.8 per cent for South Africa. The government acknowledged the fact of dumping but did not take emergency retaliatory measures because the import volume of ferrosilicon manganese declined considerably. In January 1993, the government determined that it would impose dumping duties on the Chinese imports ranging from 4.5 to 27.2 per cent. It refrained from levying duties on Norwegian and South African exporters although they were found guilty of dumping. This was because the share of Norwegian manganese in the Japanese market was negligible – 4 per cent even at its height in 1990 – while South African manganese was discounted by a small margin.

The Japanese government was cautious about imposing duties even in this case. The interim determination in June 1992 was peculiar because the government did not take provisional measures although it found that this was a case of dumping. Most countries imposed charges if the administrative authorities found a proven case of dumping. JFA criticised this 'grey' determination and submitted a proposal that required the government to take provisional measures. The final determination was to be announced in November 1992, but the announcement was delayed for two months. An official reason for this delay was that several companies concerned had not submitted requisite information. However, the government had almost finished the investigation, and delivered its decision informally to impose charges on the Chinese exporters in November 1992. The delay came from the government's cautious attitude on imposing dumping duties for the first time, and its desire to announce the decision after the GATT Uruguay Round was concluded. The dumping margin rate was also quite low. When JFA lodged the complaints with MOF, it calculated a 71.1 per cent margin for China, and a 67 per cent margin for Norway and South Africa.[31] This dumping margin was low even in terms of international comparison. In December 1994, the US government imposed a 150 per cent margin on imports of ferrosilicon manganese from China.

Despite its cautious approach, the government not only initiated an investigation for the first time but also imposed dumping duties. What implications do differences in policy outcomes between this case and the previous cases in the 1980s have for Japan's trade policy? As already explained, the existence of huge trade surpluses was often cited as a major reason why the Japanese government was reluctant to adopt a protectionist policy like antidumping in the 1980s. In fact, trade imbalances expanded in the early 1990s. Japan's trade surplus increased from US$78 billion in 1988 to US$107 billion in 1992. Japan's major trade partners continued to criticise the closed nature of the Japanese market. For instance, when the US President George Bush visited Japan in January 1992, he demanded that Japanese automakers increase the purchase of US auto vehicles and parts to help rectify Japan's trade surplus with the United States.

While the fundamental environments surrounding trade structure and trade relations remained almost unchanged, there were subtle changes in METI's stance on international trade disputes. METI gradually strengthened its reliance on the GATT dispute settlement mechanism and international trade rules. The Japanese government was long sceptical about the effectiveness of the GATT mechanism as it thought the mechanism could be abused by countries that demanded arbitration panels before exhausting bilateral negotiations (Funabashi 1995: 197). The government regarded bilateral negotiations rather than multilateral GATT negotiations as desirable for settling international trade disputes. Moreover, Japan had a disgraceful record in GATT litigation. Between

1977 and 1988, Japan was a respondent in twelve cases at the GATT panel, and Japan's measures were found inconsistent with GATT rules in major cases.[32]

However, when Japan finally brought its own complaint to GATT, the experience helped Japan change its view on the GATT dispute settlement. In October 1988, Japan brought its first complaint to the GATT panel that the EC's antidumping duties on imports of Japanese electronic parts were in violation of GATT rules. In March 1990, the GATT panel approved the Japanese allegation. This was the first time that the Japanese government emphasised multilateral negotiations rather than bilateral negotiations as a dispute settlement measure (Ishiguro 1992: 34). After this case in which the Japanese government had reason to be pleased with the outcome, the government became more willing to delegate the resolution of trade conflicts to the GATT/WTO. Japan requested seven consultations and two panels between 1991 and 1997.

The experience also motivated the Japanese government to pursue 'rule-oriented' principles in international trade relations. In January 1991, METI decided to set up a post for investigating unfair trade practices in western countries. In June 1991, the Institute for International Trade and Investment, an METI-affiliated organisation, issued a report on unfair trade practices in the United States, the EC and Canada. The following year, METI itself began to issue a report on unfair trade policies through the Subcommittee on Unfair Trade Policies and Measures of the Industrial Structural Council, an advisory body to the Minister of International Trade and Industry.[33]

The report aims to dampen a unilateral, result-oriented approach favoured by the US government after the mid-1980s by providing an objective evaluation of the trade policies and measures of Japan's major trading partners. Although the first report was criticised severely by the US government, Japan has continued to issue the report. The basic idea of the report was to promote the development of GATT and other international trade rules and the trade dispute settlement on the basis of such international rules. Thus, publication of the report implies that METI considered trade practices and disputes in terms of strict international rules, a departure from 'realistic', reconciliatory policies that aimed to avoid the deterioration of relations with trade partners.

Changes in METI's preferences for paying more respect to internationally oriented, multilateral rules are likely to affect import policies. In 1993 Yoshiro Mori, as Minister of International Trade and Industry, stated at a press conference that the imposition of dumping charges was 'a result of a fair and strict investigation based on the GATT codes, international rules and the domestic legislation'.[34] METI hoped to show that Japan supported free and fair trade in terms of both imports and exports by applying international rules strictly to imports from developing countries.

The cotton yarn case in 1993

The fifth antidumping suit was lodged by JSA in late 1993. In January 1992, JSA began an antidumping investigation of cotton yarn imports from Pakistan. At that time, JSA abandoned the petition because the Pakistani government resumed a minimum export price system on cotton yarn exports. But in 1993, low-priced exports of twenty-count cotton yarn from Pakistan became a critical issue again. In May 1993, JSA unofficially informed METI of its desire to begin an antidumping investigation, and filed a suit against Pakistani twenty-count cotton yarn on 20 December 1993. According to JSA, imports of cotton yarn from Pakistan accounted for some 80 per cent of sales in the Japanese market, and the price of twenty-count cotton yarn imported from Pakistan was 20 per cent lower than domestic prices in Pakistan.[35] Two months later, MOF and METI decided to commence an investigation of the complaint. In August 1994, the government announced that it would not take a provisional measure to restrain imports. The government postponed a final decision in February and April because the import price was unstable. In August 1995, MOF and METI decided to impose dumping margins ranging from 2.1 to 9.9 per cent. JSA did not expect the imposition of duties. Before the final decision was announced, METI's bureaucrats unofficially informed the association that the imposition of duties might be difficult. Accordingly, JSA welcomed the result, especially the fact that the government approved dumping margins of less than 10 per cent.[36] The textile industry for the first time achieved its objective of imposing dumping charges on imports after failing twice. How does this result relate to changes in METI's trade policy preferences?

First, a matter that deserves attention is that METI's responses to this issue were swift and steady by comparison with its responses in the previous cases. METI set up a dumping investigation team headed by Deputy Director-General of the Consumer Goods and Service Industries Bureau in May 1993 when JSA informally notified METI of its intention to prepare for a suit.[37] While the government did not take explicit decisions on how to handle the suits for more than three months in the three cases in the 1980s, it decided to initiate an investigation within two months in both this case and the previous ferrosilicon manganese case. The government also offered for the first time an opportunity of a 'meeting with parties with adverse interests' in the investigation process. The meeting, held with the consent of interested parties with opposing views, served to raise the transparency and fairness of the procedure.

METI showed a positive stance on antidumping in the 1993 textile report. The previous textile report released in 1988 had simply stated that antidumping duties based on GATT rules should be introduced when a sharp increase in imports was caused by unfair trade practices. The 1993 textile report included more concrete provisions for antidumping. This report explicitly spelt out that damages accompanying the imposition of dumping duties to consumers and users were mere losses of reflected interest gained through the purchase of products at unreasonably cheap prices. The report also encouraged the government to develop systems necessary for responding to antidumping suits.[38]

More significantly, in the cotton case the government did not take any action to encourage the Pakistani government to adopt a VER or other measures. On the contrary, the government decided to impose dumping margins despite a proposal by the Pakistani government to adopt a VER. This reaction was unexpected by the Pakistani government, which decided to appeal to the WTO panel on the grounds that Japan decided to take unfair measures even though the Pakistani government delivered a statement of its intent to restrain exports voluntarily.[39]

The imposition of dumping duties naturally led to the protection of the spinning industry. However, judging from overall policy orientations in the 1990s, the decision on the imposition seems to have little bearing on the protection of spinning producers. In the 1990s, METI's basic stance on industrial policy has gradually shifted to retreat from protecting industries under its jurisdiction. For instance, METI amended the Large-Scale Retail Stores Law in January 1992 and May 1994 to eliminate protection over small retailers by allowing large stores to own a larger number of outlets and facilitate their business operations. In March 1996, METI abolished the Provisional Measures Law on the Importation of Specific Petroleum Refined Products, which virtually confined the importers to the companies operating oil refineries, and consequently blocked imports of oil products. METI also became an aggressive supporter of deregulation after 1993. In May 1994, METI invited severe criticisms from other ministries when it issued two internal reports advocating deregulation in areas outside its own jurisdiction.[40]

The decision to impose dumping duties can be seen as METI's further commitment to internationally oriented rules and principles. In January 1995, the WTO was established and the WTO Antidumping Agreement came into force. During the negotiations, the Japanese government demanded tightening discipline on the calculation of dumping margins, the approval of damage and dumping investigation procedures in order to prevent the arbitrary abuse or misuse of antidumping measures. These commitments encouraged the Japanese government to apply the antidumping legislation based strictly on international rules.

A critical incident that showed METI's support for multilateral rules was the US–Japan auto and auto parts negotiations in 1994–95.[41] At the final stage of the negotiations, the US government pressured its Japanese counterpart to open the Japanese auto parts market by announcing retaliatory measures to double import tariffs on certain models of Japanese luxury vehicles. There was also domestic political pressure to search for a swift settlement of the dispute without resorting to the WTO, given that the US presidential election would be held the following year (Hosokawa 1999: 165). At that stage, the Japanese government did not form a monolithic entity, and there were divergences even within METI. While horizontal bureaus such as the International Trade Policy Bureau and the Industrial Policy Bureau favoured the strict application of WTO rules, the sector-specific bureaus such as the Machinery and Information Industries Bureau pursued a more flexible approach to maintain the interest of industries under their jurisdiction (Ikuta 1996: 6–7).

Despite these divergences, METI could adhere to the international rule-based settlement. METI presented the case at an OECD Ministerial meeting in May 1995, where almost all parties sided with the Japanese position (Pekkanen 2001: 74–5). Within few days, the Japanese government lodged a complaint with the WTO against US unilateral sanctions against Japanese auto vehicles. The appeal to the WTO and support for Japan's claim among major WTO members constituted decisive factors settling the dispute in Japan's favour (Hosokawa 1999: 164).

Thus, the settlement of the auto and auto parts dispute demonstrates that METI's officials shifted further away from a bilateral-based to a multilateral-oriented approach in resolving trade disputes. An increased emphasis on multilateralism was likely to affect import policies. METI strengthened its commitments to the international rule-oriented approach away from an ambiguous settlement such as the adoption of a VER.

As explained above, METI's support for multilateralism stemmed partly from Japan's considerable success at GATT panels. The start of the WTO in January 1995 strengthened METI's new policy orientation. Establishment of the WTO facilitated settlement of trade disputes based on international rules and principles, and strengthened METI officials' recognition of the effectiveness of utilising multilateral rules and systems (Uchiyama 1999: 41–2). In addition, the so-called 'multi faction' became more influential within METI. METI's officials gradually got accustomed to multilateral rules and systems because many young officials from various bureaus including sector-specific bureaus attended meetings during the Uruguay Round negotiations. Through their accumulated experiences, they learned how multinational negotiations work (Nihon Keizai Shimbunsha 1995: 186–7). When the Japanese government discussed the possibility of appeals to WTO panels during the 1995 US–Japan auto negotiations, older officials at METI were relatively cautious about the settlement through the WTO. In contrast, younger officials who served as directors supported the appeal to the WTO (Ikuta 1996: 5–7).

The bitter experiences of failing to settle trade disputes through bilateral arrangements also strengthened support for the multilateral approach (Schoppa 1999: 323–4). In the 1986 US–Japan Semiconductor Arrangement, the US and Japanese governments exchanged a side letter that referred to a 20 per cent market share achieved by US companies in the Japanese market. While METI officials considered the letter merely an acknowledgement of the US side's desire, it was used as a pretext for US sanctions in 1987. In the 1992 auto parts negotiations, the US government demanded the implementation of plans to purchase US-made parts despite the fact that the Japanese government had clarified that these plans were voluntary. Schoppa (1999) argues that these incidents reduced trust in US–Japan trade negotiations. They also made METI bureaucrats recognise the risks involved in bilateral negotiations relative to the risks in multilateral negotiations.

The polyester staple fibre case in 2001

The sixth antidumping suit was lodged by textile producers. In late February 2001, Teijin, Toray Industries, Kuraray, Toyobo and Unitika Fibers petitioned MOF to levy an antidumping duty on certain types of polyester staple fibres imported from South Korea and Taiwan. According to the firms, imports of polyester staple fibres from South Korea and Taiwan rose 20 per cent and 83 per cent between 1997 and 1999, respectively. As a consequence, their sales volume dropped 8 per cent, retail prices fell 13 per cent and sales plunged 19 per cent.[42]

The government commenced the investigation in April, and proceeded with the necessary procedures such as the distribution of questionnaires to filed firms and field investigations in South Korea and Taiwan. In July

2002, the government decided to impose dumping duties of 6 per cent for one Korean firm, 13.5 per cent for 25 Korean firms, and 10.3 per cent for 13 Taiwanese firms.

In the new century, METI stood in a difficult position over handling the antidumping issue because Japan began negotiations with South Korea over a free trade agreement (FTA). In September 2000, the Japanese and Korean governments agreed to set up the Japan–Korea FTA Business Forum, and the forum submitted a report calling for the conclusion of an FTA in February 2002. The following month, President Kim Dae-jung and Prime Minister Junichiro Koizumi agreed to set up a joint committee comprising of the members from the government, industry and academia to study the feasibility of an FTA between two countries. Accordingly, METI hoped not to adopt a measure that would have an unfavourable effect on Japan–Korea trade relations.

Moreover, METI was apprehensive about a rise of applications from domestic industries seeking protection from cheap imports. As explained in the following chapter, the towel manufacturers lodged a safeguard suit the same month of the antidumping file. Other producers of quite a few goods including neckties, socks, eel, and *wakame* seaweed also began to prepare for a safeguard suit. Accordingly, METI was extremely nervous about the proliferation of moves towards import protection through formal trade remedy measures.

However, METI considered that the antidumping case on the polyester staple fibres was compatible with the international rules. One senior METI official stated that 'as long as we can produce valid evidence pointing to the unfair practices of exporters, imposing antidumping tariffs within the framework of the WTO cannot be considered a protectionist measure'.[43] This case showed that METI became less restrictive to use the international legal rules for unfair trade practices even under politically severe conditions.

Significantly, METI seems to have another intention in handling the polyester staple fibre case: to show the strict and transparent procedures for an antidumping case. METI went through strict and elaborate procedures for the case. METI issued detailed questionnaires during the process. The finally published report contained concrete contents. It explained the process and result of investigations in detail, attaching Korean and Taiwanese antidumping impositions on Japanese firms and international moves towards imposing antidumping duties on Korean and Taiwanese polyester staple fibres. To carry out the strict procedures had particular political implications. Japan had conflicts with the United States over antidumping measures imposed on Japan's steel

imports, and accused Washington of the arbitrary and biased procedures.[44] The Japanese government's opposition to the abuse of
antidumping measures was also shown at the WTO Ministerial meeting
in Seattle in December 1999. During the preparation process for the
meeting, the Japanese government submitted proposals for thirteen
areas. The 'Proposal on Antidumping' stipulated that resort to
antidumping measures has been a tool for protectionist purposes in
many cases, and demanded removing ambiguity and excess discretion
inherent in the Antidumping Agreement. For the ministerial conference, the Japanese government published a pamphlet that provided
information about the background of debate and data and materials
regarding antidumping cases (METI 2000a: 354).

METI stood at an equivocal position after the late 1990s in handling
antidumping problems. It faced a rising demand for strong protection
against import pressure in the domestic market on the one hand, and
pursued the more disciplined use of antidumping measures in the
international scene on the other. METI's officials became less hesitant to
use the internationally accepted antidumping rules, but maintained
preferences against the arbitrary use of antidumping measures.

Conclusion

This chapter has focused on the trade policy preferences of METI
bureaucrats as one variable that helps explain antidumping policy and
politics in Japan. In particular, it has argued that METI bureaucrats have
strengthened their preference for an international rules-oriented
approach to resolve trade disputes, and these evolving preferences have
affected trade remedy measures including antidumping policy.

In the 1980s, METI was extremely cautious about restraining imports
through antidumping measures, and these preferences had much to do
with national antidumping policy and politics. For a long time, the
institutional framework for administering an antidumping petition was
inadequate. Guidelines for antidumping procedure were not in place
formally until 1986, and METI held a passive attitude when the guidelines were formulated under the private sector's initiative. METI's
administrative organisation for accepting an antidumping suit was also
insufficient until the mid-1990s. These institutional shortcomings
discouraged the private sector from resorting to antidumping measures.

When dumping foreign products became critical issues in the
Japanese market, METI bureaucrats sought swift resolution. They often
encouraged the parties concerned to hold inter-industry meetings and

settled the cases before initiating an investigation. A critical reason for this action was that METI feared that adopting a protectionist stance would worsen Japan's relations with major trade partners and invite international criticism that such a defensive stance runs counter to Japan's espoused commitment to rectifying trade imbalances.

During this period, METI resolved this dilemma of satisfying demands to protect declining industries on the one hand and avoiding criticism of import restrictions on the other, by adopting ambiguous 'grey area' measures that fall between free and managed trade. This reconciliatory approach based on bilateral negotiations was easily adaptable to METI. Internally, METI became accustomed to reaching consensus through close linkages with industrial sectors and using informal consultation measures that include administrative guidance. Externally, METI adopted bilateral measures as a means to settle trade disputes resulting from Japan's exports to developed countries.

The Japanese government imposed dumping duties three times after the 1990s. This fact seems to support the argument that METI changed its trade policy preferences for activating antidumping measures. However, the decision on whether to impose dumping charges depended on various aspects, including recognising the case as a true case of dumping with material injury to a domestic industry. As this study revealed, METI was still cautious about imposing dumping duties even in the 1990s, fearing deterioration in relations with Japan's trade partners.

At the same time, it seems possible to hold that METI bureaucrats have changed their views on multilateral trade rules and systems over time and that these changes have influenced antidumping policy in Japan. Pekkanen (2001) argues that the Japanese bureaucracy has become active in utilising the WTO rules and procedures both at the domestic and international levels. Increasing favour for using international legal rules has affected antidumping policy and politics. The two industrial associations that petitioned an antidumping suit in the 1980s took the same action in the 1990s. While they could not achieve their objective in the 1980s, they could in the 1990s. They were more desperate in the suits in the 1990s when import pressure rose. However, there were no distinctive changes in the measures and political resources available to these associations. The policy preferences of METI bureaucrats do matter in accounting for evolutions in antidumping policy in Japan.

METI has over time paid more respect to the rules-oriented principles embodied in the GATT/WTO system. As Japan has accumulated trade disputes with developed countries and with establishment of the WTO in January 1995, METI bureaucrats have shifted away from the bilateral, reconciliatory approach towards the international rule-oriented approach. While METI strengthened its commitment to fair trade by beginning to issue a report on unfair trade policies in 1992, it has willingly utilised GATT panels as an effective way of resolving international trade disputes. METI has also shown a more positive assessment of the antidumping measures adopted in the international trade system, departing from bilateral settlements.

Importantly, METI's new orientation does not necessarily imply that it intends to use antidumping measures more frequently. METI has recognised the risk of antidumping, which could threaten the basic tenets of non-discrimination and reciprocity embodied in the GATT/WTO regime. METI has instead pursued the use of antidumping strictly to curb the abuse of antidumping as a trade remedy. This is shown in the Japanese government's strict procedures and adamant opposition to the arbitrary use of antidumping measures at the WTO and during disputes with the United States over steel trade.

3
Social Demand and State Capability in Safeguard Policy

In the 1960s and 1970s, Japan's export drive provoked successive trade frictions with developed countries. In particular, disputes between Japan and the United States occurred, involving various products including textiles, colour televisions, steels and general machinery. The friction threatened their overall diplomatic relations as well as the international trading system (Bergsten and Noland 1993; Lincoln 1999). Thirty years later, Japan stood in a defensive position against increased imports from neighbouring countries, especially China. Several basic industries that have suffered from rising import pressure have demanded that the government introduce import restrictive measures. In particular, trade friction over the invocation of safeguard measures against Chinese products became a serious issue, attracting interest as a turning point of Japan's trade policy.

One of the most critical features of Japan–China trade friction, compared with Japan–US friction, is that it occurred in an era of globalisation.[1] In Japan–US trade friction, US firms demanded protection against import pressure from Japanese firms. The business actors competing in the trade disputes – Japanese and US firms – were completely separable. In Japan–China friction, Japanese firms were deeply involved in Japan–China trade as well as production in China. The closely linked economies underpinned by enhanced corporate activities are likely to make the framework of Japan–China friction more complicated. Accordingly, we need to add new perspectives to draw an accurate picture of the friction.

In this chapter, changes in the framework of trade friction resulting from global competition and enhanced corporate operations are considered through safeguard policy and politics in Japan. It argues that globalised corporate operations have a crucial influence on the framework of both preferences of a state's policy-makers and the cohesion of society. While enhanced economic interdependence encouraged the policy-makers to strengthen preferences for making domestic industries adapt to rapidly evolving international environments, not simply following political pressure for protection, increased corporate activities divided preferences and interest among societal actors. These factors had a vital influence on the development of trade policy and politics.

In the following section, I take a brief look at the literature on the determinants of trade policy in order to draw two central hypotheses for this study. I then investigate the development of safeguard policies and politics in the textile and agricultural sectors in Japan in order to examine the hypotheses.

Globalisation, social demand and state capability

As already explained in the previous chapter, the domestic political process for formulating trade policies has been considered from the demand and supply sides. The demand side approach highlights the preferences and roles of societal interests groups that compete with each other for higher benefits or incomes through an adoption of a particular trade policy. The supply side approach stresses the preferences and behaviour of policy-makers with autonomous power to pursue particular policy goals through a trade policy, or the roles of domestic political institutions that determine the patterns and shift of trade policy.

How are the demand and supply side models applied to Japan–China trade friction? In applying the demand and supply side approaches, we need to highlight a critical feature of Japan–China trade friction. Trade between Japan and China has steadily increased since the early 1990s (Table 3.1). Currently, Japan is the primary trade partner for China and China is the secondary partner for Japan. While Japan's trade deficit with China exacerbated in the 1990s, rising imports from China have led to trade friction in several sectors including textiles and agriculture.

Compared with Japan–US trade tension, Japan–China trade disputes occurred in the trend of globalisation when corporate activities are highly internationalised. Globalisation matters in two respects. First, globalised corporate activities have made basic trade patterns more complicated. In Japan–US trade disputes in the 1960s and 1970s, global activities of Japanese firms triggered trade problems. However, the

Table 3.1 The trends of Japan–China trade (US$ million: %)

Year	Export	Increase rate	Import	Increase rate	Total	Increase rate	Balance
1990	6,130	−28.0	12,054	8.1	18,184	−7.5	−5,924
1991	8,593	40.2	14,216	17.9	22,809	25.4	−5,623
1992	11,949	39.1	16,953	19.3	28,902	26.7	−5,004
1993	17,273	44.6	20,565	21.3	37,838	30.9	−3,292
1994	18,682	8.2	27,566	34.0	46,248	22.2	−8,884
1995	21,931	17.4	35,922	30.3	57,853	25.1	−13,991
1996	21,890	−0.2	40,550	12.9	62,440	7.9	−18,660
1997	21,785	−0.5	42,066	3.7	63,851	2.3	−20,281
1998	20,022	−8.1	36,896	−12.3	56,918	−10.9	−16,874
1999	23,336	16.6	42,880	16.2	66,216	16.3	−19,545
2000	30,428	30.4	55,303	29.0	85,731	29.5	−24,876
2001	31,097	2.2	58,099	5.1	89,196	4.0	−27,002

Source: JETRO (2001b: 7).

operations of Japanese firms were limited to exports, nor did US firms advance into the Japanese market. In Japan–China trade friction, Japanese firms have intensively advanced into the Chinese market in various forms including exports, foreign direct investment and development importing.[2] Not only was the large quantity of products exported from China to Japan developed by Japanese firms but Japanese businesses were also deeply involved in exports of these products to Japan. These conditions are likely to have significant influences on frameworks for analysing trade tension between Japan and China.

Second, increased trade and capital movements make it difficult for the state to insulate a particular issue or sector in the domestic market from overall global market trends and global competition. Because of rising global competition, the state has no longer regulated freely operating working conditions or environmental criteria, which were once purely domestic issues. Global market trends have also created meshed linkages encompassing various sectors and areas, which covered those that were previously considered to be purely domestic. Policies adopted for purely domestic issues and sectors are likely to influence the state's external relations and their firms' operations in international marketplaces.

What influence, then, do interlinked economic relations and globalised corporate activities have on trade policy formation? In the demand side, globalisation creates cleavages in policy preferences of various societal groups in various countries. Enhanced internationalisation gives benefits to capitalists and skilled workers in developed countries and to unskilled workers in developing countries, while increasing threat to unskilled workers in advanced countries and owners of both physical and human capitals in developing countries (Frieden and Rogowski 1996: 40). The former press for greater liberalisation while the latter demand higher protection. Globalisation does not permeate every segment of society evenly even in a country. It creates groups that draw benefits from enhanced economic interdependence and positively respond to global trends, on the one hand, and groups that receive unfavourable effects and seek to resist global trends, on the other. In particular, serious chasms emerge over trade policy preferences between producers of tradables or multinational firms, on the one hand, and producers of non-tradables or purely national firms, on the other. While the former seek to protect the domestic market from external competi-tion, the latter that have great bearings on imports and overseas markets tend to oppose such import restrictions (Destler and Odell 1987; Milner 1988).

The application of the contention of divided policy preferences among societal groups to Japan is particularly important. The Japanese business community has cultivated a close relationship within and among industries. Japanese industries coordinate their internal matters through the activities of industrial associations and close relations with relevant government agencies (Shindo 1992; Dore 2000: ch. 6). Japanese industries have also developed particular relational contracts between them through long-term transactions and coordination by industrial associations (Tilton 1996). These factors might have a critical influence on cleavages in preferences for trade policy within and among industries.

In the supply side, global competition and global trends create complicated policy preferences of the state's policy-makers. Enhanced interdependence and resultant competitive pressure leads particular domestic industries and groups to demand the state for protection or compensation, and the state's policy-makers respond to such concen-trated demands.[3] The states are expected to provide buffers against social and economic plight caused by globalisation (Garrett 1998). However, if enhanced economic linkages make it increasingly difficult to block the domestic market from global market trends and shocks, the state's policy-makers might consider policies to maintain the overall interests of the national economy and industry, not simply following political pressure for higher protection. A capable state is expected to have capacities and willingness to promote industrial adjustment

responding to the evolving environments surrounding the state's industries. In the globalisation era, such capabilities are directed towards
maintaining the overall competitiveness of the national industries by
linking them with the regional and global economies in rapidly evolving international marketplaces.

This perspective derives from two concepts regarding the state's role
and capacity in an era of globalisation. The first is 'transformative
capability', which refers to the ability of a state to adapt to external
shocks and pressures by generating ever-new means of governing the
process of industrial changes (Weiss 1998: 4). Such a capability is particularly important in global trends where interstate competition for
acquiring higher incomes and industrial upgrading is fierce. The second
is the concept of 'competition states'. According to Cerny (1990, 1997),
competition states pursue the increased marketisation of economic and
social activities in the name of international competitiveness by transforming its internal organisations flexibly. Both concepts suggest that
the state in the globalisation age faces increasing needs to maintain
and improve the interests of the national economy and industry by
strategically responding to the evolving environments.

The application of the transformative state model to Japan has particular implications. Some observers regard Japan as a 'reactive state'
that lacks a political power centre (Calder 1988; van Walferen 1989).
In fact, Japan was extremely slow in opening its market to foreign
firms and foreign products. This propensity continued in the late
1990s, sustained by a fact that Japan decreased overall imports from
the crisis-hit Asian economies despite earnest demand from their governments. At the same time, however, it is also a fact that the Japanese
government has located the opening of Japan to Asia in various
dimensions and human resources contributions as its key strategies.
For instance, the report of the Mission for Revitalisation of the Asian
Economy (Okuda mission) emphasises 'a third "opening", an opening
to Asia on the many different levels of people, goods, money, and
information'.[4] In November 1999, the government announced a *Plan
for Enhancing Human Resources Development and Human Resources
Exchanges in East Asia*, which was based on the recommendations by
the Okuda mission. In addition, Japan showed transformative capacity to respond skilfully to crucial changes in international environments such as pressure for market liberalisation in the 1970s and
the currency appreciation in the 1980s. We might expect that the
Japanese state pursued trade policies to defend its interest strategically
by taking into account the evolving regional markets and the

inevitable integration of Japan with East Asia, not following myopic interest from societal and political pressure.

In sum, this chapter examines safeguard policy and politics in Japan by highlighting the influences that globalisation has on the state's roles and preferences, and the interests and influences of societal actors. I set forth two hypotheses for elucidating Japan–China safeguard friction:

(1) Division in policy preferences among societal groups resulting from globalised corporate activities has a crucial influence on a state's trade policy.
(2) The state in a globalisation era shows transformative capacity to formulate trade policy for maintaining the overall interest of national industries in rapidly evolving international marketplaces.

Before delving into the two case studies of Japan–China trade friction, it is useful to overview the current safeguard system under the World Trade Organisation (WTO) rules. There are three kinds of safeguards. The first is general safeguards under Article XIX of the General Agreement and Agreement on Safeguard. Since Article XIX imposed strict conditions for invoking safeguards, import competing countries tended to prefer voluntary export restraints (VERs) to safeguard measures. The Agreement on Safeguard explicitly prohibited the 'grey area' measures including VERs and relaxed conditions on invocation to some extent. Under the WTO safeguard rules, a country can curb imports if it can prove that imported goods are causing, or threaten to cause, serious damage to domestic producers involved, in terms of nine criteria such as lower domestic output and loss in jobs.

The second is transitional safeguards under the Agreement on Textile and Clothing (ATC). In textile trade, a special framework called the Multi-Fibre Arrangement (MFA) worked from 1974 to 1994. In the new arrangement ratified in April 1994, it was agreed that the MFA would be phased out by integrating it into the general GATT rules in three stages over a ten-year period.[5] During the transition phase, any country is entitled to introduce a transitional safeguard. Under this rule, the importing country is allowed to restrain imports in cases when sharp increases in imports of a particular type of product have caused or threatened to cause serious damage to the relevant domestic industry.[6]

The third is special safeguards under the Agreement on Agriculture. For items converted from non-tariff barriers to tariffs, additional duties may be applied in case shipments at prices denominated in domestic currencies below a certain reference level or in case of a surge of imports.

Safeguard politics in the textile industry

Rising imports of textile products and Japanese responses

During the pre-war period and after the Second World War, the textile industry was the leading manufacturing industry in Japan in terms of production output and exports. However, it gradually lost international competitiveness in the labour-intensive sectors after the 1970s, suffering from a rise in imports from neighbouring countries. In 1987, Japan posted its first deficit in the textile trade. Responding to such changes, textile producer associations intensified their demand for restraining imports under the provisions of the MFA. However, the government rejected the demand on the grounds that import restrictive measures ran counter to the free trade principles.

The Japanese government's stance on import restrictions slightly changed in the mid-1990s. In May 1994, the Textile Industry Council, an advisory body to the Ministry of Economy, Trade and Industry (METI), recommended that the government take necessary actions to reduce the negative effects of sharply increased imports by instituting safeguards under the MFA with several conditions. Based on this recommendation, METI published the guidelines for the procedure of textile safeguards in December 1994.

In February 1995, the first safeguard suit was lodged by the Japan Spinners' Association (JSA) and Japan Cotton and Staple Fibre Weavers' Association (JCSFWA). While the JSA requested the introduction of safeguards against imports of forty-count cotton yarn from China, Indonesia and South Korea, the JSA and JCSFWA lodged a petition to invoke safeguards against imports of poplin and broadcloth from China and Indonesia. Although three countries were included, the main target was China, which accounted for 40 per cent of imports of forty-count cotton yarn and 80 per cent of poplin and broadcloth.[7] METI began an investigation two months later, but decided to pass over the invocation of safeguards in November. METI approved that the import rise for the past three years caused damage to the domestic industry, but judged that imports for the latest one year declined due to China's VERs and depressed demand at the domestic market. In July 1996, the JSA and JCSFWA petitioned the second safeguard file against poplin and broadcloth from China. While

METI decided to launch a survey, it began negotiations with the Chinese government searching for a new system to curb exports. In November 1996, the Japanese and Chinese governments reached an agreement to adopt a new export control measure. Under the measure, only cotton fabrics that obtained permission were allowed to be exported to Japan.

In both cases, the Japanese government was extremely cautious about invoking safeguard measures. The Chinese government also preferred settlements through negotiations. These considerations led to an adoption of the VER systems. At the same time, it appeared through real petitions that flexible petitions and investigations of safeguards were impeded by procedural conditions such as the long period for an investigation and the submission of structural reform plans as a requirement for a petition.

In 1997 and 1998, imports of textile products declined slightly, reflecting the depressed domestic demand. However, import pressure intensified again after 1999 due to the expansion of imports from China. The various textile-related sectors began to demand relief measures including safeguards, intensifying reliance on political circles. In July 2000, the Federation of Japan Towel Industry Associations (FJTIA) lobbied several Liberal Democratic Party (LDP) members to discuss textile trade issues.[8] The following month, the LDP's Special Committee on Textile Measures held a meeting, and major textile associations including the Japan Textile Industry Federation (JTIF) – the umbrella body of the textile industry – the Federation of Japan Knitting Industry Associations (FJKIA) and the JSA explained the painful conditions of their industries. Katsunosuke Maeda, Chairman of the JTIF, stated at the meeting that volume of mill consumption had declined by one-quarter in Japan in the past decade while it had increased in the United States and Europe, and that Japan should adopt commercial policy similar to those adopted in the United States and Europe by utilising antidumping and safeguard measures.[9] In October 2000, the JTIF published a position paper entitled *Strength of Competitiveness of the Japanese Textile Industry*, and explained it at the LDP's Special Committee on Textile Measures. Responding to demand from textile circles, the committee decided to set up a project team to examine measures to protect textile producers from increased imports from China and other developing countries, including the possible invocation of safeguards. In early November, the JTIF and other major textile associations appealed plight resulting from rising imports at a meeting of the project team. The following month, the coalition government approved *Measures for Steep Increases in Imports of Textile Products*. In the measures, the government earmarked 600 million yen in the fiscal 2001 budget as textile industry subsidies in order to assist small firms to strengthen their capabilities of designing and developing new products.[10] Importantly, political moves to sustain the textile industry expanded to the opposition parties. The Democratic Party of Japan organised a working team on textile policy. In November 2000, the team issued recommendations entitled *Demands Regarding Sharp Increases in Imports of Textile Products and the Fostering of the Domestic Textile Industry*. In the recommendations, the party demanded that the government respond to safeguard and antidumping petitions based on the international rules. Thus, political attention to the textile industry increased sharply in late 2000. Moves in political circles had much to do with an election of the House of Councillors scheduled in the summer of 2001. Politicians in the ruling and opposition parties hoped to gain votes from the people in economically troubled districts by extending protective measures including import restrictions.

The main target of textile circles was directed towards simplifying administrative procedures for demanding safeguard import curbs. According to the guidelines for the procedure of textile safeguards, a complainant was required to submit programs for structural reform including detailed plans of structural improvement, perspectives on competitiveness three years later and effects of safeguard measures. This requirement was an independent condition that was not required in the WTO legislation. Textile producers had to incur huge costs and time for preparation, and flexible and timely applications of safeguard relieves had been hampered.

The abolition of the requirement of structural reform plans became the target of political activities. The JTIF's Maeda repeatedly pointed out problematic aspects of this requirement at the LDP's committee meetings and talks with METI officials. The LDP acknowledged the interest of textile circles. The first item of *Measures for Steep Increases in Imports of Textile Products* was to abolish the requirement for structural reform plans.

In December 2000, the Textile Industry Council issued recommendations, which included the revisions of the guidelines regarding safeguard measures: first, an abolition of a requirement for submitting structural reform plans; second, the creation of a system under which a filed industry cooperates with relevant industries that provide raw materials; and third, clear respect for the internationally established interpretation regarding the ATC. The following month, the guidelines were formally revised, not to require the submission of structural reform plans. Furthermore, the phrase of technical and political considerations in deciding on the adoption of safeguards was also removed. Thus, lobbying of political parties and the government by textile circles successfully changed domestic institutions in favour of safeguards.

The unrealised attempt to petition a safeguard file

In response to the revision of the safeguard procedures, textile producer associations in various segments began to prepare for a file. In early December 2000, at a meeting of the LDP's Special Committee on Textile Measures, Katsunosuke Maeda showed a prospect that eleven items were eligible for a suit. The items included towels, shirts, blouses, sweaters, knitted shirts, trousers, and others.

However, action for a file did not go smoothly in most items. This was typical in the knitting industry, a segment that suffered serious damages from an import rise. In autumn 1999, the FJKIA took the lead in pushing for a campaign for keeping domestic production of textile goods by blocking disorderly imports. However, the federation showed unstable attitudes towards safeguard issues. In August 2000, the federation published *View of the FJKIA on Import Issues*. It stated that the Japanese were involved in imports of knitted products from China, and thereby the import issues should not be handled as an issue between the states. The federation did not intend to petition a safeguard file by itself but expressed approval to files by other associations. The following month, however, the federation decided to conduct questionnaire surveys to its members concerning import problems. The result showed that nearly 50 per cent of respondents agreed to petition a safeguard file.[11] The federation still kept the previous position – not to demand a safeguard petition.

The passive attitude of the federation towards a safeguard file derived from two reasons. First, the federation regarded safeguard measures as having minimal effects on curbing imports. Even if a safeguard measure is adopted, it allows imports in the first year at the same level as that of the previous year and to a 6 per cent increase per year in the second and third years. Given that the import ratio reached more than 80 per cent, safeguard curbs would have meagre effects. Second, a requirement to submit structural reform plans was a heavy burden for knitting producers, most of which were small and medium scale firms.[12]

In late 2000, the federation revealed a new policy that it would decide on a formal policy towards safeguard measures on the basis of questionnaire surveys to its member firms about the possibility of the invocation of safeguards. This policy derived from the deregulation of administrative procedures for safeguards and strong encouragement by the JTIF. After relaxations of procedures for safeguard applications were decided, the JTIF urged its member associations to consider the possibility of safeguard files and make a speedy preparation for it. The knitting sector was the main target of this encouragement.

In March 2001, the state of knit imports in 2000 was revealed. In 2000, imports increased 21.6 per cent in knitted sweaters, 36.5 per cent in knitted outer shirts and 27.6 per cent in knitted underwear. The import ratio was 95.1 per cent for knitted sweaters, 86.2 per cent for knitted outer shirts and 81.5 per cent for knitted underwear.[13] Despite the apparent increases in imports, in May 2001 the federation formally decided to abandon petitioning a safeguard file. The most crucial reason was that the knitted sector could not meet a criterion for it. The federation conducted questionnaire surveys to investigate damage caused by imports. However, only 15 per cent of the total firms (170 out of 1176 firms) responded to the survey.[14] As a consequence, the FJKIA could collect data concerning 9.6 per cent of total domestic production in knitted sweaters and 19.1 per cent in knitted outer shirts.[15] These figures were far below a criterion in the guidelines requiring that producers with more than 50 per cent of domestic production should be damaged by imports. Firms with transactions in various forms in China refused to respond to the survey. Some 40 per cent of the federation members had transactions with China in development importing and other forms.[16] These firms particularly feared that the adoption of safeguard measures would invite the Chinese government's discriminatory policies, which would curtail exports from Japanese-related firms, maintaining those from Chinese state-owned enterprises. These firms gave their approval to a safeguard file in the general surveys but exerted a veto power at the final stage.

Thus, the FJKIA maintained its stance not to invoke safeguard measures despite deregulations of the procedures and strong encouragement by its upper federation. The knitting federation regarded import issues as conflict among the Japanese, and asked METI to restore orderly imports by regulating the behaviour of Japanese importers. The unstable stance on safeguards stemmed from divided views among the member firms. The firms that forged connections with China hoped to restrain disorderly imports but opposed the invocation of safeguards, which would disturb their own imports from China.

A safeguard file by towel manufacturers

While most textile sectors found difficulty in reaching an actual suit, towel producers could proceed with a safeguard petition. On 16 February 2001, the FJTIA held an emergency meeting and decided to petition a file. Just ten days after the meeting, FJTIA formally lodged a petition with METI to invoke the safeguard clauses against import of towels from China and

Vietnam. According to industrial statistics, domestic outputs of towels fell to 42,797 tons in 1999, 13.2 per cent down from 49,313 tons in 1996, while imports grew 30.8 per cent from 43,062 tons to 56,312 tons in the same period. In 1999, China accounted for 77.9 per cent of total imports.[17] In April 2001, METI decided to investigate a claim by the FJTIA.

Three factors explain why the towel industry could file a safeguard suit. First, the number of producers was relatively small and highly concentrated. Total producers were 460 concentrating mainly on two districts: Osaka and Ehime prefectures. As of December 2000, 200 and 218 manufacturers were located in Senshu, southern part of Osaka, and Imabari city, Ehime. The industrial structure with the small number of producers in concentrated areas enabled the industry to form a common front rather easily. Second, the number of firms operating overseas was also small. Only ten out of 460 producers advanced into China. Third, the import ratio of towel products was relatively low compared with other textile products. In 1999, the import ratio of towel products was 57.1 per cent while that of overall cottons and wools were 85.5 per cent and 72.1 per cent, respectively. The towel producers had strong incentives to block a further surge of imports.

The petition by the FJTIA provoked controversy. In March 2001, the Japan Chain Store Association revealed a view to oppose import restrictions on the grounds that it would impede firms' self-efforts, restrain the opportunities of selection for consumers and exacerbate depressed consumption.[18] Many apparel makers and retailers such as Fast Retailing, famous for its Uniqlo brand name, strongly opposed moves by textile producers to encourage the government to take emergency steps to restrain imports. These firms advanced into China in order to export cheap products manufactured with locally produced textiles and local workers to Japan. They offered technical guidance and production management and know-how, which were necessary for manufacturing low-priced, high quality textile products. The start of local production of synthetic fibres by Japanese fibre producers facilitated apparel makers to procure high quality intermediate products locally. Chinese products retained higher quality than in the past and were widely accepted by consumers shown by the Uliqlo phenomenon.

A more serious opposition came from within the towel industry. Seven towel manufacturers in Ehime prefecture opposed the petition. These firms made inroads into China responding to the sharp appreciation of the yen after 1985, and actively pursued a regional strategy: development and design of products in Japan and manufacturing in China. Although the number was small, they amounted to 22 per cent of total outputs and

36 per cent of total sales in Ehime in 2000. They also accounted for 25 per cent in terms of volume and 38 per cent in terms of value of Japan's towel imports from China. In December 2000, these producers who were also the members of the FJTIA organised the Liaison Council of Firms Advancing into China. The council implemented various activities against the file. On 26 February when the FJTIA petitioned the file, the group submitted proposals to oppose the file to the Imabari municipal government and assembly. On 9 March, the council submitted a formal petition with the government not to invoke a safeguard measure with 5700 signatures. Their activities were published by major media and helped generate public interest in the towel import problem.

These firms feared negative influences of safeguard measures on shipments of products manufactured at factories in China to Japan. Toshihiro Yagi, Chairman of the council, argued that 'To cater to needs of consumers, we cannot avoid venturing overseas. China will make adjustments so that exports from its state-owned enterprises remain the same while exports quotas are set on Japanese manufacturers there.'[19] The adoption of safeguard measures would lead to the situation that challenging firms that launched production in China would be on the verge of survival in exchange of protecting domestically oriented firms lagging behind in such efforts. In the towel industry, a safeguard issue became an explicit conflict between firms staying in Japan and those advancing into China.

METI had long considered it undesirable to protect the domestic industry by import restrictions. In addition, moves to resort to safeguard measures gained momentum in spring 2001. While the Japanese government decided to invoke provisional safeguards against imports of three farm products in April 2001, producers of quite a few goods including socks, neckties, eel, and *wakame* seaweed began to prepare for a safeguard petition. Responding to such climates, METI's attitudes towards safeguards became strict. In May 2001, METI published a paper regarding safeguard measures at the Subcommittee of Special Trade Measures under the Industrial Structure Council. The paper stipulated that in deciding on whether to impose safeguard measures against a particular product, it should sufficiently investigate perspectives on the structural adjustment of the industry that produces the product. METI officials also encouraged towel producers to formulate comprehensive structural adjustment programs when they visited Imabari city in April.[20] Thus, although METI approved that the submission of structural reform plans was not a condition for petitioning a safeguard file, it adhered to showing perspectives on structural reform before receiving import protection.

In October 2001, the Japanese government decided to postpone by six months its judgement of whether to impose safeguard restrictions on towel imports. METI raised two reasons for this decision. One was that it was wise to wait for China's entry into the WTO in order to reduce the possibility of retaliation. As explained later, China imposed a 100 per cent special customs duty on imports of Japanese motor vehicles, mobile phones and air-conditioners as retaliations against the invocation of safeguard against three farm products. The other was that import trends of towels were slowing. While towel imports grew by 16.5 per cent in 1999 and 15.4 per cent in 2000, imports rose by 8.5 per cent for a year from September 2000 to August 2001.[21] However, these reasons were not convincing because there was no need to consider the most recent increase, and the overall import ratio of domestic consumption steadily rose after the petition.

The decision to postpone the final judgement derived from METI's strategic calculations responding to rapidly changing environments surrounding Japanese industries. METI officials considered reactions to the towel problems from overall trade relation with China in the near future. While some bureaucrats asserted that it was unwise to take safeguard measures in a rather small sector like towels, and the measures should be kept for more technology-intensive products such as consumer electronic and computer-related goods, others argued that the invocation of a safeguard measure in the towel sector is necessary in preparation for possible future disputes in other sectors.[22]

These considerations were sustained by METI's rising interest in the rapid growth of the Chinese economy. For instance, in Chapter 1 of the 2001 *White Paper on International Trade*, METI examined the advent of the mega-competition age in East Asia (METI 2001a: 3–38). More than one-third of the chapter was allocated to the analysis of the Chinese economy. It admits that China is rapidly improving international competitiveness in the relatively technology-intensive sectors including consumer electronics and computers as well as in the labour-intensive sectors such as textiles (METI 2001a: 16–17, 31–2). A paper presented at the New Growth Policy Committee under the Industrial Structure Council referred to threats of the emerging Chinese economy more directly. In the paper, METI raises 'responses to the emergence of China' and 'the strength of protecting intellectual property rights' among five issues for establishing a desirable international division of labour with Asian countries (METI 2001b: 50).

To summarise, enhanced corporate activities of textile producers created diverse interest between internationalised firms and purely domestic ones. Opposition activities from the former impeded the industry from proceeding with a filing action smoothly. The Japanese government adhered to showing structural reform programs before receiving trade protection and made the final decision taking into account the rising influence of the Chinese economy.

Safeguard politics in the agricultural sector

Increases in imports of vegetables and Japanese responses

Japan produced more than 90 per cent of vegetables for the domestic market until the 1980s. However, bad harvests in 1993 and 1998 induced spot imports of vegetables, and this opened the road to expanded vegetable imports. Imports of fresh vegetables increased from 657,000 tons in 1996 to 971,000 tons in 2000. China shared the large portion of imports, accounting for 36.3 per cent of total vegetable imports in 2000 (Ruan 2001: 33). In particular, China accounted for more than 90 per cent of imports for vegetables used for Japanese diets such as burdocks, welsh onions and *shiitake* mushrooms.

There were two main factors behind the expansion of vegetable imports from China. The first were the changes in Chinese policy. In China, the income gap between urban industrial workers and rural farmers expanded after the mid-1990s. The Chinese government regarded a shift from crop growing to the production of high-priced vegetables as a curial way of increasing jobs and incomes in rural areas where the WTO accession would be likely to have serious unfavourable impacts. The local governments provided vegetable producers with incentives such as tax reductions and subsidies to frozen and processing facilities. With the support of the governments, the production and export of vegetables expanded after the mid-1990s in China. Vegetable production increased from 260 million tons in 1995 to 440 million tons in 2000 at an average annual growth rate of 11.3 per cent (Ruan 2001: 36). The export volume of vegetables also expanded from 1.60 million tons in 1995 to 2.48 million tons in 2000. In 2000, Japan accounted for 39.3 per cent of total vegetable exports in terms of volume and 60.6 per cent in terms of value.[23]

The second was the role played by Japanese firms such as trading houses, seed companies and food distributors in increasing imports of vegetables from China. The trading houses engaged in development importing in order to utilise extensive agricultural land scale and cheap labour costs in China. They dispatched experts to China to improve quality throughout the production and distribution processes, and encouraged Chinese farmers to use Japanese spores, seeds and cultivation methods. The seed companies increased sales of vegetable seeds that met Japanese tastes in China. The export of seeds to China expanded by 144 per cent from 85 tons to 207 tons between 1996 and 2000 while overall exports increased by only 6 per cent in the same period.[24] The food distributors pushed for the development in China of farm products that could be imported on a stable price basis amid the intensification of price wars (Domon 2002: 159). These Japanese commitments successfully lessened the quality gap in a short time.

In late 2000, the Japanese government began to discuss measures to react to increases in imports of vegetables. In late November 2000, Yoichi Tani, the Minister of the Ministry of Agriculture, Forestry and Fisheries (MAFF), formally asked the Ministry of Finance (MOF) to begin an investigation of invoking safeguard measures on selected vegetables in response to rising low-priced imports from China and South Korea. The investigation was to assess the impact on growers, of imports of targeted products such as bulb onions, welsh onions, tomatoes, green peppers, *shiitake* mushrooms, and rushes for use in *tatami* mats.

In late December 2000, the Japanese government formally announced that it decided to study the advisability of invoking safeguards against imports of welsh onions, fresh *shiitake* mushrooms and *tatami* rushes. In the mean time, MAFF adopted measures to curb imports of vegetables from China. In late March 2001, the ministry tightened checks on imported vegetables at quarantine stations nation-wide, setting daily limits on the amount of fresh vegetables. This policy change virtually curbed imports of vegetables from China. The following month, MAFF decided to conduct administrative guidance to Japanese seed companies to restrain exports of vegetable seeds to China.[25]

In a cabinet meeting on 17 April, the Japanese government decided to impose provisional safeguard curbs on imports of three farm products: welsh onions, *shiitake* mushrooms and *tatami* rushes. For the first time, Japan took such a measure under the WTO's ordinary safeguard mechanism. The government adopted the tariff quota system. The current tariff rates on the three commodities would be applied up to a certain volume, beyond which an extra tariff rate would be added: for welsh onions (current rate 3 per cent), an extra tariff rate of 256 per cent would be added after 5383 tons, for *shiitake* mushrooms (current rate 4.3 per cent), an extra tariff rate of 266 per cent would be added after 8003 tons; and for *tatami* rushes (current rate 6 per cent), an extra tariff rate of 106 per cent would be added after 7949 tons (Table 3.2). In-quota volume was decided on the basis of average

Table 3.2   The quota tariff system for three products

Commodity	Quota within previous tariff (ton)	Extra tariff (yen/kg)	Extra tariff rate (%)	Previous tariff rate (%)
Welsh onions	5,383	225	256	3
Shiitake mushrooms	8,003	635	266	4.3
Tatami rushes	7,949	306	106	6

Source: Compiled from government reports by the author.

import volume in the three years from 1997 to 1999. The measure would be applied for 200 days until 8 November. Although the Japanese government asserted that the measures did not target China alone, around 90 per cent of the selected products were imported from the country.

During discussions leading to the decision on the invocation of safeguard measures, some officials in MOF and METI showed a glimpse of their hopes for avoiding the measures. For instance, Finance Minister Kiichi Miyazawa hoped to settle the issue through VERs by China on the grounds that Japan achieved economic growth through export expansion and it would not be advisable to reverse its basic stand by restraining imports. The adoption of the tariff quota system was a compromise between MAFF and MOF. The system, under which the current tariff rate was maintained by a certain import level, was expected to impede a sharp rise in prices, and thereby mitigate negative reactions from the Chinese government and consumers. MOF first asserted that the three years should include the year 2000, but MAFF pushed back this assertion.[26]

Advisory panels attached to MOF and METI were also cautious about invoking the safeguard measures. The Committee on Special Tariffs under the Council on Customs, Tariff, Foreign Exchange and Other Transactions failed to reach consensus on whether Japan should invoke import curbs, questioning whether damages to farmers reached a level that warrants emergency measures.[27] At the Subcommittee of Special Trade Measures under the Industrial Structure Council, most members were critical of the measures on the grounds that the measures were decided without structural reform plans by domestic producers.[28] The members also complained that the council became a place to just endorse the decision. In other words, moves to the decision were so swift that METI could not find time to refer the matter to the subcommittee.

The political process towards safeguard measures

The adoption of safeguard measures was led by political movements. The first appeal for safeguards was made in late August 2000 in Gunma prefecture. The Board of JA (Japan Agricultural Cooperatives) Sawa-Isezaki decided to ask administrative agencies to implement safeguard measures in order to arrest increases in imports of vegetables. Moves demanding safeguards spread across the country in the second half of the year. In 2000, local assemblies at 35 out of 47 prefectures and 1329 out of some 3200 municipal governments passed a resolution calling for the invocation of safeguards.[29]

The national associations of agricultural groups changed such moves in the local communities into political pressure in Tokyo. In September 2000, the Central Union of Agricultural Cooperatives of Japan (*Zenchu*) organised an emergency meeting demanding the implementation of safeguards. From late November through early December, *Zenchu* asked the Chief Cabinet Secretary and the Ministers of MAFF, MOF, and METI to introduce safeguard as soon as possible.[30] After the government formally decided to begin an investigation, *Zenchu* organised an emergency meeting on 15 and 27 March to demand the immediate implementation of safeguard measures and delivered its demand to the METI and MAFF.[31]

At first, MAFF was reluctant to take up safeguard issues. For instance, Aoi Ishihara, Director-General of the Economic Bureau in MAFF, stated at the LDP's Special Committee on Agriculture, Forestry and Fishery Trade held in early September that 'a main cause of price down of vegetables lay in the expansion of domestic production, and the current climate does not meet conditions for invoking safeguards' (Hosoya 2001: 25). MAFF's passive attitude towards safeguard measures stemmed from a bitter experience. In 1996, the ministry sought to invoke safeguard measures against increases in imports of garlic and ginger. However, during negotiations with MOF and METI, MAFF's intent was blocked by METI's assertion that Japan as a country drawing the most benefits from free trade should not adopt measures against free trade. Eventually, MAFF could not begin an investigation and draw VERs from China.

The actor that forced the reluctant MAFF to carry forward was the LDP. The LDP members who came from rural areas received adamant demands from their supporters to take measures against rising imports of vegetables. Some LDP's *norin zoku* (agricultural tribes) acted in response to such demands.[32] Toshikatsu Matsuoka, a representative *norin zoku*, presented a safeguard issue at the Research Commission on

Comprehensive Agriculture in September 2000, and demanded that officials concerned in MAFF, METI, MOF, and MOFA examine the possibility of activating safeguards (Takii 2001: 105).

Responding to pressure from the LDP, MAFF changed its stance. In late November 2000, the ministry decided to ask METI and MOF to conduct a survey to assess the impact of cheap vegetable imports on domestic producers. However, the real procedures were not so easy. MOF and METI asserted that data regarding the most recent trends of shipment, prices, and import volume were not prepared. MAFF, which was less eager to invoke safeguards, did not collect sufficient data showing damages to domestic producers. The ministry adopted a bold measure in this climate. MAFF Minister Yoichi Tani directly asked the Ministers of MOF and METI to conduct surveys on six commodities that met independent standards for beginning an investigation, skipping negotiations at the working level (Hosoya 2001: 27). The LDP sustained this move. On 22 and 24 November, the LDP held a meeting of the Research Commission on Comprehensive Agriculture where the LDP's *norin zoku* strongly demanded that the government begin to assess the impact of surging imports of farm products on the domestic market with a view to invoking safeguard measures immediately. In particular, they criticised MAFF bureaucrats for their lukewarm attitudes.[33]

The selection of items was also a problematic issue. *Tatami* rushes and *shiitake* mushrooms were selected without problem. However, targeting vegetables was difficult because their imports accounted for a small portion of the domestic market. However, the agricultural groups demanded safeguard against vegetable imports, and a situation that no vegetables would be selected was unacceptable. MAFF with the support of the LDP put welsh onions on the list (Hosoya 2001: 28). The import share of welsh onions was only 5 per cent of domestic consumption in 1999, and domestic production volume scarcely declined. But, MAFF selected welsh onions on the grounds that import volume expanded fourteen times between 1997 and 1999.

Between early March and mid-April 2001, the LDP's Research Commission on Comprehensive Agriculture conducted hearings from agricultural groups, importers, seed companies, consumer groups, and so on. Some *norin zoku* prodded senior executives of trading houses and seed companies to stop development importing, demanding that they think about the national interest.[34] At the same time, the LDP intensified direct pressure on the government. In late March, the major *norin zoku* criticised attitudes of the METI and MOF that sought to conduct sufficient investigations on the basis of the WTO rules, and asked directly the Ministers of MAFF, METI and MOF to invoke safeguard measures.[35] The three ministers reached a basic agreement to impose the provisional emergency curbs on imports of three farm products just after demand from the LDP.

There was a special factor behind the LDP's urgent and serious actions. The LDP deemed to defeat in the Upper House election in the summer of 2001 largely due to the unpopularity of Prime Minister Yoshiro Mori. The LDP speculated that the protection of farmers hard hit by import surges would help the party regain its popularity among Japanese farmers, thus boosting votes in the election. The LDP had a bitter experience. In the Upper House election in July 1989, the party experienced a devastating defeat, which led to its loss of a sole majority for the first time since the party's foundation.[36] One of the most serious causes of this setback was the dissatisfaction of farmers with the liberalisation of imports of oranges and beef in June 1988 and the LDP's ambivalent attitude towards the rice issue. The LDP was desperate to avoid the repetition of the nightmare at any costs.

The three commodities – welsh onions, *shiitake* mushrooms, *tatami* rushes – were produced in the region where major *norin zoku* had constituency. For instance, Yoshio Yatsu who became MAFF Minister in December 2000 came from Gunma prefecture where moves towards invoking safeguards began and which is a major production area of *shiitake* mushrooms. Toshikatsu Matsuoka who became senior vice-minister for agriculture had an electoral district in Kumamoto. Kumamoto produces more than 80 per cent of *tatami* rushes as well as being a major production centre of *shiitake* mushrooms.

Like the textile case, the Japan Chain Store Association criticised the government's decision to invoke safeguard measures.[37] However, the trading houses, the most likely opponents to the measures, did not implement overt opposition activities. When the government announced the invocation of provisional safeguard measures, the Chairman of the Japan Foreign Trade Council, the main association of the trading houses, showed an understanding towards the decision, commenting that although the government's decision was regrettable from the standpoint of free trade, the formal cabinet decision was reached after sufficient investigations and examinations of the stance of domestic producers and consumers' interest. The trading houses did not form political coalitions with other actors such as seed companies, super market chains, or *Nippon Keidanren* (Japan Business Federation), which had long demanded the reform of the agricultural sector (Yoshimatsu 1998).

The actions of the trading houses can be explained by two factors. First, the trading houses had transactions with domestic farmers and agricultural cooperatives. They hoped to avoid clarifying a confrontational stance on the sensitive safeguard issues in which the agricultural group had vital interest. This action is consonant with the argument that groups with a seemingly great stake in liberalisation are reluctant to embrace reforms that undermine the institutional advantages resulting from close long-term relations with other business partners (Vogel 2001). Second, basic policies on agriculture have been determined within the sub-government formed by MAFF, the agricultural group and the LDP's *norin zoku*.[38] It is extremely difficult for actors outside this sub-government to affect the policy-making process. This makes a contrast with the textile case where producers within the industry opposed to the adoption of safeguard measures.

The expanded imports of farm products from China occurred as a consequence of intensified economic linkages between Japan and China. Chinese farmers produced vegetables that met the Japanese tastes in a short time with the help of Japanese business. Japanese agriculture has absolute disadvantages in terms of deteriorating productivity, a lack of successors and the problem of ageing farmers. Such a sector inevitably faces intensive import pressure given the existence of neighbouring countries with vast land and cheaper labour mixed with rapid improvement in technology and transport measures. In fact, vegetables other than the three commodities, such as broccolis and green peppers, were rapidly grown in South Korea as well as in China.

Given close economic linkages with neighbouring countries and intensified commitments of Japanese business to the regional economies, the Japanese government should have examined the import problems from the viewpoint of overall structural reforms caused by increased economic interdependence with East Asian countries. However, MAFF's considerations to the increasing changes in regional environments were weak, giving in to pressure from the agricultural groups and their political supporters demanding the protection of myopic interests.

Chinese responses to the safeguard measures

Immediately after the Japanese decision on slapping the emergency import curbs, the Chinese government took retaliatory actions. In late April 2001, the Chinese government tightened quarantine inspections on Japanese imports packed in wooden crates, which disrupted the supply of some machinery parts from Japan to China.

The Chinese government criticised Japan's decision as targeting items mostly imported from China, and the proof of causation between import increase and damages to domestic producers was insufficient (Hattori 2001: 36). In addition, the Chinese government considered that trade tension over farm products was a kind of dispute among the Japanese: between Japanese domestic producers and Japanese companies that asked the Chinese to produce vegetables for Japanese consumers. The three commodities targeted in the safeguard measures were not originally raised in China. Japanese trading houses and seed companies brought seeds and technology to China with an eye to exporting back to Japan.

Accordingly, the Chinese government repeatedly proposed that the friction should be settled through talks at the private sector level. For instance, in April 2001 Toshikatsu Matsuoka, senior vice-minister for agriculture, had negotiations with his counterpart Long Yongtu, Vice-Minister of the Ministry of Foreign Trade and Economic Cooperation. Long proposed that guidelines between private actors, not voluntary restraints between the states, should be considered.[39] The recognition of the Chinese government clearly showed that trade friction between China and Japan should not be considered in the framework of state versus state.

The Japanese government rejected the Chinese government's proposal on the grounds that exports would not decrease without governmental commitments. There was a bitter experience for Japan. In 1996, a trade dispute over imports of ginger and garlic from China was settled by a promise that Chinese exporters would not increase exports. But, this promise was not kept and exports expanded. Japan's demand for governmental commitments to secure export restraints reminds us of US–Japan trade negotiations. In semiconductor and automobile disputes, the US government demanded governmental commitments to secure the expansion of purchases of US products by Japanese firms. The Japanese government resisted the demand on the grounds that the government would not manage private activities. The Japanese government made a similar demand on China when it stood in a defensive position.

The Japanese government intended to draw VERs from China. Before the government decided on the imposition of import curbs in April 2001, it repeatedly asked China to restrain voluntarily exports of farm products at bilateral talks. Since Beijing had accepted voluntary restraints in the textile cases, Tokyo naturally expected a similar response. However, the Chinese government was reluctant to accept VERs on the grounds that they were prohibited by the WTO rules.

The Japanese government also miscalculated the possibility of China's retaliatory actions. On 22 June, China levied a 100 per cent special customs duty on imports of Japanese motor vehicles, mobile phones and air-conditioners. Apparently, China targeted the most symbolic and internationally competitive items exported from Japan.[40] Tokyo should have expected retaliation from China because Beijing indicated that it would take retaliatory steps if Japan invoked safeguard measures. In fact, the Chinese government took a retaliatory action in trade disputes with South Korea. When South Korea invoked full safeguard measures against imports of garlic in June 2000, the Chinese government imposed punitive tariffs on imports of mobile phones and polyethylene. While import value of garlic was only US$15 million, import value of retaliatory products amounted to US$500 million (Mikamo 2001: 32). The Korean government immediately retracted the measures.

Interestingly, unlike trade friction with South Korea, the Chinese government took retaliatory actions when Japan adopted provisional, not full measures. This difference had something to do with the form of imports. In trade friction with South Korea, Chinese farmers were engaged in exports of garlic. The targeted products in friction with Japan were heavily managed by the Japanese. From the Chinese perspective, Japan's decision on safeguards was selfish because China never forced farm products on Japan in the first place and it was the Japanese who sowed the seed of trouble. This difference motivated the Chinese government to adopt a stricter policy towards Japan (Hattori 2001: 35).

The farm trade dispute settled on 21 December 2001, the deadline when Japan could have moved to impose full measures. Both the governments reached agreements that the Japanese side would not impose safeguards on Chinese agricultural goods while the Chinese side would scrap punitive tariffs on Japanese industrial products. They also agreed to set up a trade consultation panel under which the governments and private sector groups would negotiate proper trade levels of the three farm products.

In summary, Japanese businesses were deeply involved in imports of Chinese farm products but this fact did not disturb the adoption of safeguard measures. The trading houses and seed companies did not undertake overt opposition activities. The government invoked safeguard curbs responding quickly to demand from the agricultural group and political circles. This quick response meant that the government paid little attention to the inevitable integration of the Japanese market with Asia.

Conclusion

The central question of this chapter was how globalisation has influenced a state's trade policy and politics by changing the demand and supply side variables determining trade policy. In order to address this question, two hypotheses were presented regarding Japan–China trade friction over safeguards: the state is more inclined to formulate trade policy by taking into account the evolving environments surrounding the sectors concerned, and the division of policy preferences among societal actors is accelerated due to globalised corporate activities.

The two case studies showed variations in the development of safeguard policy in the textile and agricultural sectors under similar import pressure. The Japanese government imposed strict conditions for activating textile safeguards in order to avoid import restrictions, and gradually deregulated them responding to demands from textile circles. Even after towel producers petitioned a file, the government maintained a cautious stance, stressing the need for structural reform. In contrast, the government quickly reacted to a petition for activating safeguards in the agricultural case. The government invoked emergency import curbs within half a year after an import surge became a serious problem although there were criticisms of its urgency even at the government's councils.

Difference in the government's response between the two cases derived from two factors. The first was relevant to the degree of political support. In both cases, political commitments were key to realising actual safeguard petitions. However, the degree of commitments from politicians was different. There were strong supporters in the ruling party in the agriculture sector. The LDP's *norin zoku* took the lead in pressuring the government to adopt the safeguard measures. The textile industry did not have influential and solid supporters in political circles although it could draw ad hoc support from the political parties.

The second was difference in preferences of ministries concerned. METI, which had jurisdiction over industrial sectors, dealt with trade issues from a broader perspective. The ministry considered how to locate Japanese industry in the rapidly evolving Asian economy. Given the rising influence of Chinese industry in Asia including Japan, METI made the final decision on safeguard issues with due consideration to further trade tensions with China. MAFF paid little attention to the influence of decision on safeguards on Japan's overall relations with China and the integration of Japanese agriculture with the Asian economies. MAFF's approach to agricultural trade issues was quite similar to its approach to domestic issues. The ministry protected the interest of farmers responding to pressure from agricultural groups and the LDP's *norin zoku* in rice price issues and others (Mulgan 2000a). The same approach was repeated in this case. Thus, this study did not show that the Japanese state as a whole had transformative capacities to consider trade policy by taking into account the rapidly evolving Asian economies. Domestic politics such as policy networks, policy legacies and the nature of policy-making had a crucial influence on the capabilities of the state agencies to respond to demand for safeguard protection.

Cleavages in policy preferences and political actions among societal actors were also seen in the two cases. In both cases, the Japanese were deeply involved in the development and imports of products that were targeted in the safeguard files. In the textile case, producers within the textile industry were major actors engaging in operations in China. Strong opposition from these producers impeded a petition itself or helped create public opinions against import restrictions. Importantly, the degree of overseas operations had much to do with commitments to import restriction. The knitting sector whose firms were deeply involved in operations in China could not petition a file itself, while the towel sector, some portion of which undertook businesses in China, could lodge a petition but faced adamant opposition from the internationally oriented firms.

In the agricultural case, trading houses and seed companies were the main actors in the development and import operations. The trading houses did not implement overt opposition activities. This stance derived largely from their calculation of interests in maintaining sound relations with the agricultural groups. Thus, enhanced economic activities created divided preferences for trade policy, but these preferences were not straightforwardly transformed into political actions. We need to elucidate international and domestic linkages that the societal actors have developed.

It is useful to explore some implications of the findings in the case studies for broader theoretical perspectives. First, the study showed limitations of the state-based frameworks of trade friction. The states were receivers of appeals from industries suffering from import surges and were the initiators of import curbs. The friction was settled by the state's decision or through bilateral negotiations between the states. However, enhanced corporate activities had increasing bearings on the development and solution of trade friction. In the textile case, some producers asserted that since trade friction occurred among the

Japanese, the Japanese government should implement industry policy, not trade policy. The Chinese government also regarded agricultural trade friction as battles between the Japanese, and proposed settlement by coordination at the private sector level, not by negotiations at the state level. Thus, the relative importance of non-state actors increased in resolving trade friction in the era of globalisation, which suggests the limitations of analysis focusing on inter-state relations alone.

Second, China–Japan trade friction was dealt with on the basis of the WTO rules. Indeed, China's retaliatory actions ran counter to the WTO rules because the WTO does not allow retaliation against provisional actions, and the Japanese government charged China from this viewpoint. However, the Chinese government, as a whole, proceeded with its responses to the safeguard measures on the basis of the WTO rules. The government did not accept Japan's proposals of VERs on the grounds that they were prohibited by the WTO rules. The government also accused Japan's imposition of safeguard measures on the grounds that it did not meet the WTO rules to show causation between import increases and damages to domestic producers. Thus, the harmonisation with international norms of the multilateral trading system constituted a main code of conduct for China even before its formal entry into the WTO.

4

Japan and the Asian Financial Crisis: The Developmental Initiatives

The Asian financial and economic crisis had a great influence on development policies for East Asian countries and the development philosophy of the international community. The East Asian countries, whose economic growth was admired as the East Asian 'miracle', suddenly plunged into unprecedented economic turmoil. Furthermore, their economic management was accused of having much to do with the crisis. The major aspects of the developmental state, which was pioneered by Japan and was emulated by other East Asian countries, were regarded as the causes of the crisis. While close public–private collaboration provided the bases of crony capitalism and endemic corruption, the government-initiated export-oriented industrialisation was inherently fragile. It is argued that the Asian financial crisis marked 'the end of the Asian developmental state' (Pang 2000).

The Asian financial crisis had significant implications for Japan's commercial policy towards East Asia. The Japanese government, acknowledging the negative impact of the crisis on the Japanese economy and Japanese firms, launched successive measures partly responding to requests from the crisis-stricken countries and partly with its own decision. While the government provided the huge amount of financial assistance to rescue countries hard hit by the crisis, it attempted to create frameworks to block the recurrence of the currency crisis in the region.

A crucial issue concerning Japan's responses to the Asian financial crisis is how the Japanese government committed itself to the developmental state concept during and after the crisis. Indeed, the government followed the International Monetary Fund (IMF) led structural adjustment programs applied to the crisis-hit countries. Yet, the government had paid particular attention to industrial development in major East

Asian countries after the late 1980s, making various proposals to improve the bases of manufacturing industries in these countries (Hatch and Yamamura 1996: ch. 8; Doner 1997). In addition, fragile industrial bases constituted a cause of the crisis in several countries. Accordingly, Japanese government officials might have different ideas about the restructuring of the crisis-hit economies.

This chapter explores Japan's commitments to the developmental state approach after the Asian financial and economic crisis. It argues that the Japanese government maintained and partially intensified the developmental state approach in its cooperation with industrial restructuring programs in major East Asian countries after the crisis. Japanese government officials considered that the developmental state approach was useful for rehabilitating the growth model in East Asia through the upgrading of the real sector.

I will examine this argument from two dimensions. First, I explore changes in policies and institutions regarding industrial cooperation conducted by the Ministry of Economy, Trade and Industry (METI). Second, I delve into Japan's industrial cooperation policies towards Thailand. Before undertaking these tasks, the chapter begins with a review of the literature regarding the developmental state concept and its relations with Japan's external cooperation.

The developmental state concept, Asian crisis, and Japan

The main theoretical perspective examined in this study is the developmental state. The basic assertion of the developmental state paradigm is that the states play the central role in guiding economic development, leading, not following, the market. The concept of the developmental state became influential in explaining economic development in Japan, South Korea and other East Asian countries. The neoclassical orthodoxy accounts for the rapid and successful development of major East Asian countries as a result of market-driven, export-led industrialisation coupled with cheap labour, realistic exchange rates and minimal government interference. In contrast, the developmental state interpretation stresses particular and decisive roles of the states in creating efficient and competitive industrial structure that would not have arisen merely following market signals (Johnson 1982; Amsden 1989; Wade 1990).

The developmental states have several essential characteristics. First, the states have relatively autonomous power to decide on their own policy objectives and pursue them, resisting pressure from societal groups. The efficient and coherent policies adopted in the developmental states are sustained by highly talented and disciplined elite bureaucrats. These bureaucrats, being motivated to pursue export-led economic development, are less prone to the problems of inefficiency and incompetence (Johnson 1987: 152; Wade 1990: 217–24). Second, the states select particular industries as strategic sectors and foster them with a wide range of industrial policies. While the states control tariff and non-tariff barriers and limit foreign direct and portfolio investments, they encourage the private sector to allocate credit to the strategic sectors. Third, despite the autonomous character, the developmental states are deeply embedded in a society (Evans 1995; Weiss and Hobson 1995; Moon and Prasad 1998). In particular, the states work closely with sectors and trade associations to promote rapid industrialisation. The intimate relationship facilitates information sharing for economic management and sectoral development, and guides capital channelling into favoured industries. The states and business also set up institutional arrangements represented by advisory councils in order to dampen the likelihood of government failure (World Bank 1993).

After the Asian currency and financial crisis occurred, the developmental state became a source of criticisms among economists, public officials and other commentators. The critics argue that various aspects of state-led developmentalism were responsible for the onset of the Asian financial crisis. In general, close government–business partnership beneath the developmental state was accused of the hotbed of moral hazard, favouritism, corruption and crony capitalism, which constituted the basic causes of the crisis (Arogyaswamy 1998; Moon 1999; Moon and Rhyu 2000). More specifically, the bank-centred fund funnel approach and the imprudent banking system, which major East Asian countries borrowed from Japan, were considered as the main causes of the crisis (Lincoln 1997; Alexander 1998). Other observers hold that the export-oriented development model was inherently fragile and lacking in sustainability because the East Asian countries had to rely on the United States as the market of last resort for their manufactured goods (Bevacqua 1998; Wolf 1998).

Accusation was also directed at Japan's attitudes towards the state-initiated developmentalism. Some critics argue that Japan did not defend effectively its own model of the developmental state after the Asian crisis occurred (Hughes 2000: 220–1). Japan failed to show East Asian countries how to restore their growth routes on the basis of the developmental state paradigm, just lending credence to IMF-led neoliberal rescue packages. In July 1997, Thai Finance Minister Tarrin Nimmanahaeminda sounded out the possibility of arranging a rescue package outside of an IMF accord, but the Japanese financial authorities only encouraged him to seek an agreement with the fund (Sakakibara 2000: 176–7). Moreover, Japan dampened the validity of the developmental state. The numerous corruption scandals in the late 1990s demonstrated that mutually beneficial relationships between public officials and private business became entrenched over time.

The central interest of this chapter is to reconsider Japan's commitments to sustaining the validity of its own development style after the Asian financial crisis. In the 1990s, the Japanese government sought to revitalise its depressed economy by adopting neoliberal reform programs, departing from the developmental state paradigm. It has pursued successive deregulation and privatisation measures, reducing the scope of government intervention in the market and creating more transparent business–government relations. This was because undue state intervention and tight relationship with the government impeded the private sector from displaying vigour for new innovation and breakthrough ideas in the matured economies like Japan.

The adoption of neoliberal reform in the domestic market did not necessarily mean that the Japanese government considers the developmental state approach useless. On the contrary, the Japanese government with confidence in its state-guided development style intensified efforts to legitimate its development philosophy after the late 1980s. The Ministry of Finance encouraged the World Bank to conduct the first comprehensive study of economic development in East Asia by offering more than US$2 million funds for the study (Wade 1996). Although the resultant report, *East Asian Miracle*, did not find direct correlation between economic growth in East Asia and industrial policy, it became the first comprehensive study of state intervention in economic development of major East Asian countries (World Bank 1993). Japanese aid institutions strengthened an independent development approach, which was different from universally oriented, strict macroeconomic adjustment programs favoured by international financial institutions such as the World Bank and IMF. In October 1991, the Overseas Economic Cooperation Fund, the most representative aid institution in Japan, issued a paper entitled 'Issues related to the World Bank's approach to structural adjustment: proposal from a major partner' (*OECF Occasional Paper* 1). This paper was sceptical about the World Bank's universal, efficiency-oriented neoclassical approach to development and advocated positive involvement in investment and industrial development (Wan 2001: 147).

Some East Asian countries deliberately introduced the Japanese development model. For instance, the Korean government introduced Japanese development styles such as the protection and encouragement of particular export-oriented sectors, and the use of industrial policies such as policy finance, subsidies and tax incentives (Castley 1996). At the same time, the Japanese government intentionally assisted the East Asian countries to learn and adopt state-guided economic development. The first example of such efforts was the new Asian Industries Development (AID) plan. The plan, announced in 1987, aimed to promote industrial development through government programs such as a comprehensive master plan and the guidelines for sector-specific development. Unlike the previous aid programs directed towards development in economic infrastructure and humanitarian objectives, the new AID plan sought to link aid directly to the fostering of export industries by offering Japan's expertise and know-how in industrial development (Arase 1995: 129–34; Hatch and Yamamura 1996: 138–9).

In the 1990s, the Japanese government paid attention to the transitional economies as cases for showing the validity of its development philosophy. METI translated the voluminous history of industrial policy into the Chinese language (METI 1992: 144). The objective of this translation was to transfer basic ideas about industrial policy-based development to China. In 1995, the Vietnamese government asked its Japanese counterpart to design a 1996–2000 five-year development program (Terry 1996). The program, which covered industrial development, investment and financial and monetary policies, was approved in June 1996.

As for industrial development in the Association of Southeast Asian Nations (ASEAN) countries, the Japanese regarded fragile industrial bases, weak supporting industries in particular, as impeding the upgrading of industrialisation.[1] Japanese officials considered that such impediments could be overcome by state initiatives and industrial policy. This stance was explicitly shown in a report entitled *Prospects and Challenges for the Upgrading of Industries in the ASEAN Region* with the subtitle of *Recommendation of Industrial Policy*. The report, issued in 1993, encouraged the ASEAN countries to introduce industrial policy-based development strategies for supporting industries (METI 1994a). The Minister of METI announced the report at a meeting with ASEAN Economic Ministers.

Indeed, heavy reliance on imported parts and intermediate goods due to weak industrial bases and the resultant trade deficits were beneath the financial crisis in East Asia. For instance, trade deficits of East Asian countries against Japan expanded in machinery sectors. Between 1985 and 1995, trade deficits of the NIEs and ASEAN4 – Thailand, Indonesia, Malaysia and the Philippines – in total machinery grew from US$12.0 billion to US$59.8 billion, and US$4.6 billion to US$31.9 billion, respectively. The expansion was particularly salient in the parts segment. In the same period, the trade deficits in electronic parts of the NIEs jumped from US$1.3 billion to US$13.8 billion, while those of ASEAN4 grew from US$0.08 billion to US$4.6 billion (Takayasu *et al*. 1997: 27).

Japanese officials were likely to have incentives to continue or strengthen the developmental state approach that sustained steady industrial transformation in Japan's economic growth era in its cooperation with industrial upgrading in East Asia. The adoption of this approach was also desirable for Japan because it would make original contributions to East Asia independent of the IMF's structural adjustment programs, and because it would serve the interests of Japanese firms that penetrated the real sector in major East Asian countries.

As explained above, the developmental state has several unique characteristics. Given that the key objective of this chapter is to assess Japan's commitments to industrial upgrading in East Asia after the Asian financial crisis, it highlights the characteristics of the developmental state, which are directly relevant to industrial transformation. First, the states play decisive roles in promoting industrial restructuring and industrial upgrading. The states guide the private sector to create competent industrial sectors, particularly export-oriented sectors.

Second, the states utilise industrial policy designed to upgrade the competitiveness of the targeted sectors. In East Asian countries, supporting industries and small- and medium-sized enterprises (SMEs) have particular developmental importance. Industrial success in Japan was sustained by the development of machinery sectors and the formation of the subcontracting system between big companies and SMEs. In other East Asian countries, industrialisation and export expansion were also reliant on machinery sectors whose development presupposed the existence of capable SMEs. As already explained, the expansion of machinery production led to increased trade deficits due to weak supporting industries and underdeveloped SMEs in major East Asian countries. Accordingly, the East Asian states have particular incentives to implement policies for fostering competent SMEs. Besides, state support tends to be crucial for SME promotion because SMEs often possess smaller capitals, less technological capabilities and management know-how. The financial and technical assistances from the states are often indispensable for creating competent SMEs.

Third, the states develop quasi-public institutions and trade associations by utilising a close relationship with the business sector. These institutions and associations play a role in bridging state agencies and individual firms, and facilitate information sharing and the recognition of policy objectives and policy efficiency. In other words, they function as joint promoters of industrial policy.

In this chapter, I seek to investigate how the Japanese government has maintained and transferred core elements of the developmental state approach in its efforts to assist industrial restructuring in East Asia. In order to accomplish this research objective, it is necessary to capture nuanced changes in economic diplomacy by exploring detailed policy development. I investigate such changes from two dimensions: domestic and external. First, I examine the evolution of domestic institutional systems and policies regarding Japan's economic diplomacy towards East Asia. I then explore detailed external economic policies and relations by highlighting Japan's industrial cooperation with Thailand as a case study.

Thailand was selected for two reasons. First, the Japanese government has maintained a close relationship with its Thai counterpart in promoting Thai industries and developing programs for Indochina. As explained later, the Japanese government has assisted industrial reform in Thailand by sending government officials and experts since the early 1990s. Moreover, the Japanese and Thai government jointly set up a forum to sustain economic development of countries in Indochina.[2] Second, Thailand is the country that triggered the Asian currency crisis in July 1997, and fragile industrial bases including weak SMEs constituted a background of the crisis. The development of competent SMEs became a main policy objective for the Thai authority after the crisis. Accordingly, the country is a suitable case for examining the influence of the developmental state concept on its industrial restructuring policy.

Japan's industrial cooperation after the late 1990s

The sound development of the economic relationship with East Asian countries has been a pillar of Japan's post-war foreign economic diplomacy. From this standpoint, METI has implemented various commercial policies including official development assistance (ODA), trade insurance and investment finance. In the late 1990s, there were subtle changes in the basic stance of METI's commercial policy. In June 1999, the Industrial Structure Council, an advisory body to the Minister of

METI, unveiled a report entitled *Challenges and Prospects for Economic and Industrial Policy in the 21st Century*. This report, issued as the fundamental policy guidelines for the newly named METI, encouraged the Japanese government to assist supply-side restructuring reforms in East Asian countries and the harmonisation of the intra-regional systems.

The evolved policy stance was reflected on *The Priorities in Commercial and Industrial Policy*. This annual report compiles the main items of METI's policies for a year showing the budget for each policy. The 2000 report, released in August 1999, showed a clear-cut vision of new policies towards Asia under the section of 'The development of strategic commercial policy' with the budget of 10.8 billion yen increasing from 6.6 billion yen in the previous year. In this section, METI stressed support for supply-side structural reforms in the Asian region. It then stated that Japan should foster a common awareness of needs for structural reforms and create environments in which countries cooperate together on the development of institutional infrastructure for industrial activities (METI 1999b: 39–40).

The stress on supply-side structural reforms in Asia was aimed at making original contributions to recovery from the Asian financial crisis, independent of the IMF's adjustment macro-policy that emphasised demand control for avoiding inflation and budget deficits. It also aimed to assist the recovery of the real sector through the improved competitiveness of the manufacturing sectors, independent of the IMF's programs designed to promote neoliberal reforms in the financial sector.

After the Asian financial crisis occurred, there were changes in institutions that undertook Japan's industrial cooperation towards East Asia. The most important was the evolution of institutions linking METI and the ASEAN economic authorities. In 1992, METI and its ASEAN counterparts institutionalised the ASEAN Economic Ministers and the Minister of Economy, Trade and Industry of Japan (AEM–METI) meeting. The meetings have functioned as a basic forum to discuss issues concerning trade, investment and economic development, proposing detailed activities for industrial cooperation. At the 1994 AEM–METI meeting, the Economic Ministers agreed to set up the Working Group on Economic Cooperation in Cambodia, Laos and Myanmar (CLM-WG). The group aimed to discuss industrial cooperation, development in human resources and institutional reforms, which were indispensable for economic growth in Cambodia, Laos and Myanmar.

In December 1997, the Minister of METI and the ASEAN Economic Ministers agreed to transform the CLM-WG into the AEM–METI Economic and Industrial Cooperation Committee (AMEICC). The three objectives of the committee were to enhance industrial cooperation, improve competitiveness of industries in ASEAN and provide development cooperation assistance to the new ASEAN members. The formation of the AMEICC derived from METI's strategic intent. The ASEAN Economic Ministers developed official economic forums with their counterparts of Australia, New Zealand and the European countries.[3] The AEM–METI, like other institutions, has functioned as a *trade* ministers' forum. However, METI hoped to have an *industrial* ministers' forum through which Japan would transfer basic ideas about industrial development and concrete measures for it to the developed ASEAN members in addition to the new developing members. METI created such a forum (the AMEICC) by transforming the CLM-WG and raising its organisational status from the ministries' director-general level to the ministerial level.[4] Reflecting this orientation, the activities of the committee were directed towards industrial development in the ASEAN countries, such as the development of common infrastructure, improvement in business environments, and industrial and trade financing. The committee paid little attention to trade and investment liberalisation, which was often the main objective of a conventional trade forum.

However, the formation of the AMEICC did not necessarily progress smoothly. Although METI intended to create an industrial ministers' forum before the Asian financial crisis, the ASEAN members were passive about this idea. Yet, the Asian financial crisis made the development of industrial restructuring a critical policy agenda for the ASEAN countries. This was because fragile industrial bases and resultant trade deficits were beneath the crisis. When METI proposed the transformation of the CLM-WG at an AEM–METI meeting in October 1997, some ASEAN members were still sceptical about this proposal. Since the CLM-WG was initiated by joint leadership between Japan and Thailand, Malaysia was apprehensive that the new institution would be used for enhancing the interest of Thai industries. Singapore was cautious about the AMEICC in light of the perception that discussions about industries at official meetings would disturb free competition. Eventually, the then Japanese Prime Minister Ryutaro Hashimoto proposed the establishment of the AMEICC at a Japan–ASEAN summit meeting in December 1997, and drew agreements from the ASEAN leaders (Otsuji 2001: 334). The fact that METI used a summit meeting for establishing the AMEICC demonstrates its vital interest in the committee and industrial cooperation with the ASEAN countries through it.

Under the CLM-WG, two kinds of expert groups were organised. One was sector-specific groups in seven sectors: automobiles, consumer electronics, tourism, financial systems, transportation, telecommunications, and textile and garments. The other was policy-oriented groups in particular areas: human resources development, the development of mineral resources, accounting systems, the development of infrastructure, and so on. An organisational feature of the groups was that they were formed jointly by government officials and private representatives. In this sense, these were advisory councils which were common apparatuses in policy-making in Japan. The sector-specific expert groups have played a catalytic role in integrating the interests of the relevant sectors in ASEAN and Japan, according to the degree of the development of each sector. The automobile expert group has analysed the state and problems of the automobile industries in ASEAN, and suggested and implemented activities to resolve the problems. For instance, the group issued a report proposing that the automobile industry in each country should be involved in activities of the ASEAN Automobile Federation, and that the Japan Automobile Manufacturers Association (JAMA) should assist such activities by setting up a representative office in Southeast Asia.[5] In the consumer electronics sector, the expert group has assisted the new ASEAN members to organise trade associations in the electronics sector, and such an association was formed in Vietnam.

As the CLM-WG was restructured into the AMEICC, the expert groups were positioned under the AMEICC. After the Asian financial crisis, functions of expert groups strengthened. Several new expert groups were formed. While a group was formed in the chemical sector for discussing issues of oversupply based on the demand–supply perspectives in the region, a newly formed expert group on supporting industries, SMEs and rural industrialisation aimed to develop SMEs in supporting industries and to expand industrial cooperation through industrial networks. Moreover, the sector-specific expert groups in automobiles, consumer electronics and chemicals were encouraged to develop a set of market prospects in order to enhance confidence in investment. Thus, the expert groups deepened and broadened their activities after the crisis.

Changes in policy were also seen in METI-affiliated organisations. In 1996, the Japan External Trade Organisation (JETRO) began the Asian Industrial Network Program. This program has supported the promotion of industrial linkages between Japan and major East Asian countries through the dispatch of industrial specialists, the holding of seminars, and the development of databases regarding the provision and procurement of parts. Significantly, one of the main objectives of the program was to help local industries foster *gyokai* and vitalise *gyokai* activities.[6] For this objective, the JETRO invited key figures for developing *gyokai* to seminars and conferences, and sent Japanese experts with know-how and experiences in *gyokai* activities to Asia. Between 1996 and 2000, the JETRO organised six industrial exchange conferences targeting the electronics sector, and invited totally 64 representatives from the electronics industry in Southeast Asia to these conferences.[7]

The Japan Overseas Development Corporation (JODC), another METI-affiliated organisation, presents further examples of policy changes. The JODC, established in 1970, has implemented JODC Expert Service Abroad programs by using subsidies from METI's ODA budgets and contributions from the private sector. Between 1979 and 2000, the JODC dispatched 3874 experts to developing countries for technical training and guidance, and more than 90 per cent of total experts went to Asia (JODC 2001). Importantly, the JODC revised its expert dispatch programs in 1999. Previously, all the programs were directed towards assisting individual enterprises in developing countries to modernise and rationalise their business. Under the new program, the organisation began to dispatch experts to support efforts of trade associations, public institutions and their affiliates to restructure their industrial systems. While the recipients had to bear a quarter of total expenses in the previous programs, the JODC assumed all expenses in the new program. In 2000, the JODC began a consulting firm-type program, which aimed to send a consulting team to organisations such as trade associations, chambers of commerce and industry and state-owned enterprises in order to assist them to formulate economic and industrial restructuring plans.

The transformation of the programs reflects the recognition of the Japanese government that industrial restructuring should be sustained through coordination by trade associations and public institutions and their close linkages with government agencies. In Japan, industrial development has been sustained by close collaboration between trade associations in each industry and government agencies. METI strove to assist the development of such associations in the ASEAN countries in order to aggregate the interests of companies in each industrial sector and upgrade overall industrial bases.

The above changes in Japan's cooperation policies and institutions have two implications. First, METI has strengthened policies and institutions to promote industrial cooperation with Southeast Asia during and after the Asian financial crisis. The major target of cooperation was the supply-side structural reform. Second, METI has utilised apparatuses of the developmental state for promoting economic cooperation strategies. It strengthened business–government collaboration such as the expert groups, and highlighted public institutions and trade associations as intermediary bodies bridging the government and industrial sectors and the promoters of industrial policy.

Industrial restructuring in Thailand and Japan's commitments

Japan and industrialisation in Thailand before the crisis

Japan's bilateral commitments to industrial development in major East Asian countries date back to the new AID plan. As already explained, the new AID plan aimed to attain industrial development under the state-guided programs. The major East Asian countries including Thailand achieved impressive economic growth in the late 1980s, and the presence of the new AID plan was almost forgotten even among METI officials in the mid-1990s (Shiraishi 1997: 190–1). Yet, the plan provided original ideas about the necessity of and concrete measures for industrial transformation in major East Asian countries.

METI sponsored a comprehensive survey on major manufacturing industries in Thailand in 1987–90 based on the new AID plan. The three-volume survey report contained recommendations on improvement in the competitiveness of exporting industries such as toys, textiles/garment and furniture, and sector-specific industrial policies and institutions for this objective (JICA 1988, 1989, 1990). Then, METI began regular policy talks with the Thai Ministry of Industry (MOI). Based on the talks, METI sent specialists to various agencies including the Board of Investment (BOI) and the Department of Industrial Promotion (DIP) under the MOI. The start of policy talks and the dispatch of specialists had two implications. First, the beginning of policy talks had much to do with a departure from the request-based aid process in Japan's ODA policy. The Japanese government stressed recipient initiatives as a way of urging self-help of recipient countries. In the 1990s, this method was gradually replaced by policy talks as Japan became the world's largest aid sponsor (Takahashi 1998: 88–90). This change enabled the Japanese government to reflect its idea more directly on development policy in recipient countries. Second, policy talks aimed to transfer expertise and know-how for economic growth including policies and institutions for industrial development. This reflected a more confident projection of its own policies and institutional practices as well as Japan's emerging strategic vision independent of the United States (Doner 1997: 225).

The Japanese government strengthened its commitments to industrial transformation in Thailand. In 1993–94, the Japan International Cooperation Agency (JICA) conducted a survey on auto parts and electronic parts industries in Thailand, and compiled a report in May 1995 entitled *Study on Supporting Industries Development in the Kingdom of Thailand*. The report observed that the development of supporting industries would not be achieved through BOI incentives to foreign investment alone, and the fostering of local SMEs was crucial. From this viewpoint, the report made concrete proposals to restructure the DIP as a department in charge of SME promotion and to formulate a master plan for supporting industries (Unico International Corporation 1995). Although the Thai government implemented several measures designed to promote supporting industries such as the BOI Unit for Industrial Linkage Development (BUILD) programs, there was no comprehensive SME policy in Thailand. The recommendations aimed to enhance the capabilities of the DIP as a main policy-making body for SMEs, transferring service activities to relevant organisations. The Metalworking and Machinery Industries Development Institute was established in 1989 with grant aid from Japan. The main objective of the institute was to instruct enterprises in improving their production and management skills. Based on the 1995 JICA report, the institute was reorganised into the Bureau of Supporting Industry Development under the MOI in 1996. The bureau aimed to create competent supporting industries comprising broad local SMEs that sustained assembly industries (Suehiro 2000: 55).

In brief, even before the currency crisis, the Japanese government provided financial and technical assistance to industrial development in Thailand. In particular, Japanese METI and Thai MOI created institutional systems through which they conducted policy talks regarding the current state of major manufacturing industries in Thailand and the transfer of Japanese experiences in industrial development. The technocrats at the Thai MOI acknowledged the importance of the development of supporting industries comprising SMEs.

The industrial restructuring plan, *sathaban* and Japan

After the currency crisis occurred in Thailand in July 1997, the Japanese government reacted quickly to the crisis. Tokyo collaborated with the IMF in formulating a US$17.2 billion rescue package, becoming the single largest donor with a US$4 billion contribution. The Japanese government offered further assistance to Thailand at the bilateral level. In September 1997, the OECF announced a new package of ODA loans for Thailand, totalling 106 billion yen. Moreover, when Thai Prime Minister Chavalit Yongchaiyudh visited Tokyo in early October, his Japanese counterpart Ryutaro Hashimoto announced additional assistance measures: a US$8 billion package of trade insurance designed to encourage new Japanese investment in Thailand and a plan to send up to 1000 technical experts to sustain industrial restructuring efforts in the country. Hashimoto sent a decisive message that 'Japan will stand by Thailand during the time of need' (Ota 1998: 2).

In August 1997, the Thai MOI set up the National Industry Development Committee in order to discuss the problems of Thai industries and measures to improve their international competitiveness. The Industrial Restructuring Plan (IRP) was produced in the discussions. The cabinet approved the IRP in January 1998, and its action plan five months later. The IRP contained different characteristics from structural adjustment programs initiated by the IMF. The IMF programs aimed to establish neoliberal economic rules and institutions in the financial sector and corporate management. The IRP sought to improve productivity, product development and market development in the real sector. Under the IRP, the government selected thirteen sectors, most of which were export-oriented industries.[8] The government implemented programs such as the provision of low-interest loans, dispatch of experts, and assistance to human resources development and technical training. Thus, the IRP aimed to improve the competitiveness of Thai industries through industrial policies for the targeted sectors. The attempt to pick up winner industries meant a challenge for sector-specific policies which were prevalent in Japan and whose effectiveness was questioned in the 1993 World Bank *Miracle* report.

The detailed projects of the IRP were undertaken through the establishment of *sathaban*. *Sathaban* are normally translated into 'institutes' in English. However, they have broader functions and roles including the formulation of specific policies and the receipt of government subsidies. The utilisation of *sathaban* meant a new attempt for industrial development. In Thailand, consultation between the public and private sectors was seen at the upper level. The representative is the Joint Public and Private Sector Consultative Committee, which comprises the most senior officials and representatives of the three peak business federations (the Thai Chamber of Commerce, the Association of Thai Industries, and Thai Bankers Association). In the 1980s, the committee played a crucial role in drawing the government's support for promoting exports and reflecting business interests in public policy (Laothamatas 1992: 80–5; Muscat 1994: 196–7). However, consultation at the sectoral level did not develop in Thailand largely due to the lack of cohesion in industrial sectors and a shallow density of trade associations (Deyo and Doner 2001: 112).

Indeed, *sathaban* were not created in the IRP for the fist time. Several policy-oriented *sathaban* were founded in the mid-1990s.[9] However, the IRP sought to strengthen the function of *sathaban* and utilise them for sector-specific industrial policy. Between 1996 and 1998, six sector-specific *sathaban* were established in the fields of textiles, food processing, automobiles, electrical and electronics, cane and sugar, and iron and steel. Importantly, suggestion by Japanese officials motivated Thai officials to establish sector-specific *sathaban*. They encouraged the Thai government to adopt the advisory council system as a way of developing particular industrial sectors (Suehiro 2000: 50). A main characteristic of the advisory councils is the participation of government officials and private representatives. This organisational style draws close collaboration between the private and public sectors and facilitates information sharing and policy coordination.

The Thai Automobile Institute (TAI) and Electrical and Electronics Institute are two *sathaban* that are directly relevant to the development of supporting industries. These *sathaban*, established in September 1998, have launched various programs designed to enhance the competitiveness of the Thai assembly industries through the development of SMEs. For instance, the TAI has implemented five programs: the supporting industry development program; the 100 per cent localisation support program; the human resources development program; the certificate development program; and the testing and certification capability-building program. The Japanese government and business have been deeply involved in these programs. In the supporting industry development program, four JICA senior volunteers, eight JODC experts and ten JETRO experts engaged in technical guidance.[10] The JAMA has committed to selecting these engineers from auto and auto parts manufacturers. The team comprising three Thai engineers with each of Japanese experts visited individual parts suppliers for one week until such suppliers reach the level of international standards.[11] The 100 per cent localisation support program began in June 2000 as a joint project between the TAI and three Japanese automakers: Toyota, Isuzu and Honda. The program aimed to transfer the inspection of locally made parts and materials from Japan to Thailand, and thereby reduce lead-time for development and production costs.[12] The Japanese government and firms shared a common interest in developing

Thailand as a main production centre of auto-related products in Southeast Asia, and strove jointly to achieve this objective. The sector-specific *sathaban* accepted such efforts of close collaboration between the government and industrial sectors.

The SME development policy and Japan's involvement

One of the principal strategies in the IRP was the Program for Incubation and Strengthening of Small and Medium Supporting Industries 1998–2002. The program aimed to increase the international competitiveness of industries and the dispersion of industrial employment to local areas. In Thailand, the development of SMEs attracted little political attention. The DIP drafted laws to promote SMEs in the late 1980s, but the proposed legislation failed to gain support from parliament.[13] Until late 1998, there was no unified definition of SMEs.[14] However, SME development became a critical policy agenda both because of the worsened distress of SMEs resulting from the currency crisis and because of sudden interest in SMEs by political parties, both by the ruling parties (the Democratic Party and Chart Pattana Party) and by the opposition Thai Rak Thai Party (Regnier 2000: 89–90; Sevilla and Soonthornthada 2000: 12–13).

The Thai government sought to achieve SME promotion by asking the Japanese government to provide funds and know-how. When officials of the JETRO Bangkok visited Suwat Liptapallop, the Minister of Industry, in November 1998, Suwat stressed support for SMEs, revealing the basic guidelines such as the establishment of the SME Promotion Committee and SME Promotion Fund. He then asked the Japanese officials to provide cooperation in dispatching experts (Suehiro 2000: 58). Furthermore, when Japanese Minister of METI, Kaoru Yosano, visited Bangkok in the same month, Thai Prime Minister Chuan Leekpai and Finance Minister Tarrin Nimmanahaeminda requested Yosano to send a specialist who would help formulate the first comprehensive master plan for SMEs.

Yosano decided to dispatch a team headed by Shiro Mizutani, a former Director-General of the Consumer and Services Industries Bureau in METI. Indeed, Thailand was not the only country that METI sent a special mission to upgrade industrial bases in Southeast Asia. In 2000, it sponsored the dispatch of a team headed by Shujiro Urata, a Professor at Waseda University, to Indonesia. Urata became a policy adviser to the Coordinating Minister for Economy, Finance and Industry in order to assist foster local SMEs. In the case of Thailand, METI sent its own ex-senior bureaucrat.

Mizutani visited Thailand for around ten days every month from January to July 1999 as a high-level policy adviser to the Ministers of Industry and Finance. Mizutani and his team comprising young bureaucrats from METI, worked intensively towards formulating basic policy guidelines for SMEs. In July 1999, the Mizutani team published the Conceptual Master Plan for SME promotion. The seven-item plan outlined the role of SMEs, structural problems of SMEs in Thailand, solutions to the problems, and so on. The plan stressed the urgency of formulating SME policies in Thailand from two viewpoints: the formation of social safety networks linked to the agricultural sector, and the strength of international competitiveness of labour-intensive industries and supporting industries. The strength of international competitiveness aimed to return to growth trends in the real sector through export expansion. The plan then proposed five policies for strengthening SMEs: first, the introduction of the enterprise evaluation system; second, the strength of SME financing including a credit guarantee system, the restructuring of special financing institutions and an equity finance promotion system; third, the upgrading of technical and management capabilities; fourth, the fostering of human resources; and fifth, development of business infrastructure.

The Mizutani plan was incorporated into government policies in various forms. The Thai government implemented several proposals in the plan immediately after its announcement. In August 1999, the government unveiled the economic stimulus package totalling 106 billion baht. A pillar of the package was the strength of SME finance institutions designed to overcome the liquidity crunch problems of SMEs. The Small Industrial Finance Corporation (SIFC) raised the upper limit of fixed assets for eligible firms from 50 to 100 million baht and doubled the maximum loan amount from 25 to 50 million baht.[15] In addition, the Small Industry Credit Guarantee Corporation (SICGC) increased the upper limit of fixed assets for guarantee from 50 to 100 million baht and the maximum additional collateral from 10 to 20 billion baht.[16]

The Thai government had mapped out the SME Development Master Plan, which was approved in April 2000. The plan consisted of seven basic strategies such as the upgrading of the technical and management capabilities of SMEs, development in entrepreneurs and human resources of SMEs, and the strength of the financial support system for SMEs. According to the MOI, 80–90 per cent of the master plan was based on the Mizutani plan and the JICA's 1999 survey report (JBIC 2001: 35).

In January 2000, the SME Promotion Act came into effect. The law contained legal foundations for the National SME Promotion Committee, the SME Promotion Office and the SME Promotion Fund. The committee, chaired by the Prime Minister, was the primary decision-making body in charge of SME policy. The 22-member committee comprised the Ministers of Industry, Commerce, Agriculture and Finance as well as representatives from the private sector including SMEs. The SME Promotion Office was an independent agency in charge of formulating detailed SME promotion policies and measures. The office was expected to be an agency like the Small and Medium Enterprise Agency in Japan.

The Mizutani plan reflected the critical elements of the developmental state approach on Thai SME policies. The most controversial issue regarding the plan was the government's role in SME finance. In Thailand, there were specialised financial institutions such as the SIFC and SICGC that provided funds for SMEs. However, these were different from policy finance institutions because half of the stocks were held by the private sector and their funds depended on loans from overseas aid organisations, not by the government. The Thai Ministry of Finance considered that government intervention in the financial sector would invite moral hazard, and that the development of the financial system should be based on the market principles. However, the Japanese side persuaded the Thai finance authorities that loans and credit guarantee to SMEs would not be offered by the private sector alone and that opportunities for SME growth would be created by the government's efforts to develop infrastructure (Higashi 2001: 186). The Thai officials, acknowledging the importance of the role played by the government in SME finance, agreed to strengthen functions of SME finance institutions through re-capitalisation by the government. The Finance Ministry announced in the 1999 economic stimulus package that it would inject 2.5 billion baht into the SIFC in 1999 and an additional 5 billion baht in 2003.[17]

An eye-catcher of the plan was the introduction of the enterprise evaluation (*shindan*) system. According to the plan, the Bureau of Supporting Industry Development and Thai Productivity Institute together with the Technology Promotion Association of Japan began the first project in June 1999. Some 100 associates for SME management evaluators were trained and around 200 SMEs underwent business check-ups. Importantly, the enterprise evaluation system, which had functioned effectively in Japan for the past forty years, was different from the conventional management consulting structure. A management evaluator registered by the Minister of METI under the Small and Medium Enterprise Guidance Law examined an enterprise's management, finance and labour relations in light of the government's policies for SMEs.

The Mizutani plan also proposed the government-initiated programs for developing entrepreneurs and human resources of SMEs. In June 1999, the Thai government set up the Institute for SME Development, modelled on the Japan Institute for Small Business Management and Technology. The institute functions through networks between the DIP, Thammasat University, and local universities in provincial cities such as Chiang Mai, Khon Kaen, Suranaree and Songkhla. The primary objectives of the institute were to train SME owners and executives, exchange information among different business sectors, and provide opportunities for networking. The government hoped to promote the modernisation of SME management and raise transparency in their accounting systems.

The fundamental stance underlying the above policies was that the manipulation of resource allocations from a long-term perspective was necessary for SME promotion: otherwise undercapitalised, weak SMEs would not enhance their technological and management capabilities. The government was expected to play a particular and decisive role in this process. The importance of government intervention in SME promotion was clearly stated by Mizutani. Mizutani recalls that an underlying idea in discussing the responsibility of the government was that since the market surely fails, the role of the government is required for preventing such market failures (Mizutani 1999: 4).

The activities of the Mizutani team were intensively sustained by the Japanese government. The government extended a 3.5 billion yen loan for the SIFC in 1997 and a 12 billion yen loan for the Industrial Finance Corporation of Thailand in 1998. After the US$30 billion New Miyazawa Initiative was announced in October 1998, Thailand asked for US$2.25 billion for supporting SMEs, education, and so on.[18] Hiroshi Ota, the Japanese ambassador to Thailand, endorsed an idea that SMEs were the most appropriate sector to benefit from Japan's recovery program.[19] The JICA undertook a survey on SMEs in Thailand as a follow-up of a survey on Thai supporting industries in 1993–94 (Unico International Corporation 1999). This six-month survey was conducted in concert with Mizutani's activities.[20] The survey covered the impact of the currency crisis on SME management through interviews to 97 firms and questionnaires to 244 firms. The final report, entitled *Follow-up Study on Supporting Industries Development in the Kingdom of Thailand,* included valuable information about SMEs in Thailand and contained seventeen recommendations in seven fields. Since these recommendations were based on concrete and narrowly focused surveys, they provided basic data for drafting the SME Development Master Plan (Regnier 2000: 38).

In addition to the financial support, the Japanese government has implemented 'soft' human resource cooperation for institution building. The dispatch of experts of SME management and SME finance was undertaken by the JICA, JETRO and JODC. The JICA arranged to send experts of Japanese SME financial institutions such as the Japan Finance Corporation for Small Business and Shoko Chukin Bank, to relevant institutions in Thailand. Other METI-affiliated organisations – the Association for Overseas Technical Scholarship (AOTS) and New Energy and Industrial Technology Development Organisation (NEDO) – also implemented cooperative programs. In February–June 1999, the AOTS sponsored basic courses for technology and management at fifteen places for roughly 3000 people in Thailand. The NEDO provided the Supporting Industry Promotion Centre with assistance to research in the field of engineer plastics (JBIC 2001: 41). Thus, in addition to the JETRO and JICA, the JODC, AOTS and NEDO – all METI-affiliated organisations in charge of ODA programs – were involved in support for SME development in Thailand.

In summary, the IRP and SME policies adopted by the Thai government had developmental importance. The government, through the policies, sought to create the upgraded industrial structure. Importantly, the government adopted developmental methods based on state initiatives and industrial policy in order to achieve this policy objective. The Japanese government has been deeply involved in such efforts, transferring ideas and institutions for developmentalism to Thailand.

Conclusion

In this chapter, I have examined how the Japanese government has changed its economic diplomacy towards East Asia after the Asian financial and economic crisis. I have argued that the government has maintained and partially intensified the developmental state paradigm in its industrial cooperation programs towards East Asia after the crisis.

The Japanese government began to transfer the core elements of its development philosophy to East Asia as strategies to sustain export-led industrialisation before the Asian crisis. This was typically shown in the new AID plan and the following surveys on major export industries in East Asia. The Asian financial crisis played a catalytic role in accelerating the speed of Japan's economic strategies for major East Asian countries and deepened the degree of developmental orientation in the strategies. METI set up the AMEICC as a liaison forum to transfer detailed ideas about industrial development from Japan to Southeast Asia. In detailed cooperation programs, support for the development of public institutions and trade associations emerged as a key policy because they were regarded as bases for implementing and coordinating the government's policies.

Thailand accepted the IMF's structural adjustment programs in overall macroeconomic policies, financial reforms and corporate management. At the same time, the Thai government implemented industrial restructuring program. The programs contained elements of developmentalism such as explicit industrial targeting and the utilisation of *sathaban*, joint public–private institutions. In addition, state intervention increased in the field of SME promotion. While the government sought to change private, independent financial institutions for SMEs into public policy finance institutions, it launched a wide range of state-initiated programs for SME promotion. Thus, as Deyo (2000) suggests, there was a re-emergence of state-initiated developmentalism in SME policies after the crisis in Thailand.

The policy initiatives of the Thai government were intensively sustained by its Japanese counterpart. The Japanese government sent senior officials in order to assist Thailand to formulate the guidelines for SMEs, and provided human and financial resources to implement these guidelines. Significantly, the Japanese government made its Thai counterpart acknowledge the necessity of state intervention in fostering SMEs, and sought to transfer know-how of institution building such as the advisory council system, the policy finance system, and industrial development coordinated by trade associations.

The Japanese commitments might be seen as efforts to integrate the Thai industrial structure with that of the Japanese for the benefits of Japanese multinationals. The development of SMEs in the automobile industry surely gave benefits to Japanese producers that made inroads into Thailand most actively in Southeast Asia. However, intensive commitments after the Asian currency crisis had strong orientations to develop overall industrial bases beyond sectors directly relevant to Japanese interests. Furthermore, the IRP and SME promotion incorporated the fundamental methods of developmentalism such as the policy finance system and the use of quasi-public institutions.

This study has shown that the Japanese government partially intensified developmental state orientation in its efforts to assist industrial restructuring in Thailand. This is not, of course, to suggest that the Japanese government single-mindedly pursued the developmental state approach in its cooperation with East Asia. For instance, when the Japanese Ministry of Finance took the lead in establishing the ASEAN Plus Three Chiang Mai Initiative, it accepted that bilateral swap agreements were linked to the consent of the IMF for drawing down loans. However, the developmental state approach was apparent in Japan's cooperation in the fields of industrial transformation and the development of the real sector in Thailand.

The assertion found in this study does not apply to other East Asian countries straightforwardly, either. The validity of the argument depends on the degree of industrial bases and policy preferences in each country. While the argument can apply to Malaysia that maintained state-led recovery programs, it needs scrutiny in applying to the Philippines. However, Japanese officials had beliefs that government intervention was necessary in particular policy areas like SME promotion, and that uniform policy descriptions based on the neoliberal paradigm were not omnipotent, sometimes failing to meet conditions and problems peculiar to each country. These beliefs were reflected on Japan's industrial cooperation programs towards East Asia.

5

Japan and Regional Industrial Transformation: The Strategic Responses

Japan has maintained preponderant economic power in East Asia. The country has accounted for more than two-thirds of total gross domestic product (GDP) of the region, and has been a major source of capital, technology and foreign aid. Its trade and investment combined with official aid have sustained economic growth and industrialisation in most East Asian countries.

However, Japan's economic prowess and influence in East Asia seems to erode in the 1990s. Internally, Japan's economic performance has lost impetus largely due to the protracted fragility of the financial system. Political circles have been in gridlock since 1993 when thirty-eight years' conservative dominance by the Liberal Democratic Party (LDP) terminated. Externally, some of the East Asian economies have eclipsed Japan's industrial and technological prowess. South Korea and Taiwan have gradually enhanced their economic and technological capabilities although South Korea suffered from serious negative impacts from the Asian financial crisis in 1997–98. China has achieved remarkable economic performance, attracting huge foreign direct investment (FDI) from all over the world. The main interest of this chapter is how the Japanese government has responded to the recent economic and industrial transformation in East Asia.

In the late 1990s, the Japanese government has shown new initiatives in commercial policy. A representative of such initiatives is a shift in trade policy from a multilateral-centred to a multi-layered approach in which bilateral and regional arrangements are considered in addition to multilateral frameworks. The Japanese government has shown increasing interest in the regional framework comprising the Association of Southeast Asian Nations (ASEAN) countries, Japan, China and South Korea. The government took the lead in launching the Chiang Mai

Initiative, a scheme to promote financial cooperation among the ASEAN Plus Three (APT) countries. The government has also strengthened bilateral commitments by signing the Economic Partnership Agreement with Singapore in January 2002, the first free trade agreement for Japan.

In addition to these positive and cooperative initiatives, the Japanese government is likely to adopt policies and measures designed to defend its commercial interest against the relative decline of its industry in the region and rising competitive pressure from some of the neighbouring countries. I elucidate the background, development, and constraints of these policies and measures by using the concept of 'strategic mercantilism'.

This chapter argues that Japan could achieve mercantile objectives under favourable domestic and regional conditions until the early 1990s, but these conditions have gradually decayed since the mid-1990s. While Japan's capabilities as a techno-economic state and Japanese firms-centred regional networks gradually eroded, other East Asian counties have grown as economic rivals to Japan. Responding to such changes, the Japanese government has strengthened 'strategic' nature in commercial policies aiming to preserve the interests of its industries and secure its economic position in East Asia.

The organisation of this chapter is as follows. The following section examines relevant literature on Japan's external economic policy and presents strategic mercantilism as a framework to explain Japan's recent commitments to East Asia. The third section 'Structural changes in the late 1990s' elaborates how conditions that sustained Japan's mercantile objectives changed in the late 1990s. The fourth section 'Strategic mercantile policies towards East Asia' examines two distinctive policies that help achieve mercantile objectives; the fifth examines limitations to the new initiatives.

Japan's external economic policy and strategic mercantilism

How has Japan's post-war economic policy been characterised? The most conventional perspective is neo-mercantilism. Under the Yoshida doctrine that divided the security and economic matters, Japan single-mindedly pursued economic growth and rapid industrialisation, depending on the United States for security affairs. In the 1960s and 1970s, the Japanese government targeted several strategic industries allocating credit to them with an eye, at first, to utilising scarce domestic resources effectively. The government fostered these industries with a wide range of industrial policies including subsidies, policy finance, and active technology infusions from the western countries. While the domestic market was protected with tariffs and non-tariff barriers and limited entry of foreign capital, Japanese corporations advanced into overseas markets through aggressive export drive (Nester 1991).

In the 1980s, Japanese corporations expanded offshore operations by increasing FDI. Some scholars argue that the Japanese government assisted trade and investment expansion of Japanese corporations into the overseas markets by combining official commitments (Arase 1995; Hatch and Yamamura 1996). For instance, Hatch and Yamamura hold that 'it is in these industries [automobiles and electronics] that Japanese multinationals, fully supported by the Japanese government, have established the most effective vertical *keiretsu* networks in Asia' (Hatch and Yamamura 1996: 60–1). Importantly, 'protectionist' mercantilism in the 1960s and 1970s and even 'expansionist' mercantilism in the 1980s were embedded into institutional systems of the insulation of the domestic market from foreign competition and the government's orchestration of national economic policies as well as the socio-economic systems characterised by a coalition among big business, smaller businesses and agriculture for supporting the conservative regime (Pempel 1998: 48–73).

Other scholars have stressed international, liberal nature in Japan's external economic policy. Kato (1998) argues that the Japanese government pursued development cooperation policy on the basis of the liberal paradigm after the 1980s, given Japan's systemic vulnerability that it had to rely on the liberal international economic order. This systemic vulnerability also led Japan adhere to multilateral trading frameworks, avoiding regional or bilateral arrangements. Wan (1995) holds that Japan's foreign economic policy shifted from a mercantilist to international orientation in the mid-1980s, making much of the 'spending strategies' of burden sharing rather than the 'earning strategies' of linking aid with overseas trade and investment. Japan's liberal stance was seen in its regional economic diplomacy. The Japanese government had espoused to the concept of 'open regionalism' at the Asia-Pacific Economic Cooperation (APEC) forum although it showed negative attitudes towards US-induced haste and legalistic market liberalisation.

A group of scholars have presented a geo-economic perspective in explaining Japan's external economic policy. A representative is the concept of 'mercantile realism' presented by Heginbotham and Samuels (1999). According to them, 'policies designed to enhance the technological and economic fortunes of states may be pursued to increase a state's political leverage and independence even in the absence of military-security considerations' (Heginbotham and Samuels 1999: 197–8). The main factor that differentiates mercantile realism from the conventional neo-mercantilism lies in its stress on techno-economic power as a means to maintain security and augment national interest. Heginbotham and Samuels argue that Japan's post-war foreign policy was not fully explained by the structural realist theory, but consistent with predictions of the mercantile realist theory. In the similar vein, Huntington (1993: 72) holds that 'Japan has accepted all the assumptions of realism but applied them purely in the economic realm'.

The main objective of this chapter is to explain Japan's external economic policy towards East Asia after the mid-1990s. How can the above three perspectives be utilised for this objective? The concept of mercantile realism was applied to Japan's position in the world with special attention to its relations with the western countries, and confined its analysis to the period until the early 1990s. The geo-economic models including mercantile realism seem to lose their theoretical appeal after the mid-1990s both because the United States returned to its post-war norm of granting priority to international security concerns and because Japan's economic challenge against the United States, which induced the rise of the geo-economic models, is likely to end in failure (Mastanduno 1999: 26–8). In addition, main factors that characterise Japan as a mercantile realist state have evolved over the past three decades. For instance, Huntington (1993) raises producer dominance, industry targeting, corporate pursuit for market share, import restriction and sustained surplus as components of Japan's economic power maximisation. While some of these components still remained unchanged, industrial targeting and corporate behaviour of market share have shown drastic changes.

The liberal perspective can grasp Japan's changing position in the 1980s as well as its inherent vulnerability in the international arena. However, recent evolutions make it less appropriate to picture Japan's external policy from this perspective. The relative decline of the Japanese economy in the 1990s has induced the Japanese government to interweave national interest more tightly into its external economic policy. This was reflected on policy trends in official development assistance (ODA). The ODA Charter approved in June 1992 incorporated liberal and international perspectives, raising the promotion of democratisation, the introduction of a market-oriented economy, and the securing of basic human rights, as one of the four principles in considering whether to provide foreign aid. In the late 1990s, demand for using ODA more strategically for the sake of Japan's commercial interest has gained momentum as the domestic economy plunged into a long recession.[1]

In this chapter, I argue that Japan's external economic policy towards East Asia after the late 1990s is explicable in terms of mercantilism. However, mercantilism in this period is different in nature from those seen through the 1960s and 1980s. Japan's mercantile policy after the late 1990s, unlike that in the previous decades, has strengthened 'strategic' nature. The rapid growth of industries in neighbouring countries, mixed with the protracted economic slump in Japan has induced the Japanese government to intensify policies and measures to maintain its favourable economic position in East Asia as well as commercial interest of Japanese firms and industries in the region.

In order to examine this argument, three propositions are paid special attention. The first is to augment economic welfare and national interest by continuously maintaining economic and technological capabilities. This implies that Japan pursues to be a main source of technology, innovation, capital, and so on in East Asia. The second is to secure the dominant economic power in the region. This proposition implies that Japan cares for relative gain and relative position in East Asia. The third is to maintain commercial interest of its own national firms. This proposition means that Japan seeks to increase national welfare and interests depending mainly on Japanese firms. For a long time, Japan could enjoy the favourable regional climates for satisfying these three conditions.

First, Japan could maintain its national interest by becoming a source of economic and technological capabilities in East Asia. Japan pursued rapid economic growth and set up the solid 'full-set' industrial structure (Seki 1993). It also sustained economic development and steady industrialisation in the major East Asian countries by providing necessary capital and technology. A perspective that accounted for Japan's commitments to East Asia was the flying geese metaphor, which was long favoured by Japanese officials. This metaphor suggests that East Asian countries follow one another in a developmental trajectory in which the latecomers replicate the developmental experience of the countries ahead of them in the formation (Bernard and Ravenhill 1995). In this formation, Japan maintains the 'head goose' position, which can provide technology to the following geese.

Second, there were no rivals competing with Japan in economic and technological capabilities in East Asia. Japan as the only developed country in Asia had preponderant economic power. Indeed, the major

East Asian countries exhibited outstanding economic performance, but their growth was heavily dependent on Japanese technology and capital except for China. Under such climates, Japan did not feel the necessity of balancing techno-economic power against other states in the region.

Third, Japan's economic thrust into East Asia was achieved on the basis of Japanese firms-centred networks. Japanese firms developed the tight inter-corporate relationship in the domestic market, and this relationship was transferred to offshore operations. When core firms advanced into the Asian markets, they encouraged their subcontracting firms to follow them. They forged *keiretsu*-based tight production networks in East Asia, impeding non-Japanese firms entering business relationship (Hatch and Yamamura 1996). A strict adherence to quality often led to transactions with Japanese affiliates in the local economies. Under the tight Japanese firms-centred networks, technology transfer to local firms did not go smoothly and provoked criticisms from local governments and firms.[2]

The above conditions enabled Japan to attain the mercantile objectives mainly through market activities of Japanese corporations. This contention does not necessarily mean that Japan's official interest in and commitments to East Asia were unimportant. On the contrary, the Japanese government showed vital interest in economic development in East Asia. The government has provided huge financial and technical support in order to upgrade industrial bases in East Asian countries. The government has also sought to transfer the Japanese development style such as the state-guided industrialisation and close government–business relationship (Arase 1995). These policies clearly aimed to enhance commercial interest of Japanese firms and mercantile objectives of the Japanese state. However, these commitments were provided in the hierarchical structure and asymmetrical interdependence, not necessarily aiming to defend the national interest in symmetrical interdependence.

In brief, Japan enjoyed the favourable regional environments where no countries competed with the country for a position of economic and technological superpower in East Asia. Furthermore, Japan formulated particular ways to diffuse its technology by depending on Japanese firms-centred networks. These conditions enabled Japan to strengthen 'benign' mercantilism in which the Japanese government mixed the development of the East Asian economies through ODA programs or other measures with the promotion of the commercial interest of Japanese firms. These conditions began to change after the late 1990s.

Structural changes in the late 1990s

In the late 1990s, environments that sustained Japan's mercantile economic dominance in East Asia have gradually changed in all the above three conditions. First of all, Japan's economic and technological capabilities have gradually declined in the 1990s. One indicator is the increase ratio of labour productivity. Japan's ratio declined from 3.3 per cent in the 1980s to 2.4 per cent in 1990–94 and to 1.6 per cent in 1995–98 (Table 5.1). Indeed, other major developed countries showed a similar trend except for the United States, but Japan's fall is salient.

The decline of Japan's industrial competitiveness and technological prowess is shown in other indicators. Japan's technological power has declined in terms of the number of applications of patents. Until 1989, Japan was the largest patent application country in the world, exceeding the United States and European Union (EU) countries. However, the growth rate of the number stagnated in the 1990s. In 1999, the number of application was 0.91 million for Japan while 2.59 million for the United States and 2.56 million for the EU countries (MEXT 2002: 144). A critical feature of Japanese patents is that their overseas application is relatively low. In 1999, the ratio of overseas patent application for Japan was 60.2 per cent compared with 94.0 per cent for the United States and 90.9 per cent for Germany (MEXT 2002: 146). This implies that Japanese patents and Japan's technological development are domestically oriented.

Japan's declining international competitiveness reflects a gradual erosion of overall manufacturing bases. Although the manufacturing industry accounted for 21 per cent of GDP and 21 per cent of employment in 1999, it amounted to 87 per cent of total exports. The growing number of manufacturing firms has transferred the substantial process of production to East Asian countries, inviting the 'hollowing out' of the domestic industry. For instance, the number of manufacturing establishments decreased by 11 per cent from 387,700 in 1995 to 345,500

Table 5.1   The annual increase ratio of labour productivity in major developed countries (%)

	Japan	US	Germany	UK	France
1980s	3.3	1.3	2.6	3.0	3.3
1990–94	2.4	1.0	2.2	2.1	2.1
1995–98	1.6	2.2	1.9	1.6	1.9

Source: METI (2001c: 4).

in 1999. The average overseas production ratio in the manufacturing industry rose from 9.0 per cent in 1995 to 14.5 per cent in 2000 including 25.2 per cent for electrical machinery and 33.2 per cent for transport machinery (METI 2002: 30–1). Indeed, the level of outward FDI in Japan was not necessarily high compared with other developed countries such as the United States and United Kingdom. The transfer of business operations overseas might yield favourable effects if it leads to the withdrawal of firms and sectors with low productivity and profitability while stimulating the emergence of high profitable, innovative firms and sectors. However, Japan's hollowing out has occurred in a rather short-time span, not necessarily creating alternative industries in the domestic market.

The decline of Japan as a source of technology and innovation comes from the gradual collapse of an international division of labour between Japan and East Asia. Japanese firms developed an integrated production system based on an international division of labour, seeking, in their domestic production, to specialise in high value-added technology-intensive goods and to transfer manufacturing of low and medium value-added products to East Asia. However, recent manufacturing and procurement trends are departing from the past patterns. The growing number of firms has transferred the core process of production or the manufacturing of relatively high-end products to East Asian countries. This was partly because lead time to begin overseas production rapidly shortened. The production of video tape recorders began in Japan in 1976 and production shifted to overseas in 1984, eight years later. In case of CD players, production began in 1982 and shifted to overseas production in 1984. In case of digital televisions (TVs), the production began simultaneously in the Japanese and overseas markets. This means that other countries have increased their capabilities to begin the production of high value-added products, and the relative strength of Japanese firms in developing and manufacturing new products is declining.

Japanese subsidiaries in East Asia have gradually increased regional sourcing, reducing dependence on imports from Japan. This was because dependence on Japanese products became a less feasible strategy as price competitiveness from East Asian rival firms intensified. According to the Ministry of Economy, Trade and Industry's (METI) survey data on procurement sources of Japanese subsidiaries in Asia in electrical machinery, procurement from Japan declined from 46.7 per cent in 1992 to 37.7 per cent in 1999. In contrast, procurement from Asia increased from 15.4 per cent to 20.4 per cent in the same period (METI 1994b: 202, 2002: 145).

Increases in overseas production and regional procurement have led to the shrinkage of domestic manufacturing operations. Decline in domestic production has negative influences on the competitiveness of Japanese manufacturing industry. This is particularly important because technological development capabilities of Japanese manufacturing firms lay partly in high creativity in linking the established basic technology to product development through persistent and continuous efforts, and learning from mistakes on the floor mixed with knowledge of engineers and workers.

The second change is drastic evolutions in external environments surrounding Japanese industry. Some East Asian countries have caught up with Japan in terms of technological level and manufacturing capabilities. Taiwan and South Korea have become crucial industrial bases for information technology (IT) related products. Taiwan has emerged as the world's leading production centre of major IT hardware. In 1998, Taiwan producers accounted for substantial share of personal computers (PCs) and their peripherals: 40 per cent of notebook PCs, 58 per cent of monitors, 61 per cent of motherboards, and 84 per cent of scanners (Koryu Kyokai 2000: 13). Korean firms raised their presence in the production of semiconductors and thin film transistor-liquid crystal displays (TFT-LCDs). The share of Asia in total semiconductor production in the world grew from 25 per cent in 1991 to 36 per cent in 1998 including 11 per cent of South Korea, while that of Japan declined from 39 per cent to 22 per cent in the same period (Amano 1999: 24). Japanese producers accounted for 90 per cent of the TFT-LCD market in the world before 1996. However, their share declined to 37 per cent in 2001, while Korean producers represented by Samsung Electronics and LG Electronics accounted for 41 per cent.[3] In the 2000s, Japanese producers learn know-how of production efficiency from their East Asian rivals. A typical example is Nippon Steel Semiconductor, which was taken over by Taiwan's United Microelectronic Corp. (UMC) group. The renamed Nippon Foundry revived as a specialist foundry producer, and many Japanese semiconductor producers visited this company to learn production know-how.

Significantly, Taiwan and South Korea have rapidly improved their competitiveness in basic industries, as well. A typical example is found in the die mould industry. Between 1995 and 1998, South Korea and Taiwan increased production of die mould by 28 per cent and 31 per cent, respectively (Mizuno 2001: 5; Saito 2001: 9). For a long time, South Korea had large trade deficits with Japan in the die mould sector, but has expanded its surplus since 1997. Their growth had much to do with the IT development. Excellent computer-aided design (CAD) and computer-mediated manufacturing (CAM) software, as well as design and manufacturing tools that contained high skills and know-how, have been developed since the mid-1990s. East Asian firms increased design capabilities by introducing and mastering these software and tools.

In addition to South Korea and Taiwan, China emerged as a potential techno-economic power in East Asia in the late 1990s. In 1999, China was the world's primary production centre of sixteen products including crude steels, chemical fibres, colour TVs, air-conditioners, and so on. In 2000, China became the third largest producer of IT hardware (PCs and related products), following the United States and Japan (JETRO 2001a: 49). Japan was the factory of the world in the 1970s and 1980s. China is succeeding this status in the new century.

Like the ASEAN countries, export expansion in China was heavily dependent on foreign multinationals. In 2000, foreign multinationals accounted for 27.1 per cent of total industrial output, 47.9 per cent of total exports and 17.3 per cent of total tax revenue (Niwano 2002: 49). Unlike the ASEAN countries, however, industrialisation in China has been promoted on the solid accumulation of basic and supporting industries. According to the JETRO's survey in 2001, the share of Japanese-affiliated firms whose local procurement ratio was more than half was 50 per cent in China, but 38 per cent in ASEAN (Maruya and Abe 2002: 12–13). Chinese local brands crowded out foreign made products. For instance, the local brands shared the top three rankings in refrigerators, air-conditioners, video compact discs, PCs and telephones (JETRO 2001a: 52). This makes a sharp contrast with Southeast Asia where Japanese brands account for substantial share in these products.

The expansion of the Chinese economy and its rising influence in East Asia are shown in micro and macro data. China has rapidly expanded exports of relatively high-end products to East Asian countries. For instance, Chinese motorbikes and electronic products including refrigerators, washing machines and air-conditioners have driven out Japanese products in Indonesia, Vietnam and the Philippines. In Indonesia, for instance, Chinese products amounted to more than 30 per cent of colour TVs, 10–20 per cent of air-conditioners and refrigerators, and 20 per cent of motorcycles (Maruya and Ishikawa 2001: 7). Some Chinese electronics firms began local production in Indonesia and Vietnam. While TCL started operations of a TV plant in Vietnam in 1999, Changhong and Konka opened a TV plant in Indonesia in 2000 (Maruya and Abe 2002: 20). Indeed, outward FDI is still minimal compared with inward FDI, but the penetration of Chinese firms into Southeast Asia will likely expand to other countries over more sophisticated products.[4]

The rising influence of China in East Asia is shown in macro data as well. Intra-regional trade in East Asia increased from US$125 billion in 1990 to US$315 billion in 1995 to US$447 billion in 2000. Trade between China and the rest of East Asia accounted for 26.5 per cent of total intra-regional trade in 1995, but climbed to 43.7 per cent in 2000. The China-centred trade contributed to 85.1 per cent of increases in total intra-regional trade between 1995 and 2000 (Maruya and Ishikawa 2001: 6). China has collected huge investment from the world. Inward FDI into China increased from US$6.6 billion in 1990 to US$58.1 billion in 1992, and has maintained a high level afterwards. The main investors into China came from Hong Kong and Taiwan until the mid-1990s, while those into ASEAN were Japanese and westerns. However, Japanese and western firms aimed at China after the late 1990s. Thus, trade and investment networks in East Asia have been formed centred on China. Japan's limited capacity to expand imports from East Asia and minimal inward FDI intensify this possibility.

The third change is evolving patterns in corporate networks and Japanese firms-centred technology transfer. The growing number of Japanese manufacturing firms has transferred core technology to East Asian firms as corporate strategies. For instance, major electronics firms forged alliances with Taiwanese firms and transferred the technology of LCDs.[5] The alliance strategy aimed at reducing investment burdens and concentrating capital and human resources on the development of next-generation LCDs. In particular, increased competitive pressure from Korean firms forced Japanese firms to adopt this alliance strategy. Some electronics firms have accelerated technology transfer to China. In 1999, Matsushita began the integrated production of DVDs from parts manufacturing and final assembly in Dalian, Liaoning Province. In October 2000, Matsushita announced that it established a joint venture, Shanghai Matsushita Plasma Display with three local companies. The new joint venture company was designated as the first Chinese national project for plasma display panel (PDP) production by the Chinese central government.

Importantly, in addition to technology transfer as corporate strategies, there are several informal routes of transfer. First, production equipment manufacturers have contributed to technology transfer. In Japan, electronics producers and production equipment manufacturers jointly developed manufacturing machines. When Japanese manufacturing machines were sold to foreign firms, technical know-how was shipped with the machines. For instance, the LCD business in South Korea began with the introduction of Japanese LCD machines, which contained technical know-how of Japanese LCD producers (Itani 2001: 4).

Second, Japanese venture firms have strengthened linkages with Korean and Taiwanese producers, and transferred the technology of semiconductors and LCDs. These venture businesses, established often by engineers retired from major electronics firms, faced difficulty in expanding business with major Japanese electronics firms largely because the latter were reluctant to begin transactions with these small enterprises that had no established reputation. In contrast, Korean and Taiwanese firms willingly introduced new ideas and technology from these venture firms. In October 2000, 57 venture firms founded the Japan Semiconductor Ventures Association. More than half of the member firms implemented business in Korea or Taiwan.[6]

Third, technology transfer by individual engineers has become critical. Some engineers of major semiconductor companies worked in Korean firms as part-timers on weekends and vacations, and transferred the technology of dynamic random access memory (DRAM) production. The provision of technical information and expertise by Japanese engineers and active investment based on it contributed to technical strength and price competitiveness of Korean DRAMs. In the late 1990s, technology transfer by individual engineers became more salient. Korean and Taiwanese firms recruited engineers who were fired by Japanese firms through corporate restructuring, or those dissatisfied with working conditions there. These engineers willingly transferred technological know-how regarding production of devices, LCDs or even PDPs, products with critical growth potential.[7]

Thus, Japan's core technology ran out overseas through various routes after the late 1990s because tight linkages among Japanese firms and between Japanese firms and their employees, which constituted a source of Japan's technological supremacy, gradually eroded. The weak management of corporate trade secrets within Japanese firms and weak legal systems to protect property rights exacerbated unintended technology transfer.

In summary, the three conditions that sustained Japan's mercantile interests have eroded especially since the late 1990s. While Japan's technological and production capabilities gradually declined, some East Asian countries have caught up with Japan in technology and production levels. The routes of technology transfer became diverse, loosening Japanese firms-centred management of technology. In response to these situations, the Japanese government has gradually intensified initiatives to protect Japan's commercial interest by the state-led policies.

Strategic mercantile policies towards East Asia

Since the late 1990s, the Japanese government has strengthened two policy directions towards East Asia with an eye to attaining mercantile objectives. The first set of policies is the maintenance of close linkages with and support for the Southeast Asian countries. The second set of policies is increased interest in the protection of intellectual property rights.

Renewed commitments to Southeast Asia

Japan has sought to forge close ties with the Southeast Asian countries since Prime Minister Takeo Fukuda called for a 'heart-to-heart' partnership in the so-called Fukuda doctrine in 1977. Southeast Asia is an area where Japan showed one of the outstanding achievements of the post-war diplomacy (Curtis 1994: 222). Moreover, Southeast Asia is a region where Japanese firms made inroads intensively and gained higher profits than other regions. Accordingly, the Japanese government and business paid particular attention to the upgrading of industrial bases in the region after the mid-1980s. For instance, under the new Asian Industries Development (AID) plan, METI conducted research on reviews and problems in the representative supporting industries, jointly with the industry-relevant ministries in Thailand, Indonesia, Malaysia and the Philippines (Yamazawa 1994: 22). In addition, at the 1993 APEC summit meeting in Seattle, METI proposed the start of a ministerial meeting on support for small- and medium-sized enterprises (SMEs). The meeting's major target was Southeast Asia. Commitments to developing industrial bases in Southeast Asia became more substantial and systematic after the late 1990s.

As already explained in the previous chapter, the Japanese government has developed particular institutional settings to sustain steady industrialisation and economic integration in Southeast Asia. While the ASEAN Economic Ministers (AEM) and the Minister of METI institutionalised the AEM–METI in 1992, they set up the Working Group on Economic Cooperation in Cambodia, Laos and Myanmar (CLM-WG) two years later. In 1997, they transformed the CLM-WG into the AEM–METI Economic and Industrial Cooperation Committee (AMEICC). On the basis of the AEM–METI and AMEICC, the Japanese government has shown various initiatives aiming at the upgrading of industrial bases and market integration in Southeast Asia.

A representative of such initiatives was the Centre of Excellence program, which was approved at an AEM–METI meeting in May 2000. Previously, METI assisted human resources development mainly through internships or training programs at the Association for Overseas Technical Scholarship (AOTS) in Japan (Otsuji 2001: 337). The program aimed to enhance the capabilities of ASEAN to develop human resources by selecting one or two core institutions in each country and dispatching experts and deploying equipment to these institutions. Another example is the Working Group on Small and Medium Enterprises, Supporting Industries and Rural Industries. The activities of the group included training on the promotion of SME supply chain management and industrial production techniques, and the development of the SME management consulting system. These commitments directly aimed to improve the capabilities of ASEAN to foster engineers and managers as well as SMEs in supporting industries from a mid- and long-term perspective.

As for support for the enlargement of ASEAN as a single market, METI has implemented the West–East Corridor program.[8] Under the program, the Japanese government has provided assistance to the development of 'soft' infrastructures such as the formulation of a master plan for tourism in Indochina, a feasibility study for the development of the light industry in the border area between Cambodia and Thailand, and strength in the functions of trade promotion centres. Indeed, several projects had been implemented for the development of Indochina and the Mekong river area.[9] But, most of the projects aimed to develop hard infrastructure. The West–East Corridor program aimed to enhance 'soft' capabilities for the development.[10]

Moreover, METI has sustained the harmonisation of institutions such as patent rights, legal systems, standards and certification systems, and statistics in Southeast Asia. When the ASEAN countries held a meeting regarding these institutions, a meeting to discuss harmonisation issues was organised with relevant Japanese agencies such as the Patent Office and Agency of Industrial Science and Technology (Otsuji 2001: 336). The institutional harmonisation was important for promoting cross-border transactions and the region-wide complementation of industrial activities. Based on such a complementation, each ASEAN country was expected to specialise in a particular industrial sector. For instance, Thailand would be a regional centre of automobile production, while Malaysia would develop a competitive edge in the electronics industry.

The development of industrial bases and the enlargement of the integrated market in Southeast Asia were supposed to contribute to Japan's mercantile interest in several ways. First, these initiatives were expected to enhance commercial interests of Japanese firms. Given that official commitments to market integration have intensified in Southeast Asia through the ASEAN Free Trade Area (AFTA) and ASEAN Investment Area (AIA) programs, Japanese firms were forced to restructure their operations in Southeast Asia, aiming at more systematic linkages among manufacturing bases in the region. Support for local SMEs and the integrated market were consonant with such strategies. Furthermore, the harmonisation of institutions, rules and systems with the Japanese ones contributed to the expansion of Japanese standards. In the computer and telecommunications equipment fields, Japanese electronics firms failed to expand business operations largely because standards used in Japan were not adaptable to overseas markets (Dedrick and Kraemer 1998: 114; Yoshimatsu 1999: 9–10). The diffusion of Japanese standards would lead to the expansion of business in Southeast Asia. Second, these initiatives were expected to neutralise the appeal of the Chinese economy in East Asia. As already explained, China has collected huge investment from all over the world, reducing investment inflow into Southeast Asia. While development in institutions, rules and systems will improve ASEAN's overall attractiveness, the upgrading of supporting industries and the development of excellent human resources will rectify ASEAN's competitive disadvantages against China.

Another initiative for stronger linkages with Southeast Asia is the promotion of a formal economic arrangement between Japan and ASEAN. Prime Minister Junichiro Koizumi proposed an Initiative for the ASEAN–Japan Closer Economic Partnership (AJCEP) during his visit to Southeast Asia in January 2002. The vaguely defined proposals for greater economic integration did not meet the expectation of the ASEAN countries. However, the Japanese government sought to promote the initiative rather swiftly. Two weeks after Koizumi's proposal, the AJCEP Expert Group had the first meeting in Bangkok.[11] The AJCEP aimed to discuss cooperation on investment, tourism, intellectual property and competition policy, as well as trade liberalisation in goods and services. In September 2002, the group submitted a report to an AEM–METI meeting. The group recommended that the implementation of measures for the realisation of partnership, including elements of a possible FTA, should be completed as soon as possible within ten years, and that a committee consisting of senior economic officials should be established by the year 2003.

Indeed, negotiations between Japan and ASEAN over the AJCEP did not go smoothly. At the discussion of the AJCEP Expert Group, a Singapore delegate argued that a fixed timeframe should be included in the AJCEP, stating that ASEAN and China, whose economies were mutually competitive, had decided to form a free trade area within ten years, and questioning why ASEAN and Japan, whose economies were mutually complementary, could not determine the deadline.[12] As explained in the following chapter, Japan's indecisive attitudes towards an FTA with ASEAN derived from consideration for the agricultural issues. At the same time, Japan has strength in promoting closer economic ties with ASEAN because it will be able to combine programs for economic cooperation with trade liberalisation. This is exactly the objective of the comprehensive economic partnership.

The above description of Japanese policies and commitments does not imply that the Japanese government has single-mindedly pursued intensive relationship with Southeast Asia. The overall policy direction is the formation of multi-layered commercial networks. From this standpoint, the Japanese government has striven to promote regional cooperation in a broader APT framework as well as bilateral trade arrangements. However, Southeast Asia has a particular strategic importance for Japan's commercial policy.

Increasing interest in intellectual property rights

The second set of policies with a mercantile perspective is increased interest in the protection of intellectual property rights (IPRs). The government agencies, ruling parties and private firms have showed renewed interests in IPRs, setting up groups to discuss intellectual property issues and publishing recommendations regarding them. In October 2001, METI set up a study group of Industrial Competitiveness and Intellectual Property Rights as a consultative body to Director Generals of the Economic and Industrial Policy Bureau and the Patent Office. In June 2002, the 23-member group, consisting of business leaders and academia, issued a report, which recommended four strategies including the strength of protection of IPRs in overseas markets and the active utilisation of IPRs in corporate management.

In February 2002, the Strategic Council on Intellectual Property was established within the Cabinet Office. Four months later, the council published the Intellectual Property Policy Outline. The outline identified present situations and basic directions, and proposed specific action plans listing seven measures to strengthen the protection of intellectual property such as the establishment of a 'patent court' function, the reinforcement of measures against counterfeits and pirated copies, and the promotion of cooperation and international harmonisation of the intellectual property system.

Importantly, the government's moves towards stronger intellectual property policy have been sustained by political and business circles. In May 2002, the LDP's Subcommittee of Intellectual Property Policy under the Trade and Industry Division and other two committees issued a report entitled *Announcement of a Nation Built on Intellectual Property*. The report stressed a swift and accurate registration and the rigid protection of intellectual property and the development of human resources to sustain the spiral of intellectual creation. In January 2002, *Nippon Keidanren* (Japan Business Federation) issued a position paper entitled *Strength of Industrial Competitiveness Centred on Intellectual Property*. This paper outlined basic ideas about intellectual property policy from a viewpoint of the industrial sector. In June 2002 just before the council issued the outline, *Keidanren* published another paper entitled *Ideas about Intellectual Property Strategy*. Thus, the three political powers in Japan took concerted action in protecting IPRs in the early 2000s.

Concrete measures and policies would be implemented on the basis of the outline. Yet, a further step to cope with counterfeits began earlier. In April 2002, the International Intellectual Property Protection Forum was founded as a consequence of joint efforts by the public and private sectors. The forum comprising 69 associations and 87 firms aimed to promote cooperation and liaison among government agencies, relevant associations and firms in order to implement effective anti-counterfeiting measures.

The strength of intellectual property protection does not lead to the augmentation of Japan's mercantile interest straightforwardly. In addition, quite a few developed countries have focused on intellectual property as a way of improving industrial competitiveness. However, Japan's recent engagements in intellectual property have particular implications for achieving strategic mercantile objectives. First, strength in intellectual property protection induces firms to show further commitments to technological developments and innovations by giving greater protection for fruits from these operations. The Japanese government has given greater stress on the science and technology development.[13] The protection of intellectual property is a prerequisite that enables Japanese firms to shift to more innovative and sophisticated activities. This was apparent by the fact that the Council for Science and Technology Policy, established in January 2001 within the Cabinet Office, was also concerned with intellectual property policy.[14] The protection of intellectual property was also expected to preserve the competitive advantages of Japanese industry and mitigate the hollowing out of the manufacturing industry.

Second, the protection of intellectual property of Japanese firms will contain economic power of rapidly emerging East Asian rivals. Japanese firms have suffered from counterfeits in China, Taiwan and South Korea. The copying of Japanese products and infringement of Japanese patents were particularly rife in China. According to surveys by the Japan Patent Office, in 2001 the number of cases whose value of copyright and patent infringement was more than 1 billion yen and between 0.1 and 1 billion yen was 22 and 54, respectively. China accounted for 33.0 per cent of counterfeits of Japanese products in terms of production area, followed by South Korea (18.1 per cent) and Taiwan (17.6 per cent). In 1989, the shares of Taiwan and China were 37.6 per cent and 3.8 per cent, respectively (Japan Patent Office 2002). The rapid industrialisation in China for the past ten years was accompanied by the growing counterfeits and pirated copies.

The injuries of property rights in China were particularly serious in consumer electronic products and motorcycles. For instance, in 1999 roughly 400 companies produced 11 million motorcycles, 1.25 million of which were manufactured by 19 companies that obtained licenses from Japanese firms. Given that most Chinese manufacturers did not retain sufficient development capabilities, nearly 70 per cent of the remaining 9.75 million units were believed to be counterfeits sporting the designs and trademarks of Japanese products.[15]

In a sense, stronger intellectual property protection followed the US experience. When competition from East Asian countries intensified in the 1980s, the US government and industries placed greater stress on patents especially after the publication of the Young report in 1985. China's growth as a major economic rival drew a similar response from the Japanese government and industries.

Third, the intensive intellectual property protection would improve internal management of corporate trade secrets within Japanese firms. As explained above, engineers' job-hopping led partially to illegal technology transfer. Frequent job-hopping does not necessarily lead to decline in industrial competitiveness. New innovation and industrial competitiveness in the Silicon Valley and Hsinchu and Tainan science parks in Taiwan have been reliant partly on such practices. The main problem for Japan lay in the fact that since the country long maintained tight linkages between firms and their employees, it did not establish the effective management of corporate trade secrets and legal systems to protect IPRs. It was particularly important to regulate illegal technology transfer by individual engineers as a crime given that Japanese manufacturing industry has maintained competitiveness in shop-floor operations. Accordingly, the government intended to revise the Unfair Competition Prevention Law, making a leak of corporate trade secrets a crime and imposing penalty on individuals who violate corporate property rights.

Two constraints on the new initiatives

The above section argued that Japan has strengthened initiatives designed to secure mercantile interests in East Asia. However, such policies are undermined by at least two factors. The first is the influence of diverse interests within the state. The mercantile perspective presupposes that the state as a whole pursues the augmentation of national wealth and enrichment. However, the Japanese state has not created a common front for achieving this objective. For instance, the Japanese ministries have competed over initiatives and policies over development assistance to Southeast Asia. As mentioned above, METI institutionalised the CLM-WG in September 1994. This group was set up partially with an intention to compete with the Forum for Comprehensive Development of Indochina whose establishment was announced by the then Prime Minister Kiichi Miyazawa in January 1993. This Ministry of Foreign Affairs (MOFA)-initiated forum aimed to be a gathering for debates and exchange of views on the balanced development of Indochina. METI hoped to create its own networks and channels for development in Indochina (Shiraishi 1998: 62). Furthermore, METI decided in December 1997 to transform the CLM-WG into the AMEICC in order to promote the ASEAN-wide industrial cooperation. In the same year, MOFA also set up a similar organisation called the Japan–ASEAN Development Round Table whose first meeting was held in Okinawa in May 1998. This organisation was development oriented, but its detailed operations such as the development of human resources were similar to METI's industrial cooperation.

METI and MOFA also adopted different approaches to FTAs with Southeast Asia. The two ministries forged a common front on the basic policy of giving priority to FTAs with South Korea, ASEAN and Mexico. However, MOFA's strategy for ASEAN was to promote bilateral FTAs with Thailand, the Philippines and others, and then expand the agreements to the whole ASEAN. METI has sought to pursue an FTA with ASEAN as a whole. METI's policy orientation was understandable given that it has striven to assist economic integration and industrial cooperation in ASEAN.

The influence of diverse interest within the state is seen in intellectual property policy. As already mentioned, the Japanese government set up the Strategic Council on Intellectual Property in February 2002. The council consisted of nine ministers concerned, but originally did not include the Ministers of Finance and Foreign Affairs. The absence of these two ministries was peculiar given that the protection of intellectual property overseas was closely relevant to foreign relations and that tax reforms and tax incentives would likely become a pillar for stimulating firms' research and development (R&D) activities.[16] Intellectual property is under the jurisdiction of various agencies including METI, Ministry of Agriculture, Forestry and Fisheries, Ministry of Education, Culture, Sports, Science and Technology, as well as Ministry of Public Management, Home Affairs, and Posts and Telecommunications. The government did not strive to coordinate policies and measures of these agencies in formulating the Intellectual Property Policy Outline. The council had only four meetings before publishing the outline. This means that the government abandoned the formulation of the comprehensive policy, just listing up various policies presented by each ministry.

The second constraint concerns the influence of preferences and activities of non-state actors on the state's policy. The mercantile perspective tends to stress the role of the state as the central actor in economic affairs, paying little attention to non-state actors in discussing a state's external relations. However, even if the state seeks to pursue a particular external policy, its effectiveness is often dependent on preferences and actions of non-state actors. There is a high possibility that actions of non-state actors undermine the state's strategic intentions and policies.

This was the case in Japan's mercantile policy towards East Asia. While the Japanese state seeks to revitalise its economy by enhancing R&D capabilities and creating innovative bases in Japan, Japanese firms have their own corporate strategies and calculations, which are incompatible with the state's policy objectives. This chasm was clearly shown in hearings at a meeting of the Information Subcommittee of the LDP's Trade and Industry Division in December 2001. The chairman of the subcommittee stated that 'we expect that Japanese firms will continuously strive to locate R&D capabilities in Japan, but some firms are likely to transfer R&D facilities offshore. This is our most serious concern for the future'. Tatsuo Tanaka, an executive director of the Japan Electronics and Information Technology Industries Association, the major industrial association of Japanese electronics firms, responded that 'we hope to take the leadership in the world by conducting R&D activities, mainly in Japan. But, a crucial point is to secure international competitiveness in the greatly evolving industrial world. We think it necessary to compensate our weak fields by establishing facilities in a country with strength in these fields'.[17]

According to the mercantile perspective, rapid transfer of R&D to China is not desirable while commitments to industrial upgrading and market integration in ASEAN are advisable. However, Japanese firms have aggressively strengthened R&D and design capabilities in China. In particular, Zhongguancun, a sub-district area in northwestern Beijing's Haidian District, became the main locus of R&D activities. The area has shown remarkable performance in software development and IT-related research as China's 'Silicon Valley'. The major Japanese electronics firms have established R&D facilities there in order to get benefits from the accumulation of human and technology resources. For instance, Matsushita opened an R&D centre in June 2001. Twenty-four out of 53 employees had the degree of MA or PhD and planed to increase the number of employees to 120 within one and a half year.[18] Other major Japanese electronics firms including Fujitsu, Mitsubishi Electric, NEC, Toshiba also retain an R&D facility in Beijing.

As China has achieved high economic growth improving industrial competitiveness, Taiwanese firms have transferred their production bases from the ASEAN countries to China. Such moves were not prominent among Japanese firms largely because most Japanese firms adopted a strategy to maintain business bases both in China and ASEAN (Ishikawa 2002: 74–5). However, Japanese electronics producers began to establish plants for LCD panels and PDPs in China, not setting up such plants in the ASEAN countries first. In April 2002, NEC announced that it would establish a joint venture with the SVA Group to carry out product planning, development and manufacturing of TFT-LCD panels in Shanghai. The joint venture, NEC's first affiliate to manufacture TFT-LCD panels in Asia, aimed at the growth of PCs in the Chinese market.

As for the counterfeit problem, some Japanese firms adopted different approaches from the government's initiatives. In April 2001, Honda Motor established Sundiro Honda Motorcycle by merging its subsidy China Tianjin Honda Motors with Hainan Sundiro Motorcycle. This merge attracted great interest because Hainan Sundiro achieved high growth by counterfeiting the design of Japanese motorcycles. Instead of filing a lawsuit, Honda adopted a strategy to utilise the company's competitive edge in manufacturing models in low and middle price ranges as well as procurement and sales networks in China.[19]

Thus, actual corporate strategies and behaviour, which were not consonant with the government's policies, have undermined the state's mercantile objectives. Similar problems occurred in the 1970s in the United States when US multinationals transferred operations overseas, and US officials were apprehensive about the decline in competitiveness of domestic manufacturing industry. Given geographical proximity between Japan and East Asia and intensive trends towards globalisation, the harmonisation of the state's policy objectives and corporate strategies might be more difficult for the Japanese state and firms.

Conclusion

The central interest of this chapter was what external economic policies the Japanese state has adopted in order to respond to the evolving regional environments surrounding the Japanese economy and industry in general, and increasing competitive pressure from the East Asian countries in particular. The argument derived from a shift in regional distribution of economic power. Japan could afford to pursue rather benign external economic policies before the mid-1990s when the country retained preponderant techno-economic power in East Asia. In the late 1990s, Japanese firms' power and influence gradually decayed in the domestic and international markets. Consequently, the Japanese government has strengthened strategic initiatives to secure the commercial interest of Japanese industry.

There have been outstanding evolutions surrounding Japanese industry since the mid-1990s. Japan's capabilities to be a single producer of high-technology goods in East Asia have gradually declined, as South Korea and Taiwan have caught up with Japan even in the relatively high-technology fields. In addition, China's potential as a manufacturing base and a centre of regional economic networks was a great threat to Japan. Closed Japanese corporate networks and resultant rigid technology transfer also became loose partly because the major firms were forced to transfer core technology to East Asian firms and partly because various sorts of informal technology transfer became salient. Thus, favourable conditions that sustained Japan's techno-economic dominance in East Asia eroded after the late 1990s.

Being confronted with such changes, the Japanese government was motivated to propel renewed initiatives designed to preserve its techno-economic power in East Asia. The government has intensified assistance to industrial upgrading and market integration in the ASEAN countries.

These initiatives aimed to protect the commercial interest of Japanese firms in Southeast Asia where they had advanced intensively, and to maintain Southeast Asia as a counterweight to China. The Japanese government has also attempted to strengthen the disciplines of IPRs. This initiative aimed to increase R&D capabilities of Japanese industry, protect Japanese firms' intellectual assets against East Asian rivals, and prevent illegal technology transfer by individual employees.

Importantly, Japan's mercantile policies were constrained by at least two factors. The Japanese state has not necessarily formulated the rational and integrated policies to attain the mercantile objectives due to the failure to coordinate basic interests and stance of ministries concerned. The government has not necessarily formulated cohesive and persistent policies towards ASEAN largely due to conflict between METI and MOFA over initiatives and methods of economic cooperation. Stress on domestic R&D and production policies was likely undermined by the global and regional orientation of corporate strategies. Japanese corporations with their own preferences and calculations do not necessarily follow the state's interest and policy directions.

This chapter elucidated Japan's strategic responses to regional evolutions. As indicated in various parts in this chapter, the Japanese government has also strengthened policies to promote regionalism and regional integration in East Asia. The following two chapters focus directly on Japan's commitments to regional cooperation and integration.

6
The Liberal Democratic Party, Finance Ministry and Regional Cooperation

The previous two chapters have examined the relationship between the Asian financial crisis and regional industrial transformations on the one hand, and Japan's external economic policy on the other. This chapter seeks to deepen our understanding of Japan–East Asian relationship by highlighting Japan's regional cooperation policy in the rapidly evolving regional environments.

Japan, the regional economic superpower, showed little leadership in promoting regional cooperation. This constituted one of the major reasons why East Asia was behind other regions in moves towards regionalism. For a long time, Japan's foreign policies were formed on the basis of relationship with the United States. Not only has Japan maintained the Japan–US Security Treaty but it has also developed intensive economic linkages, heavily depending on the US market for exports. As a junior partner, Japan tended to adjust its policies to those of the United States even in economic affairs in East Asia where Japan increased linkages and stakes after the mid-1980s.

Japan gradually showed more independent interest in the East Asian economic affairs after the early 1990s. The Japanese government institutionalised a meeting of Economic Ministers with Association of Southeast Asian Nations (ASEAN) countries in 1992 and a meeting of Finance Ministers in 1995. Furthermore, the government sought to legitimate its own developmental model, which was emulated by other East Asian countries, in the international scene.

After the Asian financial crisis occurred in July 1997, the Japanese government proposed various schemes and policies designed to sustain the quick recovery of the crisis-hit countries and block the recurrence of a crisis. In October 1998, for instance, the government launched the New Miyazawa Initiative in order to sustain economic recovery in major

East Asian countries. Japan's rising interest in regional economic affairs was also shown in the trade field. While the Japanese government signed the Japan–Singapore Economic Partnership Agreement (JSEPA) in January 2002, it has continued studies of or negotiations over free trade agreements (FTAs) with South Korea, Thailand, ASEAN and others.

There are several questions regarding Japan's commitments to regional cooperation in East Asia after the mid-1990s. What factors have encouraged Japan to show more interest in regional economic affairs? To what extent do these commitments reflect changes in Japan's basic policy stance? Will these commitments lead to Japan's genuine leadership in East Asia? A conventional approach to answering these questions is to examine Japan's commitments to particular regions and countries or in specific issue-areas. There are quite a few studies that analysed Japan's involvements in the Asian economies by using this approach. Unlike the previous studies, this chapter seeks to address the above questions through an actor-specific approach.

This chapter examines preferences and actions of the Liberal Democratic Party (LDP) and Ministry of Finance (MOF) towards the East Asian economies and regional cooperation after the mid-1990s. In particular, it investigates any meaningful changes in their preferences and actions, and identifies factors leading to such changes. The main argument of this chapter is that regional evolutions represented by the Asian financial crisis have changed preferences of the LDP and MOF in favour of stronger regional integration and cooperation. Both actors with due consideration to the regional changes have found greater interest in promoting economic cooperation in East Asia. Before looking at the preferences and activities of the two actors in detail, the following section presents an analytical framework for this chapter.

Japan's regional cooperation policy: an analytical framework

In the study of international relations, international and domestic variables have been considered as factors that determine a state's external policy and relations. The approach that focuses on the relative attributes of units (states) in international structure regards a state's external policy and relations as a product of interactions and interrelationships in such a structure.[1] This international politics approach posits that a state's external policies are constrained by characteristics inherent in the international system. This approach, which regards the state as a coherent unit and its preferences and beliefs are consistent, has strength in its parsimony.

According to the international politics perspective, Japanese foreign policies are qualified by its relative power position, relationship with the United States in particular. Japan was long a junior partner of the United States during the Cold War period, developing close relationship with the country in the security, political and economic domains. As a consequence, Japan's foreign policy was formed in accordance with US policy stance, being highly responsive to explicit or tacit pressures from the country (Hellmann 1988; Orr 1990; Miyashita 1999). Japan showed distinctive policies towards Middle East where Japan depended on oil and positively promoted economic and political linkages with Southeast Asia, but the baseline of Japan's policy towards Asia was qualified by its relations with the United States.

The international politics approach is useful in explaining broad policy outcomes across time in different countries, or general trends in the overall international economic system. Yet, it cannot account adequately for why a particular type of policy was adapted in a state. For instance, it provides no explanation of why one sector is protected from international competition while simultaneously other sectors are willingly opening their markets.

The international politics perspective contains several problems in explaining Japan's external relations and policies. First, it misses evolving relations between Japan and the United States. It is often argued that Japan is venerable to US pressure because Tokyo is more dependent on Washington especially in terms of security and export markets. While Japan is still dependent on the United States in the security domain, Japan's relative reliance on the US market declined as its economic linkages with East Asia rose after the mid-1980s. While the US share in Japan's total exports declined from 38 per cent in 1985 to 28 per cent in 1995, that of East Asia rose from 24 per cent to 42 per cent in the same period (ICSEAD 2002: 23–4). Second, Japan often cannot show a coherent and decisive stance in issue areas where the United States does not show clear opposition. The market opening issues including the promotion of deregulation in the 1980s and early 1990s are such examples. In order to clarify these points, we need to look to the domestic politics approach.

As explained in other parts of this book, the domestic politics approach has considered various factors as explanatory variables for a state's external economic policy. One strand of the approach has focused on preferences and roles of policy-makers in realising the national interest through public policy (Krasner 1978; Nordlinger 1981; Skocpol 1985). This view postulates that policy-makers are not mere intermediaries for societal interest groups but are capable of maintaining autonomous power to formulate and pursue their own policy goals. Another strand of the approach has stressed the role of domestic political institutions in explaining a state's policy formation (Goldstein 1988; Garrett and Lange 1996). According to this institutional approach, not only do political institutions create the particular social order but also constitute the filter through which the demands from societal actors are transformed into policies. Furthermore, some scholars have highlighted preferences and behaviour of societal actors in policy formulation. This approach regards the state's external policy as the product of the ongoing struggle or competition among individuals, firms and groups, which retain particular policy preferences. The interests and preferences of societal interest groups and their abilities to form a coalition to attain specific political objectives are the primary importance of policy formation. According to this view, state officials or political institutions play neither an autonomous nor a significant intervening role in formulating public policy.

This chapter follows the domestic politics approach that focuses on preferences and actions of a state's policy-makers. But, it does not adopt a conventional research method. The previous studies of Japan's external policy tended to consider the influence of domestic politics by examining political interactions among major actors over particular issues or relations with specific countries or regions (Funabashi 1995; Mendl 1995; Sudo 2002). Unlike the previous studies, this chapter adopts an actor-specific approach. I select specific actors and explore how and why their preferences and activities for East Asian affairs have evolved. The two actors taken up in this chapter are the LDP and MOF.

The focus on the LDP and MOF in examining Japan's economic policy towards East Asia derives from two interests. First, the LDP and MOF have been the two main power centres in Japanese politics. Indeed, the LDP and MOF are not central actors in Japan's economic diplomacy, but their political influence extends over every aspect of Japanese policy-making. The LDP has reigned the power since 1955 except for 1993–94. Although the party has been obliged to form a coalition or engage in extra-cabinet cooperation with small parties since 1994, its role in policy-making has been preponderant. MOF is the most powerful ministry, often called a 'ministry above ministries' in Japan. The ministry long dominated budget and jurisdiction over the financial sector. While it reduced power due to the separation of the Financial Supervisory Agency in July 2000, it has still been a main power centre in Japan. In fact, quite a few scholars have identified either the LDP or MOF as the driving force behind changes (or no changes) in Japan (Rosenbluth 1996; Calder 1997c; Pempel 1999). In a recent study of Japan's responses to international capital pressure, Pempel argues that the LDP and MOF have been among the most persistent opponent of changes resulting from global capital pressure (Pempel 1999).

Second, despite their political power, few studies have examined relationship between the LDP or MOF and East Asia. This is understandable given that there are two actors that deal with Japan's external economic policy: the Ministry of Foreign Affairs (MOFA) and Ministry of Economy, Trade and Industry (METI). While MOFA is a ministry that deals with foreign affairs including economic diplomacy, METI has gained an influence in the field of economic diplomacy after the mid-1980s. Several studies have examined MOF's preferences and policies towards Asia since the mid-1990s. However, the main focus of these studies has been the development and economic implications of the policies, not preferences and activities of MOF.[2] The studies of the LDP's Asian policy are far more limited. Given the preponderant influence of the LDP and MOF in Japanese politics, research on their preferences and activities will enrich our understanding of Japan–East Asian relationship. In particular, we could expect that when the LDP and MOF would have paid particular attention to strength in relations and cooperation with East Asia, Japan's commitments to the region would be determined and deeply rooted.

This chapter examines the preferences the LDP and MOF have towards regional cooperation, as well as how and why these preferences have evolved since the late 1990s. For this objective, I delve into particular activities and responses of the LDP and MOF regarding regional cooperation and explore their evolving preferences and factors producing such evolutions.

Domestic interest, regional cooperation and the LDP

The LDP and the APEC EVSL initiative

One of the main issues where Japan's stance and behaviour had a significant impact on regional cooperation in the late 1990s was the Early Voluntary Sectoral Liberalisation (EVSL) Initiative at the APEC (Asia-Pacific Economic Cooperation). At the Vancouver meeting in November 1997, the APEC members agreed to take steps to liberalise trade in fifteen sectors under the EVSL program. Nine out of the fifteen sectors were identified as 'priority' sectors.[3] Japan's attitudes towards proposed tariff cuts on forestry and fishery products, two of the nine priority areas, became a critical issue at the Kuala Lumpur meeting in November 1998.

In June 1998, an APEC Trade Ministers' meeting was held in Kuching, Malaysia in order to formulate frameworks for the scope of coverage, specific measures and time line for the implementation of priority sectors. Officials from the United States, Canada, and others began to present the view that all fifteen sectors represented a package to be implemented in full by all economies (Wesley 2001: 196). METI Minister Mitsuo Horiuchi expressed his view that tariff cuts would be implemented under the APEC's 'voluntarism' principle. However, Horiuchi was isolated, not gaining support even from the Asian members.

The newly appointed METI Minister Kaoru Yosano visited Singapore, Indonesia and Malaysia in late September in order to drum up support for Japan's stance on the EVSL. However, Rahardi Ramelan, Indonesian Minister of Industry and Trade, asserted that 'exports of forestry and fishery products were critical for Indonesia. The liberalisation not including all the nine areas would be meaningless'. Malaysian Prime Minister Mahathir also just answered 'I understand' to Japan's request to support its stance.[4]

In late October, some members of the government searched for a compromise. At an APEC-related Ministers' meeting on 23 October, METI Minister Yosano asked Shoichi Nakagawa, the Minister of Ministry of Agriculture, Forestry and Fisheries (MAFF), to conduct a survey to estimate the possible impact of tariff cuts on the fishery industry. METI feared that Japan would be blamed for putting the brakes on moves towards liberalisation at APEC. Nakagawa did not reject this proposal but stated that this would be nothing to do with the acceptance of the liberalisation program.[5] Prime Minister Keizo Obuchi reportedly requested the ministers concerned to make ultimate efforts for adjustment.[6] Accepting Obuchi's request, Nakagawa visited the United States in order to have a meeting with US Trade Representative Charlene Barshefsky.

The LDP, in cooperation with relevant interest groups and MAFF, pushed back moves towards a compromise. On 28 October, the LDP's Special Committee on Trade in Agriculture, Forestry and Fishing Products and other relevant divisions directly asked Prime Minister Obuchi not to accept further tariff reductions in the forestry and fishery sectors.[7] On 4 November, the National Fisheries Cooperative Federation (*Zengyoren*) and Japan Forestry Association (*Nihon Ringyo Kyokai*) held anti-EVSL assemblies, and some thirty *norin zoku* (agricultural tribes) attended the assemblies.[8] On 5 November, the special committee held a meeting, and confirmed Shotaro Oshima, Director-General of the Economic Affairs Bureau at MOFA, that other countries recognised that Japan would not join the liberalisation of forestry and fishery products.[9] In these moves, the government consolidated its position not to accept the liberalisation.

Commitments of the LDP's *norin zoku* and relevant interest groups continued just before the APEC Ministerial meeting on 14 and 15 November at Kuala Lumpur. On 11 November, eight groups including the Central Union of Agricultural Cooperatives (*Zenchu*), *Zengyoren*, and *Nihon Ringyo Kyokai* held a joint conference at the LDP's headquarters. Some 350 people gathered to pressure the government to defend tariffs on wood and fish products. At the meeting, Arata Sakurai, the head of the LDP's Special Committee on Trade in Agriculture, Forestry and Fishing Products, stated that 'we are in the unpredictable situation because the United States conducts active lobbying. We will undertake the Dietmen's diplomacy in order to protect the forestry and fishing sectors'.[10]

In fact, Yoichi Tani, chairman of the LDP's Research Commission on Comprehensive Agricultural Administration and several other *norin zoku* visited Malaysia, and had a meeting with Prime Minister Mahathir in order to get confirmation of support for Japan's stance.[11] These *zoku* members observed the process of the Ministerial meeting. The visit of Japanese Diet members to an APEC meeting was quite exceptional. The Ministers of METI and MOFA did not have a right to negotiate but just had to stick to the policy determined in Japan. Eventually, the APEC Ministers agreed to refer the EVSL program to the World Trade Organisation (WTO) where they would try to persuade other countries to sign up and reach a WTO-level agreement on trade liberalisation in those nine sectors by the end of 1999. Japan could push through its assertion by receiving backing of major Asian countries that finally sided with Japan on the issue.

The result was interpreted as Japan's success of drawing support from other Asian countries, pushing back US pressure for rapid liberalisation.[12] However, the stance of Asian countries was more complicated. Some Southeast Asian countries such as Thailand and Indonesia had an expectation for market liberalisation under the EVSL program (Wesley 2001: 202). The Southeast Asian countries acknowledged the need to promote market liberalisation and integration in the serious economic slump under the Asian financial crisis. A Thai senior official, who attended the Kuching meeting in June 1998, criticised Japan's position, arguing that 'Asia in difficult circumstances has to promote liberalisation. Japan, as an economic power, should take the lead in implementing liberalisation'.[13] In fact, at the Sixth ASEAN Summit in December 1998, the ASEAN members issued the 'Statement on Bold Measures', which aimed to achieve the ASEAN Free Trade Area (AFTA) by 2002, one year earlier than the previous plan. The reduction of tariffs on fisheries and forest products was desirable for most Southeast Asian countries.

However, the Japanese government did not pay due respect to such preferences, and used financial packages as leverage to secure the support of the neighbouring countries. At the final stage, the Japanese government decided to offer 25 billion yen aid packages over five years to improve the fishing and lumber industry in Asian countries. This package aimed at exchange for a release to tariff reduction on Japan's fisheries and forestry products. The New Miyazawa Initiative, announced in October 1998, also became a catalyst to draw support from the Asian members.

The EVSL Initiative has been raised as an example of Japan's regressive leadership (Rapkin 2001: 391–4). Importantly, the Japanese government did not form a common front opposing market liberalisation under the EVSL program although the treatment of the sectors as a package clearly departed from Japan's understanding of and expectation for the EVSL. But, MOFA and METI strove to search for a compromise. The decisive factor that blocked moves towards a compromise was the LDP's stubborn opposition.

A critical note is that the LDP did not necessarily recognise the economic plight of the East Asian countries and the need to promote economic cooperation with them. In February 1998, the LDP dispatched a mission to investigate economic and financial conditions in Southeast Asia, and issued a policy paper entitled *Emergency Measures towards the Financial and Currency Crisis in Southeast Asia*. The paper listed numerous measures to sustain the economic recovery of the crisis-hit countries (Nakajima 1999: 92–7). In June 1998, the LDP set up a subcommittee concerning the internationalisation of the yen under the Research Commission on the Finance and Banking Systems. Four months later, the subcommittee issued a policy paper that contained detailed measures for the internationalisation of the yen. In this paper, the LDP showed the view that it is Japan's responsibility to develop environments favourable for promoting the use of the yen, given deepened economic linkages between Japan and Asian countries. Thus, in 1998, the LDP reacted to the Asian financial crisis by sending a special mission, and formulated measures for stronger financial integration with East Asia. However, when the matter was concerned with the interest of its core constituency, the behaviour of the party became reactive, not considering the effects of adopted policies on Japan's external relations.

The LDP and FTAs

A dramatic change in Japan's trade policy after the late 1990s is a shift in stress from the multilateral system to regional alternatives. Japan, as an economy with an unusually diverse range of export markets, was long cautious about discriminatory regional trade arrangements. However, this policy stance changed in the late 1990s. The origin of changes began in summer 1998 when METI's International Trade Policy Bureau commenced to investigate worldwide trends of regional economic integrations, its merits and demerits, and possible policy options for Japan (Munakata 2001: 100). The new policy stance became apparent in METI's *White Paper on International Trade*. The 1999 edition appreciated positive aspects of regional trade arrangements such as the provision of models of rule making for multilateral forums and the advancement of multilateral trade negotiations in deadlock by enabling plural countries to form one voice (METI 1999a: 293–4).

METI's policy shift was consonant with policy preferences of big business. *Nippon Keidanren* (Japan Business Federation) issued quite a few position papers concerning FTAs after 1999 (Table 6.1). In the June 2001 paper, the federation showed the scenario of market integration in East Asia: the formation of an FTA with South Korea following that with Singapore; the formation of FTAs by Japan, South Korea and Singapore with other countries in the region; and the conclusion of FTAs among the ASEAN Plus Three (APT) countries. Furthermore, Keidanren was directly involved in the formation of FTAs. After the Japanese and Korean governments agreed to set up the Japan–Korea FTA Business Forum in September 2000, Keidanren assumed a joint secretariat with other organisations such as the Japan Chamber of Commerce and Industry.

METI and Keidanren had common objectives in propelling FTAs. First, they sought to promote domestic structural adjustments through the formation of FTAs. They believed that the FTAs would be a catalyst to revive the depressed domestic economy by urging structural reforms of the internationally weak industries. Second, they hoped to protect the interest of Japanese business in worldwide moves towards regionalism. They feared that a delay in response to regionalism would give serious disadvantages to trade and investment operations of Japanese firms in the world.[14]

Table 6.1   Keidanren's recommendations concerning free trade agreements

Date	Title
20 April 1999	Report on the possible effects of a Japan–Mexico Free Trade Agreement on Japanese industry
10 April 2000	Joint statement recommending an early commencement of negotiations leading to a Free Trade Agreement between Japan and Mexico
18 July 2000	Urgent call for active promotion of Free Trade Agreements: Towards a new dimension in trade policy
2 October 2000	Expectations for the Japan–Singapore Free Trade Agreement
14 June 2001	Towards the implementation of strategic trade policies: A grand design of Japan's policy as a nation built on trade
23 October 2001	A renewed call for the early conclusion of a Japan–Mexico Free Trade Agreement
20 November 2001	Searching for a renewed development in industrial cooperation between Japan and South Korea
17 September 2002	Urgent call for implementation of the Initiative for Japan–ASEAN Comprehensive Economic Partnership
30 October 2002	Welcoming the opening of official negotiations towards a Japan–Mexico Free Trade Agreement, and expecting for an expeditious conclusion

Source: Compiled from data in Keidanren's homepage by the author.

Growing preferences for FTAs led to real policy changes. In late 1999, Singapore Prime Minister Goh Chok Tong proposed his Japanese counterpart Keizo Obuchi to begin studying the possibility of an FTA. In October 2000, Japan and Singapore agreed to start negotiations over the formation of an FTA. The two countries signed the JSEPA in January 2002. Japan has continued to examine the formation of FTAs with South Korea, Mexico, ASEAN, Thailand and others. However, Japan's posture towards FTAs was, by and large, lukewarm and indecisive. When Thai Prime Minister Thaksin Shinawatra visited Tokyo in mid-November 2001, he proposed an FTA between Japan and Thailand. Prime Minister Junichiro Koizumi gave an evasive reply to this proposal. Koizumi proposed an initiative for the Japan–ASEAN Close Economic Partnership during his visit to Southeast Asia in January 2002. However, the proposal, which did not contain a fixed target for the formation of a free trade area, was below the expectation of the ASEAN countries.

Japan's indecisive and unstable stance on FTAs had much to do with the treatment of the agricultural sector. Farm products accounted for small portion of exports from Singapore, but considerable portion from other FTA candidate countries. Since Article XXIV of the GATT requires that regional trade arrangements cover 'substantially all the trade', it is difficult to exclude farm products. However, MAFF has been cautious about including agricultural products in FTAs.

MAFF's views on FTAs were demonstrated in several official documents. In a paper regarding the JSEPA released in August 2001, MAFF stated that given the current situation of Japanese agriculture, tariffs regarding agriculture, forestry and fisheries should be discussed at the WTO negotiations, and further tariff reductions should not be made at negotiations over individual FTAs.[15] A crucial reason why Japan shifted from the multilateral-oriented to bilateral-centred trade policy was the delay of trade liberalisation at the WTO. In particular, the agricultural sector was a bottleneck at the WTO negotiations. MAFF rejected tariff reductions through FTAs with a pretext of the WTO (Nakakita 2002: 107). In July 2002, MAFF issued a formal position paper entitled *Japan's Food Security and Agricultural Trade Policy: Focusing on FTAs*.[16] In this paper, MAFF states that in committing to an FTA, it is necessary to pay due attention to food security in Japan and to avoid negative impacts on efforts to implement structural adjustments. The report also states that FTAs will give minimal direct benefits to the agricultural sector. MAFF considered benefits of FTAs in light of the agricultural sector alone, not the entire Japanese economy.

A main reason why Japan chose Singapore as the first partner for an FTA was that the country exported minimal agricultural products. Singapore's exports of agricultural products such as dairy products and cut flowers made up only 3 per cent of Japan's imports from the country. Nonetheless, the treatment of the agricultural sector became a controversial issue during the negotiations because MAFF asserted that agricultural products should be excluded from the target of an FTA. In October 2000, Yuki Takagi, Vice-Minister of MAFF, checked the negotiations, stating that agricultural issues should be negotiated at the WTO framework, not at an FTA table.[17] The Japanese government as a whole was anxious about international criticisms of excluding the whole agricultural products from the FTA with Singapore. Accordingly, the government adopted a policy to list agricultural products whose tariffs were virtually zero as 'tariff zero products'. Some 460 items became the target under this method. The main objective of concluding FTAs was to promote structural adjustments in the internationally weak industries, and the agricultural sector was a representative. However, the sector was virtually excluded from the FTA with Singapore. Interestingly, MAFF bureaucrats welcomed the JSEPA at the final stage, expecting that the agreement, which excluded the agricultural sector, would be a precedent for future FTAs.[18]

The peculiar treatment of agricultural products in the JSEPA had much to do with political pressure. In early August 2001, MAFF explained detailed policies for agricultural products at an FTA with Singapore at the LDP's Research Commission on Trade in Agriculture, Forestry and Fishing Products, and confirmed that tariffs regarding agricultural and fishing products would not change as a result of the FTA. However, the commission members argued that tariffs on agricultural products should be discussed at the WTO and that it needs to examine effects of an FTA with Singapore on negotiations over FTAs with Mexico and South Korea.[19] The LDP members had strong preferences for discussing tariffs on agricultural products at the WTO and feared that once Japan made concessions on market liberalisation at an FTA with Singapore, it would be forced to make the same concession with other countries.

Eventually, it was the same day as the third negotiations when the Japanese government intended to reach a virtual agreement with Singapore that the LDP formally approved the government policy.[20] A government official who was involved in the negotiations recalls that 'there was strong pressure from the LDP and the farm lobby on the government not to agree to make any further liberalisation of the agricultural market in negotiating an FTA with Singapore'.[21]

The LDP's policy stance was persistent in that it opposed any attempt to promote market liberalisation beyond the WTO framework. Its actions concerning FTAs were superficially the same as those seen towards the APEC meeting in November 1998. However, the LDP seemed to deepen the recognition of the need to promote economic integration with East Asia. Some LDP members gave respect to economic integration with East Asia through the conclusion of FTAs. Former Prime Minister Yasuhiro Nakasone stated at a lecture of the party that Japan should expand an FTA with Singapore aiming at the East Asian Economic Cooperation Treaty.[22] In June 2002, the LDP's Trade and Industry Division and Research Commission on Small and Medium-sized Enterprises issued a position paper entitled *Emergency Recommendations for Revitalising the Japanese Economy*. In this paper, the party proposed creating the East Asian Free Business Zone by promoting economic integration with East Asia and propelling the conclusion of FTAs. This proposal was one of the four pillars that would be the base for the reconstruction of Japan's industrial competitiveness.

A crucial factor that urged the LDP to highlight regional cooperation was China's rising influence in East Asia. The June 2002 paper raised China's prominence in parallel with the globalised world economy and information technology (IT) evolution as examples of drastic changes in economic environments surrounding Japan. Some LDP politicians expressed their anxiety about Japan's delay in moves towards regional integration compared with China. At a meeting of the Foreign Affairs Division in November 2001, one member stated that 'I was surprised at the news that China and ASEAN would form an FTA within ten years. I am concerned about China's rising economic influence on the ASEAN countries, and our country should react to this through Asian diplomacy'.[23] These facts imply that views on FTAs were divided within the party and China's economic emergence and commitments to regional integration raised the sense of the crisis that delay in moves towards regional integration would lead to serious disadvantages to Japan.

The LDP, foreign affairs, and East Asia

As economic linkages with East Asia increased after the late 1980s, Japan's economic prosperity has become increasingly dependent on the relationship with and prospect of the region. However, the LDP did not support initiatives to promote regional cooperation with East Asia when the issue was pertinent to the interest of its core constituencies. In this sense, both increased economic interdependence and the Asian financial crisis did not produce significant changes in the LDP's preferences and actions to regional cooperation.

Two factors have constrained the LDP's stance on regional integration in East Asia. The first is minimal interest of LDP politicians in foreign affairs due to little pork barrelling or relevance to election districts. The Foreign Affairs Division has been one of the most unpopular divisions, sometimes facing difficulty in finding its chairman. Indeed, some LDP members showed interest in ODA programs, but this interest did not last long. Moreover, distinctive characteristics of foreign affairs dampened the interests of politicians. In the Constitution, the management of foreign affairs is clearly attributed to one of the functions of the Cabinet.[24] The LDP politicians criticise the government policy fiercely at the meetings of the Foreign Affairs Division (Kurimoto 1999: 176). This is not because the LDP members have great interest in foreign affairs but because MOFA makes a report of policies that have been already determined.

The second factor that influenced the LDP's stance on East Asian affairs is its emphasis on alliances with the United States and resultant weak concerns with Asia. Indeed, some influential politicians paid respect to relationship with Asia. This was shown in some LDP members' attitudes towards the EAEC, a proposal that the Japanese government did not formally endorse. Noboru Takeshita, former Prime Minister and the most influential politician in the early 1990s, explicitly supported the East Asian Economic Caucus (EAEC) from its first proposal. When Takeshita attended the Davos forum in January 1992, he stated that the Asian countries excluded the imposition of the developed countries' values and referred to the EAEC in parallel with APEC.[25] Later, Prime Minister Ryutaro Hashimoto focused on improving linkages with East Asia by choosing Southeast Asia as his first foreign visit destination (Wang 2002: 119). Prime Minister Keizo Obuchi also sought to deepen the linkages between Japan and East Asia by unveiling a US$500 million package for human resources development in Asia and human exchanges between Japan and other Asian countries.

However, the LDP as a whole has given high priority to close relationship with the United States. The alliance with the country has been one of the basic tenets for the party's mainstream factions (Inoguchi 1999: 6–8). The emphasis on close linkages with the United States was natural during the Cold War period, but this policy stance continued without significant reassessments even after ten years from the end of the Cold War. In October 1997, the LDP's Research Commission on Foreign Affairs issued the guidelines regarding Japan's Asia-Pacific policy. The first pillar of the eight basic strategies was the maintenance and strength of the Japan–US alliances, and other pillars did not refer to 'Asia' or 'East Asia' (Liberal Democratic Party Foreign Affairs Division 1997: 11–20). This implies that the party has not sought to define diplomatic objectives and strategies for East Asia independent of the United States. Thus, the basic characteristics – little interest in foreign affairs and stress on relationship with the United States – impeded the party from pursuing far-sighted regional policies despite drastic changes in regional environments.

MOF and regional financial and monetary cooperation

MOF's commitments to East Asia before and during the Asian financial crisis

For a long time, MOF sought to strengthen linkages with the western countries. The ministry put emphasis on collaboration at the meetings of the G-7 Finance Ministers and Central Governors. This does not necessarily mean that the ministry paid little attention to Asia. The Japanese government took the lead in establishing the Asian Development Bank (ADB) in 1966, becoming the largest contributor to the bank. In the development of the bank, an informal practice of selecting Japanese presidents was established and six out of the seven presidents to date were MOF's ex-bureaucrats (Wan 2001: 152–3). MOF also offered intellectual contributions for the economic reconstruction of major Asian countries and assisted the return of some Asian countries to international finance (Kubota 1999: 50). What characterises these activities was Japan's unilateral commitments to Asia, contributions from an advanced country to developing countries in the region. These policies envisioned neither the strength of economic linkages with East Asia in a symmetrical relationship nor the strategic use of the linkages for enhancing Japan's interest in the world.

MOF gradually intensified efforts to promote stronger linkages with East Asian countries after the early 1990s. When Tadao Chino became a Vice-Minister of Finance for International Affairs in July 1991, he visited several Asian countries the following month. This was the first time that a newly appointed Vice-Minister of Finance for International Affairs chose Asia as the first destination.[26] MOF began to explain international financial affairs to the ASEAN members in 1995 by holding informal meetings with the ASEAN Finance Ministers. Between 1995 and 1999, the meeting was organised ten times when the finance ministers attended the annual International Monetary Fund (IMF)-World Bank meetings or the annual ADB meetings. Importantly, the first ASEAN Finance Ministers' meeting was organised in February 1997 after the meeting with Japanese Finance Minister was institutionalised (Yamakage 2001: 69).

In the mid-1990s, MOF raised its interests in the East Asian economies by establishing several research institutes. The Institute for International Monetary Affairs (IIMA) was set up in December 1995. The institute, headed by Toyoo Gyoten, a former Vice-Minister of Finance for International Affairs, was established by the Bank of Tokyo (currently the Bank of Tokyo-Mitsubishi), but it has played a critical role in leading the debates on financial and monetary issues, often undertaking research projects entrusted by MOF. Moreover, the ministry set up the Asian Development Bank Institute in December 1997. The institute, located in Tokyo, aimed to provide intellectual bases for pursuing the appropriate development paradigms for Asia, which were composed of the balanced combination of the role of market, institutions and the government. The original dean, Jesus Estanislao, a former Finance

Secretary of the Philippines, resigned after just one year in office, and Masaru Yoshitomi, a former senior official at Japan's Economic Planning Agency, took over the post.

In the early 1990s, MOF began to challenge the development paradigms adopted by western-dominated international financial institutions. The ministry with increasing confidence in the state-guided development model induced the World Bank to undertake the first comprehensive research on economic development in East Asia (Wade 1996; Wan 2001: 147–8).[27] Japanese aid institutions represented by the Overseas Economic Cooperation Fund intensified an independent development approach, which was different from universally oriented, strict macroeconomic adjustment programs pursued by the World Bank and IMF. The establishment of the research institutes aimed to deepen linkages with East Asian countries, and strengthen intellectual capabilities to study the Asian economies in order to legitimate the Asian style development approach. For instance, the ADB Institute took the lead in establishing the Asian Policy Forum in December 1999. The forum, comprising seventeen research institutes, all located in Asia, aimed to provide intellectual and analytical leadership in the Asian policy communities. Importantly, the forum represents MOF's preferences that recommendations for the Asian economies should reflect local realities in terms of each economy's institutions, history, and stage of development.

When the Asian currency crisis occurred in Thailand, MOF at first adopted a stance to follow the IMF. When Thai Finance Minister Tarrin Nimmanahaeminda sounded out the possibility of arranging a rescue package outside of the IMF in July 1997, the ministry only encouraged him to seek an arrangement with the fund (Sakakibara 2000: 176–7). However, Tokyo hosted an international meeting for Thai rescue the following month, and successfully took the lead in drawing up a rescue package totalling US$17.2 billion mainly funded by Asian countries. Inspired by this mood, MOF pushed forward an idea to establish a new regional monetary fund, the Asian Monetary Fund (AMF).

Indeed, it seems that the AMF was proposed rather abruptly at this time, but MOF had considered the necessity of a regional monetary and financial cooperation mechanism since around 1992 (Furukawa 2001: 17). This was because the United States opposed capital increase of the IMF and ADB, which would lead to the decline of its representation in these institutions. MOF was also discontent with the IMF conditionality, which comprised the drastic austerity policy and structural adjustment policy. MOF officials considered that there were cases when expansionary rather than tight macroeconomic policies were appropriate, and structural adjustment policy should be undertaken from a mid- and long-term time span.

At the annual IMF-World Bank meeting in September 1997, Japan formally proposed an AMF, which would include US$100 billion in contribution from Asian countries. However, the proposal met adamant opposition from the US Treasury and the IMF. The US government and IMF protested against the proposal on the grounds that the proposed fund would increase danger of moral hazard and its functions would overlap with those of the IMF. China did not support the proposal as well because of fear that Japan would take the lead in the region at its expense. In addition, domestic financial turmoil in autumn 1997 signified by the bankruptcies of Hokkaido Takushoku Bank and Yamaichi Securities prevented MOF from coordinating with Japanese banks and other relevant private sectors about the AMF (Katada 2001). Eventually, the AMF did not come into being, and instead the Manila Framework was agreed in November 1997.

When the currency crisis changed into the overall economic crisis in East Asia, MOF strengthened its commitments to the East Asian economies. In July 1998, the ministry set up the International Financial Market Office (literally Japanese name is the Asian Currency Office). This was the first division that deals specifically with Asian financial matters.[28] Other divisions also began to take up matters pertinent to East Asian countries, and the ministry's awareness of issues and problems that the Asian economies faced became rapidly deepened (Sakakibara 1999: 46).

In early October 1998, Finance Minister Kiichi Miyazawa announced the New Miyazawa Initiative. The US government did not oppose the initiative because there was an implicit understanding between Tokyo and Washington that Japan would not object to US rescue plans for Brazil while the United States would not oppose Japan's rescue packages for Asian countries including Malaysia (Sakakibara 2000: 76).[29] The initiative aimed to provide packages of support measures totalling US$30 billion, of which US$15 billion would be made available for the mid- to long-term development while another US$15 billion would be used for the short-term capital need during the process of implementing economic reform. Before launching this initiative, directors at MOF's International Bureau formulated concrete plans by setting up country-specific policy teams for South Korea, Thailand/Malaysia, Indonesia and the Philippines (Suehiro 2001: 250). The total amount that the Japanese government provided for assistance reached US$80 billion, US$70 billion of which was implemented by December 1999 (MOFA 2000).

The failure to establish the AMF made MOF officials cautious about taking the initiative in regional and monetary affairs. For instance, when Korean Prime Minister Kim Jong-pil proposed a regional monetary fund of US$300 billion in November 1998, the Japanese government showed no meaningful responses. However, MOF raised its interest in regional economic affairs and showed substantial commitments to resolving economic plights in major East Asian countries caused by the financial crisis.

MOF and East Asia after the Asian financial crisis

After the East Asian countries recovered from the Asian financial crisis, MOF's interest was directed towards regional and monetary cooperation to prevent the recurrence of a financial crisis. Three policy areas were particularly targeted. The first was the development of regional financial facilities. In the APT summit meeting in November 1999, the APT leaders agreed on the need to enhance self-help and support mechanism in East Asia. Then, the APT Finance Ministers agreed the Chiang Mai Initiative at the second APT Finance Ministers meeting in May 2000. The initiative, designed to strengthen the mechanism for self-help and support in the region, consisted of two pillars. The first was an extension of the existing ASEAN swap arrangement among the ASEAN-5 countries (Indonesia, Malaysia, the Philippines, Singapore and Thailand) to all ten ASEAN members, raising the total amount from US$200 million to US$1 billion. The second was a network of bilateral swap and repurchase agreement facilities, which included Japan, China and South Korea.

Interestingly, it was unclear who took the lead in establishing the Chiang Mai Initiative. However, MOF surely undertook informal negotiations behind the scenes in order to gain explicit support from the United States and other East Asian countries. Unlike the AMF proposal, the US government did not oppose the Chiang Mai Initiative. This was partly because the US government recognised the need for regional facilities as measures to prevent the repetition of a financial crisis. At the same time, the ministry successfully persuaded the United States. A senior MOF official recalls that it was tough to convince Washington that the initiative would be completely different from the AMF.[30] The Japanese government successfully gained approval of the Chiang Mai Initiative from the United States and other developed countries. In a report to the Heads of State and Government issued in July 2000, G-7 Finance Ministers reaffirmed that:

[M]ember countries may strengthen, on a regional basis, their cooperation in these areas, in a way which is supportive of the IMF's objectives and responsibilities in the global economy, taking into account their common interests in international trade and investment and shared concerns about the risk of regional contagion. Such regional cooperation can improve regional stability and thus contribute to the stability of the global economy.[31]

The networks of the swap agreements have deepened, with Japan at the centre (Figure 6.1). As of July 2002, Japan concluded the bilateral swap agreement with Korea (US$7 billion), Thailand (US$3 billion), the Philippines (US$3 billion), Malaysia (US$3.5 billion) and China (US$3 billion). In addition, Japan began negotiations with Singapore and Indonesia. China and Korea also concluded or considered swap agreements with several ASEAN countries. The cumulative value reached US$17 billion, and the total value of bilateral swap facilities stood at US$24.5 billion including amount under the New Miyazawa Initiative.

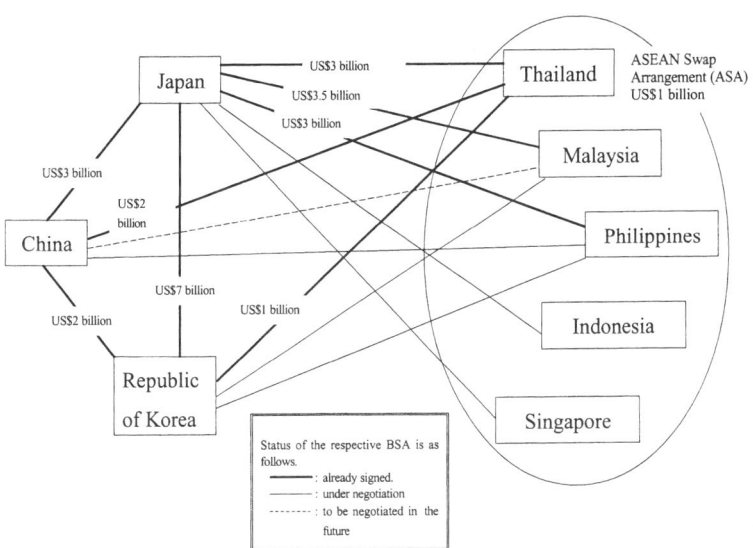

Figure 6.1   Bilateral swap agreements (BSAs) under the Chiang Mai Initiative

Note: The BSAs for Japan–Korea and Japan–Malaysia include the BSAs under the New Miyazawa Initiative. The BSA between Japan and China is a yen–rembinbi swap arrangement.
Source: CCTFEOT (2002: 30).

There was a controversial condition regarding the bilateral swap agreements. At the fourth APT Finance Ministers meeting in Honolulu in May 2001, it was concluded that 90 per cent of the bilateral swap agreement would be activated with the IMF's financial support. In other words, only up to 10 per cent of the maximum amount drawn would be provided without linkages with the IMF. This condition was regarded as retreat from Asian attempt to increase its autonomy in managing regional financial affairs. Some scholars attribute this retreat to insufficient Japanese leadership. For instance, Dieter (2001) argues that the regional liquidity agreements became a toothless tiger due to Japan, which wished to maintain its status in the region rather than providing the framework for genuine and deep integration.

However, the condition could be seen as a compromise of varying preferences of East Asian countries regarding regional financial mechanisms. Malaysia, which dealt with the 1997 crisis without the IMF's help and had a swap agreement with Japan, opposed links with the IMF. In contrast, China and Korea, which would be called upon to mobilise their reserves, favoured close linkages with the IMF programs. Given the significant reform of the IMF, MOF sought to reconcile the interest of East Asian countries adopting higher linkages with the IMF (Amyx 2002: 12–14). In fact, at the third session of the seminar on international financial cooperation between Japan, China and South Korea in late February 2001, the following common understanding had been reached:

> It is necessary to enhance regional financial cooperation to prevent financial crises. In order to make it work in an efficient way, the regional financial cooperation should be designed to supplement the existing international facilities including IMF support. The Chiang Mai Initiative is an effort in this direction and expected to be further materialized. While other means of monetary cooperation might be worthy to be discussed in the future, they have to be pursued in a cautious manner at present time.[32]

Importantly, the APT Finance Ministers agreed to review the main principles of the bilateral swap arrangement under the Chiang Mai Initiative in three years at the Honolulu meeting in May 2001. The first to be reviewed might be the 90 per cent IMF linkage.

The second area of MOF's commitments was the establishment of the reliable regional surveillance system.[33] A critical background of the Asian financial crisis lay in the fact that East Asia had not developed efficient surveillance measures and mechanisms. In addition, the high linkages with IMF at the bilateral swap agreements raised the position of the surveillance system as a way to secure regional autonomy. In October 1998, the ASEAN Finance Ministers signed a Terms of Understanding for the ASEAN Surveillance Process, following the proposals under the Manila Framework. The ASEAN Finance Ministers have met twice a year for policy coordination under the process. Furthermore, the first peer review meeting under the APT framework was held in May 2000 on the sidelines of the annual ADB meeting. The APT framework was particularly important for the ASEAN countries. This was because the broader APT mechanism would facilitate the countries to break away from the tradition of non-interference, one of the main principles of ASEAN (Manupipatpong 2002: 119).

MOF has sustained the development of the surveillance system in East Asia. Japan and other six countries (Brunei, Indonesia, Korea, the Philippines, Thailand and Vietnam) agreed on bilateral exchanges of short-term capital flow data. In order to facilitate this process, MOF established the Japan–ASEAN Financial Technical Assistance Fund at the ASEAN Secretariat in September 2001. The fund aimed to assist some ASEAN countries to improve their monitoring, collection and reporting systems on capital flows. Furthermore, MOF has sent its bureaucrats and other specialists in finance to several Southeast Asian countries under the New Miyazawa Initiative. These specialists, dispatched to the Central Bank or Finance Ministry of the recipient countries, offered assistance and guidance to develop human resources regarding financial and fiscal policies, government bond management, and so on (Kishimoto 2000: 75–7).[34]

The ADB has provided technical assistance to support collaborative efforts among the APT members to develop a regional early warning system that would help detect emerging macroeconomic, financial and corporate sector vulnerabilities (Rana 2002: 6–7). Moreover, the bank set up a study group to identify a monitoring or surveillance unit for the successful implementation of the Chiang Mai Initiative. This unit has monitored liquidity positions and economic fundamentals of its member countries, implementation of common standards agreed among the members, and so on (Rana 2002: 11). MOF's preferences were likely to be reflected on these activities because Dadao Chino assumed the presidency of the bank after January 1999. Chino took part in the creation of the bank and represented MOF at a number of international conferences as the Vice-Minister of Finance for International Affairs.

The third area was the establishment of the stable regional currency system. The initiative in this respect was showed mainly under the

Asia–Europe Meeting (ASEM) framework. In January 2001, Japan hosted the third ASEM Finance Ministers meeting in Kobe. At the meeting, the Japanese government proposed the flexible managed exchange rate system based on the currency basket of the dollar, euro and yen. In addition, a report regarding the exchange rate system was presented. The report, prepared by Japanese and French staff, proposed a managed floating exchange rate regime whereby the currency moves within a given implicit or explicit band with its centre targeted to a basket of currencies. It also states that basket currency regimes including the dollar, yen and euro would better suit the geographical structure of the balance of payments and would foster stability in Asia.[35] Furthermore, the Japanese government proposed the Kobe Research Project.[36] While the IIMA coordinated the whole project, the Japanese scholars conducted research on two topics: exchange rate regimes and strengthening financial cooperation and surveillance. The project, which attempted to collect useful information on the experiences and lessons in Europe for financial and monetary cooperation in East Asia, had a critical implication in that it deepened the understanding of Asian policy-makers about European integration and revealed the new seriousness about their own regional initiatives (Bergsten 2000a: 11).

The outcomes of the project were presented at the fourth ASEM Finance Ministers meeting in Copenhagen in July 2002. The research papers regarding exchange rate regimes for Asia, pointed out the danger of the *de facto* dollar peg system, which is susceptible to fluctuations in effective exchange rates with volatile yen–dollar and dollar–euro exchange rates. They then proposed that the East Asian economies introduce a currency basket system that links the currency's central rate to a basket to major currencies such as the dollar, yen and euro.[37]

MOF's interest in the regional currency system had much to do with the internationalisation of the yen.[38] The debate on the internationalisation of the yen began in the mid-1980s when the Yen–Dollar Committee took up this issue in 1984 and the Council on Foreign Exchange and Other Transactions (CFEOT) released a report on this issue in March 1985.[39] However, substantial progress was not seen for more than ten years afterwards.[40] This was largely because the interest groups in the financial sector and the administrative agencies that had jurisdiction over the sector feared that deregulations for promoting the internationalisation of the yen would lead to the loss of vested interests (Tadokoro 2000: 54–5).

Moves to promote the internationalisation of the yen gained momentum after 1998. In May 1998, Finance Minister Hikaru Matsunaga made it clear that Japan would seek to create better environments for improving the role of the yen at an APEC Finance Ministers meeting. This announcement became a turning point to promote the internationalisation of the yen. In July 1998, the CFEOT established the Sub-council on the Internationalisation of the Yen. The sub-council's report, issued in April 1999, analysed the background and necessity of the internationalisation of the yen, and proposed measures such as the stability in the exchange rates among the dollar, euro, and yen, the strength in correlation between the Asian currencies and the yen, and further improvements in the financial and capital markets (CFEOT 1999). The study of the internationalisation of the yen continued through a private study panel and discussions at the IIMA.

MOF's commitments to regional monetary and financial cooperation have been sustained by intensive research after the financial crisis. In October 1997, the ministry set up the Subcommittee on Asian Financial and Capital Markets at the CFEOT. The aim of the subcommittee was to discuss the causes and characteristics of the Asian financial crisis and the problems that the crisis caused in the emerging market economies, international financial institutions and Japan. In May 1998, the subcommittee issued a report entitled *Lessons from the Asian Currency Crises: Risks Related to Short-Term Capital Movement and the "21st Century-Type" Currency Crisis*.

Then, in November 1999, MOF set up the Sub-council on the Revitalization of the Asian Economy and Financial Markets. In June 2000, the sub-council issued the report entitled *The Road to the Revival of the Asian Economy and Financial System: Sustainable Growth in the 21st Century and Building of a Multilayered Regional Cooperative Network*. The report stressed the formation of comprehensive networks of regional trade and investment, mutual stability of regional currency rate, the promotion of policy talks and regional financial arrangements.

MOF continued research on the Asian economies by establishing in January 2001 an Expert Group on the Challenges of the Asian Economy and Financial Markets. The group conducted comprehensive research on the Asian economies and possible measures to prevent the re-emergence of a currency and financial crisis in Asia. In July 2002, the group issued a report entitled *Responding to the Challenges of the Asian Economy and Financial Markets: Crisis Prevention and Realization of Stable Economic Growth*. This report proposed detailed measures for developing the efficient and stable financial systems and creating the appropriate choice of foreign exchange regimes and capital flow controls.

Thus, MOF has searched for the stable financial and monetary regime in East Asia through discussions at the research bodies. The three research groups examined the causes of the Asian financial crisis, showed blueprints for recovery of the Asian economies, and proposed detailed measures to promote the sound development of the Asian economies. The successive establishment of the research bodies was a reflection of MOF's genuine interest in the East Asian economies, and the ministry's concrete activities followed various proposals and recommendations by these research groups.

The background of MOF's renewed interest in the East Asian economies

What factors have induced MOF to show renewed and substantial commitments to regional cooperation in the 1990s? Indeed, the ministry's actions were partially inspired by demands from the private sector. The business federations and major industrial associations urged the Japanese government to strengthen economic and financial linkages with East Asia after the late 1990s. In March 2000, *Keidanren* issued a report entitled *For Asia's Economic Renewal: A Proposal by Japan's Business Community*. The report proposed that Japan offer more assistance by both the public and private sectors to other Asian countries in the areas of personnel training and know-how in order to strengthen the financial system in the Asian countries, and that the Manila Framework be required to strengthen so that the Asian countries can better cope with market trends that stray too far from their economic fundamentals. In May 2000, *Keizai Doyukai* (Japan Association of Corporate Executives) issued a policy proposal entitled *A Private-Sector Perspective on the Internationalisation of the Yen: A Study on Japanese and Asian Stability and Growth*. It proposed that the internationalisation of the yen should be promoted in structuring intra-regional cooperation including free trade agreements, direct investment agreements, currency stabilisation agreements, and the Asian monetary fund or similar institutions.[41] Thus, the private sector encouraged the government to show more commitments to the Asian economies and contributed to identifying problems in the existing financial regulatory systems.

More important factors that induced MOF to show increasing interest in the regional economic issues were the Asian financial crisis and relevant incidents. Dissatisfaction with the IMF's policy prescriptions for the Asian currency crisis encouraged MOF bureaucrats to pursue independent policies towards East Asia. This is clearly shown in the May 1998 report issued by the CFEOT. The report criticises the IMF approaches, stating that the IMF needed a more flexible approach in tailoring the conditionality to the situation in individual countries, and that the requirements of a long-term agenda for structural reform can be differentiated from the urgent issues related to an ongoing liquidity crisis (CFEOT 1998). Even during the Asian financial crisis, MOF bureaucrats were critical of IMF's prescription to the crisis. For instance, MOF's senior officials had fierce disputes with Bijan Agheveli, the IMF's mission chief to Indonesia, opposing bold programs for structural reform applied to the Indonesian economy (Sakakibara 2000: 196–7).

The failure to establish the AMF did not reduce MOF's interest in the East Asian economies but changed the style of commitments to regional financial affairs. Learning from its failure, the ministry has proceeded with regional, financial and monetary cooperation carefully and strategically. While it has maintained close collaboration with other countries such as the United States and China, it has implemented activities in close collaboration with international institutions such as the ADB and ASEM. This style of commitments seems to be less assertive, but might be realistic and eventually more effective. In establishing the AMF, MOF showed an exceptionally assertive role. However, it returned to Japan's conventional leadership style, 'leading from behind' after its failure.[42] The ministry has also utilised its affiliated research institutes such as the IIMA and ADB Institute in order to develop institutional relationship with other regional countries, and deepen the ideas about desirable economic development for Asia.

Conclusion

The central argument of this chapter is that the pivotal political actors in Japan changed their preferences for stronger regional integration and cooperation, responding to changes in regional environments after the mid-1990s. In order to examine this argument, it has focused on preferences and activities of the LDP and MOF, the power centres in Japanese politics. The preceding examination has revealed different stances and roles of the two actors regarding Japan's commitments to East Asia.

There were two cases when the LDP's preferences and actions impinged on the development of regional cooperation after the late 1990s. The first was market liberalisation under the EVSL Initiative at APEC. The United States pushed for the package program under the initiative towards the Kuala Lumpur meeting in November 1998, and some Southeast Asian countries hoped to promote market liberalisation in response to the Asian financial crisis. However, the Japanese government pushed back such moves, and APEC's proposed program was eventually referred to the WTO. The Japanese government's posture was highly influenced by the LDP, which was desperate in protecting the interest of the agricultural group, one of its core constituencies.

The LDP showed similar actions with respect to moves towards FTAs between Japan and East Asian countries. The economic bureaucrats and business leaders intensified their preferences for bilateral FTAs because they expected that the agreements would become a catalyst to promote structural reforms of Japanese industry. However, the myopic interest of protecting the agricultural sector impeded such policy preferences from being translated into policy outcomes smoothly. MAFF virtually excluded the agricultural sector from the target of an FTA with Singapore, and its stance was sustained by the LDP's *norin zoku*.

Importantly, the recent regional evolutions such as the Asian financial crisis and increased economic interdependence did not necessarily have no influence on the preferences and behaviour of the LDP. The LDP sent a special mission to Southeast Asia in order to investigate economic conditions in the region. The LDP politicians at the Trade and Industry Division and Foreign Affairs Division supported the promotion of FTAs with the East Asian countries partly as a countermeasure to China's rising economic influence in the region. However, the LDP's preferences and behaviour became reactive when the matter concerned the interest of its core supporters. In this sense, recent regional evolutions surely influenced the preferences of the LDP regarding regional cooperation, but did not change the basic style of partisan politics.

In the late 1990s, MOF made significant efforts to promote regional cooperation. The ministry provided huge financial assistance to the crisis-hit countries under the New Miyazawa Initiative. MOF also took the lead in developing regional financial facilities and regional surveillance mechanisms, and searched for a desirable currency system for the region.

Indeed, MOF's commitments to regional cooperation had begun in the early and mid-1990s. While it strengthened institutional linkages with East Asian countries, it set up research institutes to search for desirable development paradigms for East Asia. However, the ministry's commitments to regional financial and monetary affairs after 1997 were more comprehensive and strategic. The Asian financial crisis and relevant incidents were the main factors drawing MOF's renewed interest in and commitments to regional affairs. The Asian financial crisis raised the interest of MOF bureaucrats in the East Asian economies. The failure to realise the AMF encouraged the ministry to promote regional cooperation more strategically in collaboration with the international organisations and its affiliated research institutes.

Stress on relationship with East Asia needs the reassessment of Japan's overall diplomacy, and the reassessment then requires the scrutiny of Japan's relationship with the United States and far-reaching strategies for the development of Japanese industry. However, the LDP's passive attitudes towards regional integration impede Japan from conducting such a reassessment and showing genuine leadership in East Asia.

As this chapter confirms, Japan's East Asian policy is surely evolving, but what is currently important is not the direction but the speed of change. This is largely because China, which has shown remarkable economic growth, has had increasing influences on regional integration in East Asia. The following chapter examines the development of regional integration in East Asia from a broader perspective, paying attention to Japan–China relationship.

7

Japan and China in Regional Cooperation

Regional cooperation and integration have been long considered to be difficult in East Asia. The region is characterised by enormous diversities and differences such as the degree of economic development, political systems and cultural backgrounds including languages and religions. The region has experienced serious political rivalries and security tensions, which are still seen in the Korean Peninsula and the Taiwan Strait. These factors have constituted imperative obstacles to any efforts towards regional cooperation and integration. In fact, there was no formal regional institution except for the Association of Southeast Asian Nations (ASEAN) in East Asia, until the Asia-Pacific Economic Cooperation (APEC) was formed in 1989.

Moves towards regional integration have gained momentum in East Asia since the late 1990s, as one scholar argues that 'East Asia may be on the brink of an historic evolution as Europe was half a century ago' (Bergsten 2000b: 22). International and regional evolutions exemplified by intensive trends towards regionalism elsewhere in the world and the Asian financial crisis in 1997–98 made policy-makers in East Asia recognise the need to protect their interest through holding their own regional cooperation frameworks. The East Asian countries began the ASEAN Plus Three (APT) summit meeting in December 1997, and sought to develop this framework as a forum to discuss economic, political and even security matters. The countries also agreed in May 2000 to build a network of bilateral swap and repurchase agreement facilities among the ASEAN countries, China, Japan, and South Korea.

This chapter examines the conditions for promoting the further development of regional integration in East Asia in terms of leadership role. One of the main factors promoting regional integration in Europe was Franco–German cooperation. The initiatives of Jean Monnet,

Robert Schuman and Konrad Adenauer in the mid-1950s paved the way for the European integration afterwards. In East Asia, Sino–Japanese cooperation is an analogy of Franco–German entente. Japan and China steadily intensified political and economic ties after the normalisation of diplomatic relations in 1972. In particular, economic interdependence between the two countries has deepened sharply since the early 1990s. Bilateral trade increased dramatically from US$18.2 billion in 1990 to US$85.7 billion in 2000. Their cooperation has become increasingly important for the smooth and sound development in regional integration in East Asia in the late 1990s. Based on this perception, this chapter seeks to address the following questions. How are regional cooperation and integration in East Asia theoretically evaluated especially in terms of experiences in Europe? How have political and economic evolutions in East Asia changed the necessary conditions for co-leadership between China and Japan? What limitations or obstacles are there to propelling Sino–Japanese collaboration for regional cooperation?

Some observers hold that Sino–Japanese entente for regional integration is unlikely given their hostility from the past, and mutual suspicion stemming from present economic and security concerns (Webber 2001: 362–3). In fact, there are additional sources of conflict such as the Taiwan problem and territorial disputes over Diaoyu/Senkaku Islands. However, practical moves towards regional integration have shown drastic developments since the Asian financial crisis in 1997–98. These moves are likely to have considerable influences on the basic stance of policy-makers in Japan and China on regional cooperation and detailed ways for collaboration.

The main arguments of this chapter are threefold. First, particular characteristics of market integration and regional cooperation in East Asia require perspectives on regional integration and cooperation that are different from those developed in Europe. Second, increased constraints on the East Asian approach to regional cooperation and the shifting regional distribution of capabilities have raised the necessity and probability of Sino–Japan collaboration for regional integration. Third, limitations at the domestic and international levels – intensive nationalistic sentiments among the public and the US policy stance on East Asia – are likely to impede the development of Sino–Japanese tie-ups.

This chapter is organised as follows. The following section overviews moves and background of regional integration in East Asia. The third section 'Regional integration and political leadership' locates political leadership in broader integration debates and draws meaningful conditions for regional integration in East Asia. The fourth section 'Necessary conditions for Sino–Japan co-leadership at the regional level' examines how preconditions for Sino–Japan leadership have evolved from the demand and supply sides. The subsequent two sections consider practical moves towards co-leadership and obstacles to be overcome.

Moves towards stronger integration in East Asia

The formal initiation of an East Asian regional grouping began with a proposal of an East Asian Economic Group (EAEG) by Malaysian Prime Minister Mahathir Mohamad in 1990. The EAEG was renamed into the softer East Asian Economic Caucus (EAEC) one year later, but the EAEC did not develop afterwards largely because of an outright hostility from the United States that feared 'drawing a line down the middle of the Pacific'. The East Asian grouping comprising the ASEAN members, China, Japan and South Korea was formally recognised as the Asian representatives of the Asia–Europe Meeting (ASEM) whose initial meeting was held in Bangkok in March 1996. Then, the first APT summit meeting was held in Kuala Lumpur in December 1997. The APT summit meeting has developed as a comprehensive forum to discuss economic, political and security issues in the region. Furthermore, the APT leaders agreed to establish an East Asia Vision Group, accepting a proposal by South Korean President Kim Dae-jung. The group submitted a report on 'an East Asian Community' to the APT leaders, which was approved at the fifth APT summit meeting in November 2001.

Importantly, the East Asian countries have promoted monetary cooperation prior to trade liberalisation. In May 2000, the East Asian countries announced the Chiang Mai Initiative, and agreed to extend the existing ASEAN Swap Arrangement and to establish a network of bilateral swap and repurchase agreement facilities among the APT members. The East Asian countries hoped to utilise the collective reserves of over US$800 billion, which was over twice those of the Eurozone countries and close to ten times those of the United States (Bowles 2002: 240). The initiative stemmed from a reflection that the past swap agreement was inefficient in cases of speculation against inappropriate exchange rates and aimed to provide short-term financial assistance in the form of swaps to countries that need short-term liquid support.

The East Asian countries have promoted talks about trade liberalisation as well. In November 2000, Chinese Prime Minister Zhu Rongji proposed the formation of a free trade agreement (FTA) between China and ASEAN at an APT summit meeting. One year later, China and ASEAN agreed to begin negotiations over the formation of a free trade area within ten years. Japan signed an FTA with Singapore in January 2002, and has continued the studies of or negotiations over bilateral FTAs with South Korea, Thailand, Taiwan, and so on.

Ministerial meetings under the APT frameworks have extended to foreign affairs and economic cooperation. The first APT Foreign Ministers meeting was held in July 2000, while that of Economic Ministers was organised in Myanmar, in May 2000.[1] In particular, the Economic Ministers in East Asia have formed meshed regional networks: the ASEAN Economic Ministers (AEM) meetings; AEM and the Japanese Minister of Economy, Trade and Industry (AEM–METI) meetings; consultation between AEM and the Minister of Foreign Trade and Economic Cooperation of China; and Economic Ministers meetings of Japan, China and South Korea. Thus, the East Asian commitments to regional cooperation have evolved substantially by deepening the content of talks at the summit meetings and by extending areas for consultation and cooperation.

In Europe, external and internal background conditions created moves towards regional integration in the 1950s. Externally, the threat of communism motivated major countries in Western Europe to strengthen regional linkages. The economic integration of Western Europe and political and security alliances in the Atlantic were paid to respond to the Soviet bloc. Internally, Europe was desperate to construct institutional frameworks so as to avoid another catastrophic war between the constituent states. In particular, subjugation of long hostilities between France and Germany was a key to prevent war. This was clearly shown in the Preamble to the Treaty for the European Coal and Steel Community, which aimed to resolve 'to substitute for age old rivalries the merging of their essential interests', and 'to create, by establishing an economic community, the basis for a broader and deeper community among peoples long divided by bloody conflicts'.[2]

In the late 1990s, similar external and internal forces constituted the background of regional integration in East Asia. Indeed, there was no comparable direct external threat in East Asia to Europe where the North Atlantic Treaty Organisation (NATO) and Warsaw Pact divided the region (Foot 1995: 229–30). However, the continued deepening and expansion of regional arrangements that occurred in North America and Europe were likely to be a serious external threat to East Asian countries. Whereas the EU steadily deepened its networks by adding new members and signing additional cooperative agreements, the United States sought to conclude agreements on a Free Trade Area of the Americas with countries in Latin America. These moves made the East Asian leaders recognise the need to form and develop their own regionalism. The need to strengthen its own regional frameworks was also reinforced by trade and investment liberalisation at a snail's pace under the auspices of the World Trade Organisation (WTO) and the failure of the 1999 WTO Ministerial Conference in Seattle. The internal factor was the Asian financial crisis in 1997–98. The crisis intensified moves towards regional integration through various ways. First, the crisis made East Asian leaders recognise that the Southeast and Northeast Asian economies were closely linked each other. For instance, Domingo Siazon, a former Foreign Affairs Secretary of the Philippines, recalls that 'the East Asian leaders intensified their interests in institutionalising the APT summit through the Asian economic crisis. We recognised with a strong conviction that what happened in Japan, China and South Korea had strong impacts on the ASEAN economies, whereas economic growth in Northeast Asia could be promoted by the development of ASEAN' (Terada 2001: 65).

Second, the crisis provoked resentment against the United States and its domination of international monetary and financial affairs (Higgott 1998). Not only did the US government underestimate the severity of the crisis at first, but it also refused providing financial assistance to Thailand. This made a sharp contrast to the Peso crisis in 1994 when the United States offered US$20 billion as part of a US$50 billion package for Mexico. The 'Washington consensus', which underpinned the International Monetary Fund (IMF) policy prescriptions for some East Asian countries, was regarded as exacerbating the problems than solving them (Bello 1998). For a long time, most East Asian countries hoped that the United States continuously exerted certain influence in the region as a balancer to two regional powers, Japan and China. However, the Asian financial crisis led to reduced expectation for Washington.

Third, economic difficulties due to the crisis raised interest in deepening regional economic integration. In Europe and Latin America, domestic economic troubles raised incentives to promote regional arrangements (Lawrence 1996: 86; Haggard 1997: 38–9). The Asian financial crisis played such a role by intensifying motivations of policy-makers in East Asia to utilise regional arrangements as a way to overcome the economic difficulties.

Regional integration and political leadership

What factors enable regional integration? Mattli (1999) identifies the demand, supply, and subsidiary conditions for successful regional integration. The demand side factor is strong market pressure for integration.

When the potential for economic gains from market exchange grows within a region through important economies of scale or the diffusion of new technologies, market players have an incentive to lobby for regional institutional arrangements that render the realisation of these gains possible (Mattli 1999: 44–50). In the process of European integration, the absence of common legal regimes, of regulatory systems and of technical standards were regarded as obstacles to the generation of wealth and collective gains (Stone Sweet and Sandholtz 1998: 11). Potential market gains from regional integration become a catalyst to create demand from market players for common regional rules and organisational capacity to regulate.

The supply side factor is 'undisputed leadership'. There must be a benevolent leading country in the region, which enables other countries to overcome collective action problems. Such a country is expected to serve as a focal point in the coordination of rules, regulations and policies, mitigating tensions that arise from the inequitable distribution of gains from integration (Mattli 1999: 50–7). Mattli's focus on undisputed leadership as a central factor for successful regional integration shares common understanding of the hegemonic stability theory of the international economic system.[3] While the hegemonic stability theory highlights leadership to provide public goods overcoming free rider problems, Mattli's interest lies in leadership to overcome distributional inequities (Mattli 1999: 56).

In addition to these two conditions, Mattli identifies the third subsidiary condition: the provision by an integration treaty for the establishment of 'commitment institutions'. Commitment institutions such as centralised monitoring and their-party enforcement improve compliance with the rules of cooperation by acting as constraints in circumstances where self-help measures alone are insufficient to prevent reneging (Mattli 1999: 42–3).

How is regional integration in East Asia evaluated in terms of Mattli's three conditions? Cross-border economic transactions in East Asia have risen sharply since the early 1990s. But, these moves have not necessarily changed into demand from market players for the increasing harmonisation of rules and institutions. There is no undisputed leadership in East Asia. Japan, an economic superpower in the region, did not demonstrate the willingness and capabilities required to lead the region to form the integrated market. Major regional institutions including ASEAN and ASEAN Regional Forum (ARF) are not based on any treaty or formal binding agreement among the participating states. Thus, East Asia has not met the three conditions that Mattli presented. However, since the late 1990s, regional integration through the APT framework 'has gained considerable momentum in a relatively short time, not only in the economic field but also in human resources development and notably in monetary and financial cooperation' (Alatas 2001: 2). How can we explain this development?

In analysing the development of regional integration in East Asia, it is necessary to realign Mattli's three conditions: strong market pressure, undisputed leadership and commitment institutions. East Asia is unique in terms of the influence of market pressure. In this region, virtual regional integration has been promoted by expanded business activities. While regional integration in Europe occurred *de jure*, the policy-driven integration through the development of institutional frameworks, regional integration in East Asia occurred *de facto*, the market-driven integration through the increased flow of trade and investment. Regional integration through trade and investment has deepened since the early 1990s. The ratio of intra-regional trade in Asia increased from 38.5 per cent in 1985 to 43.0 per cent in 1990 to 51.3 per cent in 1997. The ratio in 1997 was still below 62.4 per cent of the EU but higher than 45.1 per cent of the North American Free Trade Agreement (NAFTA) (Keijzer 2001: 14). Economic activities by the private sector have been a driving force to promote the regional integration process. The private activities also contributed to the formation of sub-regional economic zones including the Indonesia–Malaysia– Thailand growth triangle, the South China coast, and the SIJORI growth triangle involving Singapore, Johor in Malaysia and the Indonesian Riau.

The market-driven integration has been promoted by strengthened business networks such as Japanese production networks and Chinese merchant networks. The sharp appreciation of the yen after 1985 triggered a massive outflow of Japanese capital, and East Asian locations became major production bases for Japanese manufacturing firms. In the 1990s, Japanese multinationals in the machinery sectors formed integrated production networks linking their production bases in the region in order to seek the optimal international division of labour (Ernst 2000).

The ethnic Chinese who came from Guangdong, Fujian, and Hainan provinces in China dominate the local economies in most Southeast Asian countries. For instance, in Thailand all but one of the 20 largest business enterprises traded on the stock exchange are owned by overseas Chinese, while overseas Chinese owns all the largest firms except for the three Spanish-affiliated groups in the Philippines (Katzenstein *et al.* 2000: 91). Some Chinese merchants in Southeast Asia have expanded investment into China. For instance, the Charoen Pokphand Group, the largest conglomerate in Thailand, has actively invested in China, with the accumulated value of investment reaching roughly US$30 billion (Wakamatsu 2001: 64). The overseas Chinese merchants have strengthened region-wide institutional networks. A representative of such business networks is the World Chinese Entrepreneurs Convention, which was organised by the Singapore Chinese Chamber of Commerce and Industry in 1991. The latest sixth convention, held in Nanjing in September 2001, attracted more than 4500 participants all over the world. The convention has contributed to cooperation and better understanding among overseas Chinese entrepreneurs.

While extended business activities have virtually integrated the regional economies, the privately driven integration has not led to formal integration initiatives straightforwardly for two reasons. First, the formation of pan-Asia business groupings that demand the harmonisation of rules and institutions in the region is still premature. Indeed, there were some moves in the business sectors to promote formal regional integration in Southeast Asia. The ASEAN Chamber of Commerce and Industry showed support for the ASEAN Free Trade Area (AFTA) and regional integration, but its overall position on regional integration has been ambiguous (Bowles 2000: 449). Some Japanese multinationals that have extended production networks in Southeast Asia have demanded the promotion of regional market integration in order to facilitate cross-border transactions and draw benefits of economies of scale (Yoshimatsu 2002). However, these actions were seen mainly in assembly sectors, without necessarily extending to other sectors. In East Asia, market-driven *de facto* integration has not generated spillover effects that would lead to formal economic and political integration.

This makes a sharp contrast to Europe where transnational business interests played a critical role in promoting market integration. Scholars who have analysed the development of market integration in Europe conclude that industrial actors in evolving regional and international markets changed their preferences in favour of policies and institutions that promote the unified European market. For instance, Sandholtz and Zysman (1989) argue that the transnational industrial coalitions, which experienced changes in the international economic structure, allied with the European Commission to push for the 1992 market unification process.[4]

Second, persistent adherence of major East Asian states to sovereignty has hindered the development from informal to formal regional integration. There is a paradox between the state-led domestic economic development and market-driven regional integration in East Asia. The major states in East Asia have played a 'developmental' role in achieving rapid industrialisation under the authoritarian regime largely as a means to promote and maintain the national unity, the major concern for the political leaders. The seemingly market-driven integration in East Asia might be seen as the reflection of a fact that the East Asian states have been reluctant to promote official regional arrangements, which might lead to any surrender of sovereignty.

The uniqueness of East Asia is also revealed in the subsidiary condition. The East Asian countries have developed distinctive styles of regional cooperation and commitment institutions. East Asia is characterised as having enormous diversities in economic development, political systems and cultural and religious traditions. Given this characteristic, most East Asian countries give more credence to informal consensus-building and ad hoc problem-solving diplomacy than formal institutions based on legalistic and contractual paradigms (Kahler 1995: 18). Major regional organisations including ASEAN, ARF and Pacific Economic Cooperation Council adopt the organisational style as a consultative forum. Under this organisational style, the members form a loose consensus in the form of 'declaration' and implement it in voluntary, unilateral manners.[5]

According to the Asian approach to cooperation, after the basic principles are agreed, the guiding rules and detailed designs for cooperation evolve and grow in the process of informal and incremental consultation and actual practices. The Asian countries acknowledge the value of informality in raising 'the level of comfort among the participants and creates a flexible decision-making environment which allows room for shifts in national bargaining positions' (Acharya 1997: 329). This approach is often criticised as not producing expected results because of likely free riding and an inherent limitation in dealing with issues regarding fundamental national interests. However, they recognise that consultation aiming at consensus has a potential to promote negotiations at a rapid speed by fostering trustworthy relationship among the members (Funabashi 1995: 127).

The above characterisations of market integration and regional cooperation in East Asia encourage us to reconsider conditions for regional integration in East Asia. Indeed, market integration has surely promoted, but it has not led to demand for formal integration initiatives. The role of commitment institutions in promoting regional integration has not been prominent in East Asia. Consequently, undisputed political leadership is given special importance in promoting regional integration in Mattli's three conditions.

Leadership for regional cooperation is provided by one state like the United States in North America or by a duo like France and Germany in Western Europe. In East Asia, it is realistic to expect that Japan and China provide joint leadership given the two countries' preponderant power and influence in the region. Importantly, the regional environments surrounding Japan and China have shown drastic changes since the late 1990s, which raised necessary conditions for co-leadership.

Necessary conditions for Sino–Japan co-leadership at the regional level

In the late 1990s, conditions for requiring Sino–Japan leadership have been gradually matured. The necessary conditions emerged in both the demand and supply sides. In the demand side, changes in two factors that have characterised regional integration and cooperation make Sino–Japan co-leadership more plausible. The first is increasing limitations to the Asian approach of informality, consensus and gradualism in the current international settings. The informal, consensus-based incremental approach was valuable in formulating new institutional frameworks for regional cooperation in East Asia. The Asian style of cooperation facilitated unwilling countries to participate in a framework by creating a frank environment for talks and communications in a confidence-building atmosphere.

The Asian approach has played a crucial role in developing the APT. The transition from the EAEC to APT was possible with accumulated informal meetings among East Asian countries. While the ASEAN members raised the EAEC as an agenda at the ASEAN Ministerial meetings from 1991 to 1997, the luncheon meetings among the ASEAN members, China, Japan and South Korea were held from 1994. These informal commitments paved the way for the first APT summit meeting in December 1997 (Terada 2001: 64–5).

At the same time, the informal, consensus-based incremental approach has several inherent shortcomings. First, this approach is prone to retrenchment and spillback. Commitment to regional action and solidarity under this approach is much weaker than in cooperative arrangements based on international treaties and contractual obligations (Rüland 2000: 444). Second, the incremental approach takes time in making a decision, often changing an organisation's meeting into a place for collective talks, not collective actions. The slow progress put the participants in a disadvantageous position in promoting regional cooperation in the rapidly evolving international arena. In fact, the rapid and steady development of regionalism in other regions encouraged some East Asian countries to accelerate their regional integration initiatives. For instance, the ASEAN members gradually advanced the completion of the AFTA from 2008 to 2003 then to 2002.

The Asian approach is valuable in creating an atmosphere for frank consultations among members with serious heterogeneity and thereby launching a new institution. But, this is less useful in developing regional cooperation in the established institution aiming at particular policy goals in competition with other institutions with different values. In the latter case, more explicit political leadership is required to accelerate cooperation initiatives and activities in the fixed time frame.

The second is the declining role of ASEAN as the main promoter of regional integration. The association was the focal point that promoted regional cooperation until the mid-1990s. ASEAN took the lead in launching the ARF, the first forum to discuss security matters in East Asia. An idea of commencing the ASEM was first articulated by Singapore Prime Minister Goh Chok Tong in October 1994. Even the APT, currently the centre of regional integration in East Asia, could come into existence precisely because of initiatives and the diplomatic glue provided by ASEAN (Alatas 2001: 1).

However, cohesion and capability of ASEAN as an organisation deteriorated after the mid-1990s. The Asian financial crisis posed a serious challenge to ASEAN's capability and solidarity to respond adequately to a crisis of this kind and size. The ASEAN members failed to formulate decisive and effective measures against the crisis largely because the crisis-hit members were too preoccupied with their own economic recovery plans (Rüland 2000). Their awkward responses to the crisis dampened the image and credibility of ASEAN. In particular, political disarray in Indonesia, the association's most crucial member with two-fifths of its population, became a serious problem for ASEAN. The collapse of the Suharto regime in May 1998 and subsequent political instability prohibited the ASEAN members from regaining the unity among the members.

Furthermore, the ASEAN divide became serious in the late 1990s. In 1999, the association achieved the 'ASEAN ten' by the participation of Cambodia. However, the enlargement of ASEAN through the entry of the Indochina countries led to a 'two-tier' ASEAN with disparities in levels of economic development and types of political system and social structure. The chasm has also become apparent even among the developed ASEAN members. While Singapore and Thailand were positive in regional market liberalisation, Malaysia was passive largely because it hoped to protect its domestic industries.

Thus, intensified moves towards regionalism have enhanced intrinsic limitations of the Asian approach to regional cooperation, raising the relative importance of explicit political leadership. The decline of cohesion and capability of ASEAN raised the relative position of Northeast Asian countries in promoting East Asian cooperation and integration.

In the supply side, the evolving position and perception of Japan and China in the region make Sino–Japan co-leadership more likely. The perception of Japan among East Asian countries has gradually changed since the late 1990s. Most East Asian countries were reluctant to accept Japan's leadership role with mainly historical and economic reasons. Many East Asian countries, China and Korea in particular, were highly frustrated with Japan's failure to express a clear-cut apology for its aggression in the Second World War. Disparity in economic capability also made East Asian countries reluctant to accept Japan's leadership. Significantly, Japan increased its economic power and influence in Asia in the 1970s and 1980s. For instance, Germany accounted for one-fourth of Western Europe's gross domestic product (GDP) in 1970–90, while the share of the United States in North America was much higher (well over 80 per cent) but was stable during this period. In contrast, Japan's economic hegemony in East Asia increased during this period: Japan's share in East Asia's GDP rose from 54 per cent in 1970 to 72 per cent in 1990 (Grieco 1997: 177–8).

In the 1990s, the Japanese economy plunged into a long recession, while its neighbouring countries improved their industrial competitiveness. Indeed, Japan still accounts for some two-thirds of total GDP in East Asia, but it is no longer the only industrialised nation in the region. As explained in Chapter 5, Korean and Taiwanese firms have caught up with their Japanese rivals in relatively high technology sectors such as semiconductors and liquid crystal displays. China, which has increased competitiveness in both relatively technology-intensive and labour-intensive industries, is superseding Japan's position as the factory of the world.

Ironically, Japan's economic slump in the 1990s reduced fears that the regional economies would be incorporated into a Japan-centred economic bloc. In particular, Japan's lukewarm initiatives to implement necessary measures for structural adjustments changed East Asia's perception of Japan. For instance, South Korea, which implemented the restructuring of the financial system after the Asian financial crisis rather promptly, became a tutor to teach Japan necessary measures to remove financial problems.[6] The fear of too much of Japan's power in organising regional order in Asia was replaced by the fear of too little of Japan's power in dealing with its own economic problems (Katzenstein 2000: 360).

China's economic relations with East Asia have changed in the 1990s. Its economic capabilities and thrust into regional integration have grown sharply in the late 1990s. As already explained in Chapter 5, trade and investment networks in East Asia are increasingly formed around China. Most East Asian countries have strong desires to gain economic benefits from the ever-growing Chinese market. In 2002, South Korea designated reclaimed land in Kimpo between Seoul and Incheon International Airport as a special economic zone.[7] This designation aimed to establish the business hub of Northeast Asia, given China's growth as the world's manufacturing base. A critical reason why the ASEAN members agreed to forge an FTA with China in 2001 was that they hoped to get benefits from the Chinese market. China's greater interest and leadership in regional economic affairs would be desirable for other East Asian countries insofar as the country pays due attention to the overall economic development of the region.

Moves towards Sino–Japan co-leadership

The favourable conditions for Sino–Japanese leadership for regional integration in East Asia have gained momentum. But, concrete moves towards joint leadership are still preliminary. At the APT summit meeting in November 1999, the leaders from Japan, China and South Korea agreed on trilateral joint research on economic cooperation among the three countries. Three research institutes – Development Research Centre of China, National Institute for Research Advancement of Japan, and Korea Institute for International Economic Policy (KIEP) – launched a joint study in November 2000, and issued a report one year later. The report analyses trade relations between the three countries and recommended the establishment of a mechanism of annual meetings of Economic Ministers of the three countries.[8]

In August 1999, MOF began policy talks with China and South Korea about possible international financial cooperation through the government-affiliated research institutes. Three research institutes – Chinese Academy of Social Sciences, the Ministry of Finance, Policy Research Institute (MFPRI) of Japan, and KIEP – as well as the international finance bureaus of the three countries, have organised seminars regarding regional financial arrangements, stronger supervision over short-term capital flow and the establishment of the early warning systems in the region. In October 2000, the MFPRI organised the China Study Group, and the development of cooperation with China became a major agenda for the group. These initiatives, which primarily aimed to create opportunities for trustworthy relationship between Japan and China (as well as South Korea), are important because confidence building through talks and consultations at government-affiliated organisations often constitutes the first step for deeper cooperation. Direct cooperation between China and Japan under the APT framework has begun to emerge. In March 2002, the Bank of Japan and the People's Bank of China singed a Yen–RMB swap arrangement equivalent to US$3 billion. The agreement had a symbolic significance as the two countries held the key to regional cooperation (Asami 2002: 3–4). Thus, moves to strengthening the relationship between Japan and China envisioning regional cooperation just began at the official level.

Probably, more interesting and important steps derived from fierce rivalries between Tokyo and Beijing for taking the initiative in regional integration. Their initiatives have not been coordinated but mutually reinforcing. In the late 1990s, Japan that departed from its sole reliance on the multilateral trade track began talks about an FTA with Singapore as a way to pursue the multi-layered trade track. When Noboru Hatakeyama, Chairman of the Japan External Trade Organisation (JETRO), had a meeting with Shi Guangsheng, Chinese Minister of Foreign Trade and Economic Cooperation, in August 2000, Hatakeyama referred to implications of FTAs to Chinese officials (Yamada 2002: 19). Although their direct responses were not keen, the Chinese government proposed the formation of an FTA between China and ASEAN only three months later. China's swift moves towards an FTA were largely stimulated by Japan's policy switch and initiatives to form an FTA with Singapore (Otsuji and Shiraishi 2002: 12).

In November 2001, China and ASEAN agreed to begin negotiations over the formation of an FTA with a ten-year time limit. China's quick move was accepted by Japanese bureaucrats and politicians with a great surprise, and the Japanese government took counteraction.[9] In January 2002, Prime Minister Junichiro Koizumi proposed to the ASEAN leaders an Initiative for the ASEAN–Japan Closer Economic Partnership (AJCEP) during his visit to Southeast Asia. Shortly after this proposal, the AJCEP Expert Group began talks about specific measures to realise the AJCEP. Significantly, ASEAN–China negotiations over an FTA have become a pacesetter for negotiations between Japan and ASEAN, creating incentives for Japanese bureaucrats to keep up with their moves.[10]

Similar moves were seen in the financial field. In September 1998, Japanese Finance Minister Miyazawa proposed a meeting of Asian Finance Ministers and Central Bank Governors. Six Asian countries attended this meeting, but not China. In late 1998, Chinese Vice-President Hu Jintao proposed a meeting of Deputy Finance Ministers and Central Bank Vice-Governors of the ASEAN members together with China, Japan and South Korea. This proposal led to an APT Finance Ministers meeting in Hanoi in March 1999. The Japanese MOF made efforts behind the scenes to launch the Chiang Mai Initiative at the second APT Finance Ministers meeting in May 2000. The Chinese government, which opposed the Japan-initiated Asian Monetary Fund (AMF) proposal in 1997, supported the initiative.

As explained in the previous chapter, the APT Finance Ministers agreed that 90 per cent of each bilateral swap lines requires the IMF loan agreements as precondition. This agreement can be interpreted as Japan's consideration to preferences of China, which insisted that the swap agreements be closely linked to the IMF programs arguing even for 100 per cent linkage (Amyx 2002: 12). An account by a former MOF official supports this interpretation. Eisuke Sakakibara, who was credited with being the main promoter of the AMF plan, answered to the question of 'What lessons did you learn from the experience of the AMF?' as follows:

> An importance of alignments with China . . . . We did not make sufficient prior consultation and negotiations due to weak linkages between the Japanese and Chinese governments. Both MOF and I myself, out of this reflection, make great much of the relationship with China.[11]

Ravenhill (2002: 191) argues that tension between Japan and China may rebound to the benefits of regionalism if their leadership rivalry continues to be translated into competing initiatives for moving integration forward. Up until around 2002, spiral forces to stir China and Japan to provide regional public goods worked effectively, creating positive-sum games between the two countries.

The positive and benign competition between China and Japan in promoting regional cooperation has two implications. First, both Japan and China put stress on close linkages with ASEAN and needed its collaboration. The presence of ASEAN has become increasingly important for Japan and China in a triangular relationship in East Asia. Southeast Asia has long been a special region for Japanese diplomacy.

Furthermore, Japanese manufacturing firms established production networks between Japan and Southeast Asia or among Southeast Asian countries. The development of competent industries in ASEAN has been particularly important for Japanese manufacturing industries.

China, which put emphasis on international or bilateral relations for a long time, did not formulate specific regional economic or security policies (Austin and Harris 2001: 283). In the late 1990s, the country began to consider its relationship with East Asian countries more strategically. In a sense, China is destined to continue steady economic growth because slow growth will lead to social and political upheavals. Its steady economic performance through trade expansion and increased inflow of foreign investment is heavily dependent on favourable international environments. On the other hand, trade and investment expansion has raised the sense of the China threat among Southeast Asian countries. China has hoped to alleviate their apprehension by promoting economic linkages (Cheng 1999). This was typically shown in China's substantial concessions offered in proposing an FTA with ASEAN. China provided concessions including the grant of special preferential tariff treatments for some goods from Cambodia, Laos and Myanmar, and offered US$5 million to help navigation along the upper stretches of the Mekong River in Laos, Myanmar and Thailand.[12] These proposals aimed both to mitigate the threat of the Chinese economy and to develop the Yunnan Province jointly with the Indochina countries as the market of Chinese products.

Second, gaps in basic values and ideas between Japan and China do not constitute a serious obstacle to their collaboration. Japan hopes that China would be a democratic state that pays due consideration to human rights. Yet, this is not so strong to constitute the clash of ideology and value, which was apparent in US–Sino relations (Wang 2002: 140). Japan and China do not have critical differences in basic ideas about economic development. As explained in Chapter 4, Japan still supports an idea that economic development in developing countries should be sustained by government intervention. As seen in its support for the Asian members to promote economic and technical cooperation at APEC, Japan has been sceptical about a swift trade and investment liberalisation (Yoshimatsu 2000: 18–20). These stances are consonant with those of China, which has given priority to the state-led economic development.

As China achieved steady economic growth in the early 1990s, some Chinese leaders began to advocate the 'double locomotive model' for Asian economic cooperation: Japan is the front locomotive to pull and

China is a rear locomotive to push (Deng 1997: 93–7). This model for regional economic cooperation seems to gain high validity, but the position is reverse. While China formally takes the lead in promoting regional cooperation, Japan substantiates such an initiative from behind. As seen in the Asian members' reluctance to promote swift liberalisation at APEC, the East Asian countries hope to combine market liberalisation and integration with economic and technical cooperation. ASEAN, which comprises less developed Indochina countries, have strong incentives in this respect.[13] In order to promote regional integration combined with economic and technical cooperation, Japan's economic power, technological capabilities and experiences of economic cooperation are indispensable.

Problematic sufficient conditions for co-leadership at the domestic and international levels

As already explained, conditions for Sino–Japan co-leadership gained momentum at the regional level. However, obstacles to co-leadership are seen at the domestic and international levels. A main domestic obstacle in Japan is a rise of nationalism. China has been a political great power in East Asia, and China's military might was regarded as a threat to Japan. In the late 1990s, China has emerged as a critical economic competitor for Japan. Not only has China's export drive caused trade friction in Japan but it has also crowded out Japanese products from the markets in some Southeast Asian countries. A shift of manufacturing bases from Japan to China has also caused the 'hollowing out' of Japanese industry, which exacerbated the unemployment problem. Other social factors have made the Japanese antagonistic towards China. The Japanese have lost confidence during the decade-long economic stagnation with a rising unemployment pressure. Rising crimes by foreigners including the Chinese are recognised as a great threat to Japan's ordered society. These factors made the Japanese more nationalistic in defending their interests.

In the late 1990s and the early new century, the sense of the China threat has permeated among bureaucrats, politicians and the public. As explained in Chapter 3, METI has gradually regarded the economic prominence of China as the threat of other East Asian countries including Japan. There are numerous publications that fuel the China threat. *Bungei Shunju* and *Chuo Koron*, two representative monthly magazines in Japan, have had special editions of China in 2001 and 2002.[14] The sentiments of the Japanese public towards China have become worse. According to a 2002 *Asahi Shimbun* poll, the proportion of respondents who 'have friendly feelings towards China' reduced from 29 per cent in 1997 to 19 per cent in 2002 while those without such feelings also declined slightly from 19 per cent to 17 per cent in the same period.[15]

In political circles, a review of official development assistance (ODA) policy towards China became a critical issue after 1999. Chinese research ships were repeatedly sighted roaming Japanese coastal waters without any prior notification in 1999 and 2000. In late July 2000, Foreign Minister Yohei Kono made a strong protest to his Chinese counterpart, but Kono could not gain whole-hearted responses and the ship operations continued. Responding to such moves, some LDP politicians intensified their voice demanding a review of ODA provision with China. In December 2000, the LDP's Special Committee of External Economic Cooperation issued a report entitled *The Colligation and Guidelines of Economic Aid and Cooperation towards China*. The report raised concerns about recent military build-up in China, China's provision of foreign aid, operations of Chinese research ships in Japanese waters, and so on. It then stated that Japan would continuously implement economic aid and cooperation towards China, but that comprehensive reviews would be necessary in terms of objective, emphasis and scale.

For the Chinese side, a gradual rise of nationalism against Japan is also a critical obstacle to East Asian integration on the basis of Sino–Japan collaboration. Japanese cultures represented by animations, dramas and pop music have become popular among the Chinese public since the late 1990s (Watanabe 2001). However, anti-Japanese sentiments, which are deeply rooted in the Chinese, have become worse. For instance, Prime Minister Zhu Rongji's message before his visit to Japan of October 2000 that the people of Japan today and of those days do not have to assume responsibility for a war perpetrated by militarism invited severe criticisms at the Internet opinion forum 'Qiangguo Luntan' (China Forum) opened by *the People's Daily*. Zhu toned down his comments on the history issues during his stay in Japan caring for such criticisms (Kato 2001). Perceptible increases in anti-Japanese emotions among the Chinese public were confirmed by an opinion poll. In a poll of 1852 people by the Chinese Academy of Social Science, the proportion of respondents who 'do not have friendly feelings towards Japan' rose sharply from 34 per cent in 1997 to 53 per cent in 2002 while the proportion of those with such feelings was unchanged (10 per cent).[16]

Particularly anxious is increasing anti-Japanese sentiments among the Chinese intellectuals. Ryo (2000) categorises the Chinese intellectuals into five groups: the emotional anti-Japanese group; rational Japan-suspicious group; pro-US and anti-Japanese group; rational pro-Japanese group; and rational internationalist group. Currently, the first three groups constitute the mainstream among the public opinion, and the latter two groups are difficult to be accepted. The aforementioned opinion poll indicated the critical perception of Japan among the educated people. The proportion of respondents who 'do not have friendly feelings towards Japan' was 62 per cent among the people with university education (compared with 53 per cent in total) and the proportion of respondents who think that 'Japan's past compensation is insufficient' was 95 per cent (86 per cent in total).[17]

The Japanese and Chinese, who have lived as neighbours for nearly two thousand years, developed contradictory sentiments such as commonality and disparity, mutual respect and suspicion, and attraction and repulsion (Iriye 1980: 3). Moreover, in the post-war period, both countries did not need to consider seriously the influence of the existence of the other or the mutual relationship on its future prosperity. However, a new reality that Japan and China are embedded into a mutually interdependent and symmetrical relationship is emerging. The Japanese and Chinese people face difficulty in adapting to this newly emerging reality. Given this uncertainty, policy-makers in both countries are required to pay due attention to mutual perception among the people avoiding overconfidence and insensitivity.

The most crucial obstacle at the international level is reactions from the United States. Indeed, US foreign policy after 1945 established the principle of multilateralism in Europe and bilateralism in Asia (Katzenstein 1997: 23). In Europe, Franco–Germany coalition was possible with the backup of the United States, the 'hegemonic' power in world politics. The US government considered that the integration of West Germany with Europe would lead to the prosperity and stability of the region, and West Germany was embedded into regional frameworks of NATO and European Community (EC). Furthermore, under the Cold War regime, the United States had strategic rationale to accept unfavourable effects from the European integration process and even the build-up of a potential future rival: the threat of the Soviet Union.

The US approach to Western Europe made a sharp contrast to its policy towards East Asia. Unlike Western Europe, the East Asian region did not have a group of states with similar capabilities as Japan. In addition, Japan's neighbouring countries did not hope to promote regional cooperation with Japan (Grieco 1999: 338–40; Ikenberry 2001: 77). Accordingly, the United States adopted bilateral-oriented foreign policy, forging security treaties with Japan, South Korea, Taiwan and ASEAN. Japan was incorporated into bilateral relationship with the United States, not into regional frameworks.

In the late 1990s, the United States did not welcome moves towards stronger economic integration in East Asia. When Japan proposed the AMF in autumn 1997, not only did the US government oppose the proposal directly but it also encouraged China to adopt an opposition stance. China, which was at the final stage of negotiations over the WTO and had its own interest in blocking the expansion of Japan's influence in East Asia, opposed the AMF proposal. When China proposed a meeting of the APT Deputy Finance Ministers, the Japanese Prime Minister Obuchi opposed this idea at the second APT summit meeting in December 1998. Obuchi followed advice from the Ministry of Foreign Affairs, and the US government required the ministry to oppose the idea (Furukawa 2001: 15).

Under 'unipolar' politics in the new century, the US stance has a crucial influence on the development of East Asian regionalism. In a sense, there has emerged a condition that Japan could be embedded into East Asia because the newly industrialised economies including democratic South Korea and Taiwan, and China in the virtually market economy have formed the symmetrical economic relationship with Japan. In the near future, the United States will have to pay attention to China rather than Japan as an economic as well as political rival. China has capabilities to surpass Japan in terms of total GDP within several years and is likely to be a serious competitor against the United States. To embed the emergent China into regional frameworks and check its external policy and relations will contribute to the stable regional order and the US interest.

Conclusion

This chapter has examined theoretical implications, conditions and problems regarding Sino–Japan leadership for developing economic integration in East Asia. The distinctive characteristics of market integration and regional cooperation in East Asia have yielded conditions for regional integration in East Asia different from those in Europe. In East Asia, market pressure and commitment institutions had weak importance for regional cooperation. Consequently, undisputed leadership by the leading countries had critical implications. Under such conditions, a duo leadership by Japan and China has become increasingly important in the rapidly changing regional environments. The consensus-based, incremental approach to regional cooperation in East Asia has faced increasing difficulty in keeping pace with moves towards regionalism in other parts of the world. In addition, the capability of ASEAN as a promoter of regional cooperation declined after the Asian financial crisis. The relative decline of the Japanese economy diluted the fear of the Japan-dominated regional bloc, on the one hand, and the prominence of the Chinese economy raised expectation for a more prominent role of China, on the other.

While environments at the regional level for anticipating Sino–Japanese leadership have gradually matured, there are serious obstacles to the leadership at the domestic and international levels. In Japan, the sense of the China threat proliferated among bureaucrats, politicians and the public after the late 1990s. Distrust and antagonistic feelings against Japan have also increased among the Chinese public. Internationally, the development of Sino–Japan collaboration is heavily dependent on the US strategies towards the Asia-Pacific region.

As shown in Chapters 3 and 5, trade friction and economic tension between Japan and China have intensified since the late 1990s. However, the friction can be regarded as a natural consequence of increased economic interdependence between an already matured economy and a newly emerging economy, which was seen in the US–Japan relations in the 1970s and 1980s. Tokyo and Washington, despite repeated trade frictions, have deepened mutual trust and understanding. A critical factor that differentiates Sino–Japan from US–Japan relations is mutual distrust. The Chinese are suspicious about Japan's likely return to militarism as well as the Japanese people's insensitivity to war responsibility. The Japanese regard the Chinese political and social systems as being different from theirs.

In the early new millennium, both the Japanese and Chinese governments share a common objective to pursue the sound development of regional integration. However, the current positive-sum game for leadership will easily fall into sharp antagonism if both countries fail to deepen mutual understanding and trust. In order to avoid such a situation, Tokyo and Beijing need to narrow the perception gap. While Japan should support China's efforts to be a good economic player in the world, it needs to pay due attention to the perception of Japan among the Chinese people. For the latter objective, Tokyo and Beijing are required to develop multi-layered communication channels. The Franco–German collaboration in Europe became possible with intensive communications at the various levels (Webber 1999: 2). Learning from their experiences, Japan and China need to develop trustworthy relationship at political, administrative, and citizen levels.

8
Conclusions

This study has looked in detail at Japan's policy towards antidumping and safeguard issues, the Asian financial crisis, regional industrial evolutions, and regionalism in East Asia in order to explore how Japan has changed its economic policy towards and economic relationship with East Asia since the mid-1990s. The findings in this book reveal Japan's complicated and evolving relationship with East Asia. While policy preferences of major economic bureaucrats and societal actors have become in favour of strong integration with East Asia, actual policy initiatives did not go towards this direction straightforwardly in several policy areas. Japan has shown more willingness to assume a leadership role in East Asia, but its real commitments have been limited in several important issue areas. While Japan needed to develop collaborative relationship with China in order to promote regional cooperation in East Asia, it has sought to defend Japanese industry strategically from competitive pressure from the country.

The first section of this chapter examines how the central argument that the recent regional changes have produced proactive and strategic responses in Japan's economic policy towards East Asia is applied to various policy areas examined in this study. The following two sections consider how Japan's external policy and relations are explained in terms of three analytical variables – an aspiration for regional leadership, bilateral relationship with China, and domestic politics. The last section discusses the limitations of this study and explores future research issues.

Three characteristics in Japan's East Asian economic policy

The central question of this book is how Japan has transformed its economic policy towards and economic relationship with East Asia since the mid-1990s in the rapidly evolving regional environments. It is argued that the recent changes have produced proactive and strategic responses in Japan's economic policy towards East Asia. The Japanese government has shown constructive initiatives to sustain the sound development of the regional economies, on the one hand, and strategic policies to secure its economic interests in a gradual shift in the distribution of economic capabilities, on the other. This book examined this argument in three policy areas: trade remedy measures, reactions to the regional financial crisis and industrial evolutions, and commitments to East Asian regionalism.

Japan has shown two kinds of responses in handling regional economic affairs since the mid-1990s. The first set of reactions is characterised as 'proactive'. The representative case was its commitments to the Asian financial crisis. The government provided a huge amount of financial assistance to rescue the crisis-hit countries. The crisis revealed the structural fragility of most Southeast Asian economies. Accordingly, the Japanese government has strengthened intellectual support for sound economic management in these economies by sending experts in industrial reforms and policies for small- and medium-sized enterprises (SMEs). Japan's activism was also seen in commitments to regional integration. The Ministry of Finance (MOF) has taken the lead in developing institutional frameworks to block the recurrence of a financial crisis in East Asia by developing the financial facilities and surveillance systems. Given the declining influence of the Association of Southeast Asian Nations (ASEAN) as a promoter of regional cooperation in East Asia, Japan–Sino cooperation has become important for this objective. Japan's cooperation and competition with China for regional leadership have produced positive-sum games for greater economic integration in East Asia.

The second set of policies can be termed as 'strategic'. A typical example of the policies belonging to this category was found in trade remedy measures. Japan shifted its basic stance on solution of trade disputes from reliance on 'grey area measures' to stress on internationally accepted rules, and sought to apply trade remedy measures on the basis of the international rule-governed principles. Although the number of antidumping cases was extremely low compared with the United States, Australia and Canada, the Japanese government became less hesitant to utilise antidumping measures in order to give relief to domestic industries. Japan's response to textile safeguards in the towel industry was also strategic. The government did not invoke textile safeguards against towel imports largely because of the consideration of further integration with the Asian economies. Furthermore, commitments to enhancing the disciplines of intellectual property rights (IPRs) belong to this category.

The government sought to promote research and development (R&D) activities of Japanese firms by enhancing the protection of their intellectual assets. The strategic nature was found in Japan's external relations as well. The Japanese government has strengthened economic linkages with and among the ASEAN countries by sustaining the harmonisation of rules and institutions and industrial upgrading in the Indochina countries. Japan's initiatives in forming bilateral free trade agreements (FTAs) are included in this category.

In addition to these two kinds of policies and measures, there was the third set of policies, which could be characterised as 'reactive'. The typical case was a safeguard invocation in the agricultural sector. Responding to demands from the agricultural groups, the government invoked provisional safeguard curbs on imports of three farm products from China. The emergency measure was decided within half a year after an import surge became a political problem although there were criticisms of its urgency even at the government's advisory councils. Reactive nature was also found in Japan's commitments to regional cooperation. Japan was unable to show a positive position at the negotiations over the Early Voluntary Sectoral Liberalisation (EVSL) initiative under the Asia-Pacific Economic Cooperation (APEC) forum, and weak leadership shown in Japan's defection led to the subsequent APEC adrift. In addition, domestic opposition has disturbed smooth negotiations over an FTA with Singapore, and impeded the Japanese government from showing a determined stance on FTAs with other East Asian countries.

The above policies were not classified into one of the three categories without confusion. For instance, assistance to industrial development and market integration in Southeast Asia contained both proactive and strategic nature. The formation of FTAs with Asian countries sprang from a strategic intention of converting its stress on trade policy from multilateralism to bilateral FTAs. But, its negotiation process was disturbed by reactive moves. However, it is possible to identify particular characteristics embedded in these policies. Our interest is what factors have produced variations in policies and measures towards East Asia under the seemingly similar regional conditions. This is explained by considering three analytical variables: commitments to independent regional leadership, bilateral relationship with China and domestic politics.

Japan's regional leadership and Japan–China relationship

Japan's proactive policies towards East Asian affairs are likely to be explicable in terms of its desire to show a more independent leadership role in East Asia. In Chapter 1, two perspectives on Japan's leadership role were presented. One perspective holds that Japan did not show an independent leadership role due to its special relationship with the United States, while the other posits that Japan has played an increasingly independent leadership role in East Asia. What do the findings in this study tell us about Japan's leadership role?

In the financial sector, Japan's proposal to establish a regional monetary fund, an unexpected step in regional leadership, was not realised largely due to oppositions from the US Treasury and International Monetary Fund (IMF). However, the brink dismissal of the fund did not weaken Japan's willingness to show an assertive role in East Asia. The Japanese government has reclaimed the initiative by providing the largest sum of funds of all donors to the crisis-stricken countries, and by leading the development of the financial facilities and surveillance mechanisms for the region. MOF's willingness to show an independent role was also found in its commitments to discussing the Asian oriented development style through its affiliated research institutes.

In the real sector, the Japanese government has sought to play an independent role for the sound development of regional industries after the crisis. This was apparent in assistance to industrial restructuring efforts in Thailand. The Japanese government dispatched its ex-official in order to help the country formulate the guidelines for SMEs. Japanese officials considered that fragile industrial bases in the real sector were one of the main causes of Thai's economic turbulence, and that development-oriented state intervention was indispensable for returning the Thai economy to the growth trend. The Japanese government made its Thai counterpart acknowledge the necessity of state intervention in fostering SMEs, and transferred know-how of developing necessary institutions including the policy finance system, the advisory council system, and industrial development coordinated by industrial associations. Importantly, the Japanese government maintained and partially intensified its own development approach in cooperation with industrial restructuring programs in major East Asian countries.

Japan's leadership role in promoting regional cooperation and coordination has been found in several industrial sectors, which this study did not refer to directly. In the textile sector, the Ministry of Economy, Trade and Industry (METI) took the lead in launching the Asia-Pacific Textile and Clothing Industries Forum.[1] This forum aimed to coordinate the supply and demand of textile products in Asia where the rapid development of the textile industry would lead to the overproduction problems. For this objective, the forum has encouraged the member countries and economies to provide and exchange basic data on supply and demand of textiles and apparels. In the steel sector, METI has taken the lead in developing bilateral policy dialogues with the Northeast Asian economies.[2] The dialogues aimed to respond to protectionist moves in the steel industry triggered by successive antidumping petitions in the US market and to discuss likely overproduction problems in the region. These initiatives had significant implications because the solution of overproduction, one of distributive, prisoners' dilemma-type problems, needs higher leadership (Doner 1997: 202).

Thus, this study holds that the regional economic evolutions after the mid-1990s played a catalytic role in encouraging the Japanese state to show a more distinctive and influential leadership role in defining and imposing solutions to regional economic problems. In some areas, Japan engaged in behind-the-scenes mediation, leading from behind. In other areas, Japan has intensified its willingness to take the lead in creating 'rules of the game', not merely exploiting the existing system. In both cases, Japan has sought to interweave its own ideas and styles, stressing human resources-based, intellectual contributions in addition to conventional fund provisions.

Perspectives on bilateral relationship with China are relevant to Japan's strategic policies towards East Asia. The strategic policies had much to do with China's continuous economic advent. Indeed, some policies such as the utilisation of antidumping measures and positive attitudes towards FTAs originated from other policy objectives. However, negotiations over an FTA with ASEAN have been undertaken in keeping pace with those between China and ASEAN. Other initiatives such as the strength of IPRs protection and commitments to the ASEAN integration had a general objective to maintain the commercial interest of Japanese firms. However, the China factor has gradually become prominent in these initiatives. The intensive disciplines of IPRs aimed to protect Japanese firms' intellectual assets against other East Asian economies especially China. Assistance to industrial upgrading and market integration in the ASEAN countries aimed partly to maintain their economic power and influence as a counterweight to China. Thus, Japan's economic policy towards East Asia has been increasingly conditioned by the China factor.[3]

What influence, then, do Japan's strategic policies have on the overall Sino–Japan relationship? Indeed, the strength of strategic nature in Japan's external economic policy towards East Asia aimed to contain the Chinese economic power or to balance regional distribution of power against China's economic advent. But, the adoption of strategic policies was a pragmatic response, reflecting the growing recognition of China's economic potent among Japanese policy-makers. Moreover, some of the strategic policies contribute to the Chinese economy. Japan's commitments to strong disciplines of IPRs and support for the creation of the sound intellectual property system in China give benefits to the Chinese government which has implemented various measures to reduce patent violations. Japan's support for the development of industries in the ASEAN countries is also desirable for China, which has sought to tighten economic linkages with them.

Regrettably, this study cannot make a decisive argument about the overall Sino–Japan relationship largely due to the lack of sufficient analysis on China's responses to Japan's policies. However, it provides several lessons for the future relationship of the two countries. First, this study confirmed that the Sino–Japan relationship entered the new stage of strong power relations. From an historical perspective, Sino–Japan relations were basically characterised by either a 'strong (China)–weak (Japan)' or 'weak (China)–strong (Japan)' typology, but the relationship in the new millennium is characterised as a 'strong–strong' typology (Wang 2002). Given uncertainty in the current relationship, each state needs to adjust its external policy by taking into account the interest of the other. For this objective, it is important to develop multi-layered networks, making use of geographical proximity. For the time being, Japanese political leaders are required to develop close and trustworthy relationship with the newly selected Chinese leaders. The bureaucrats need to tighten linkages through various frameworks such as the ASEAN Plus Three (APT), Japan–China–Korea frameworks and bilateral talks. Several local governments in Japan have sought to develop sub-regional collaboration with China. These moves are important and desirable given the growing nationalistic emotions among the public in both countries. The development of the multi-layered networks will dampen the possibility of misunderstanding and miscalculations of each other's policy intentions, and expand the base of mutual trust.

Second, it is possible and advisable to mitigate direct friction and tension by promoting further cooperation and competition for regional leadership. Given that direct economic disputes are likely to increase in the near future and that the triangular relationships among the United States, China and Japan tend to lead to strategic conflicts, it seems useful to embed the Sino–Japan relationship into tight regional frameworks. For this objective, it is crucial to develop common interests in regional economic development through functional cooperation. Franco–German cooperation began with the establishment of the European Coal and Steel

Community. Both countries need to find such areas. The Mekong River development project provides such an opportunity because both governments have keen interests in the project. Stronger collaboration in a specific industrial sector also needs to be considered.[4]

Domestic politics as constraints on external economic policy

Japan's aspiration for an independent leadership in East Asia was partially undermined by reactive moves. Domestic political repercussions were a main reason why Japan was unable to support market liberalisation at the APEC's EVSL Initiative. The development of strategic policies has also been impeded by reactive moves in domestic politics. The initiatives to forge FTA networks with East Asian countries have been constrained by passive preferences of the Ministry of Agriculture, Forestry and Fisheries (MAFF) and its supporters in political circles.

In considering the influence of domestic politics on Japan's external polices, two variables were important: policy preferences of political and societal actors, and political institutions. An important finding of this study concerning Japan's regional economic policy is that economic bureaucrats and major societal actors have strengthened their preferences for tighter linkages with the East Asian economies. The bureaucrats at METI and MOF have taken into account the development of regional environments and redefined Japan's interest in it, pursuing policy directions to form a multi-layered relationship with the East Asian countries. The big business associations represented by *Nippon Keidanren* (Japan Business Federation) and *Keizai Doyukai* (Japan Association of Corporate Executives) supported such initiatives, and internationally oriented firms opposed moves to restrain trade with the East Asian countries. The government officials and business leaders converged their preferences towards tighter integration with East Asia, responding to changes in regional economic structure. Given the growing and inevitable economic interdependence, they sought to utilise such a trend as a catalyst to promote structural reforms of domestic industries and thereby secure the economic interest. However, their preferences were not transformed into effective policies, and reactive policies, instead of cooperative or rational policies, were sometimes adopted.

The underpinning causes of Japan's reactive policies lay in immobile and regressive political institutions. Immobile nature in political institutions that affected Japan's East Asian policies was seen in the continuous fragmented character of the state authority. Japan has a hierarchy or complex of overlapping hierarchies in the administrative structure. The vertically structured bureaucracy with few linkages between ministries has induced each ministry to pursue its own ministerial interest. The Liberal Democratic Party (LDP) has developed the division (*bukai*) system under the Policy Affairs Research Council in parallel with each ministry. The lack of either a functionally oriented administrative corps or authoritative codification of ministerial responsibilities has made it difficult to dampen bureaucratic disputes over jurisdiction (Calder 1997a: 196).

Given that foreign affairs have become dense and agendas for coordination get more crowded and complicated, decisive and firm leadership of the Prime Minister has become increasingly important. However, the Prime Minister's official residence (*kantei*) had weak capabilities with a total staff of less than 20. Most staff of the office were bureaucrats, not personal appointees, often retaining loyalties to their original ministries (Calder 1997b: 12–14; Mulgan 2000b: 195–6). In the new millennium, the Japanese political system has moved towards stronger power for the Prime Minister. In 2001, the Prime Minister's Office (*sorifu*) was reorganised into the Cabinet Office (*naikakufu*) in order to strengthen the Cabinet's functions including its capabilities to respond to emergency situations and to coordinate inter-ministerial matters. The Economic Policy Council was also established within the Cabinet Office as a measure to enhance the Prime Minister's power. However, basic institutions that have impeded the Prime Minister's leadership remained almost unchanged.

The representative of such institutions is the LDP's faction politics. Under the parliamentary cabinet system, which the existence of the cabinet is dependent on parliamentary confidence, policy preferences of the ruling parties in the Diet directly influence the government policies. Under the faction politics, the Prime Minister has been obliged to take into account demands from the major factions in order to secure his post. Indeed, the electoral reform of adopting the single-member district system in 1994 was supposed to reduce the importance of factions because the LDP candidates would not need to compete with other candidates from the party any longer. The factions within the LDP were formally dissolved at the end of 1994. However, the factional system has remained as the principal mechanism for the promotion to executive positions in the party and in cabinet (Mulgan 2000b: 189). A maverick Prime Minister Junichiro Koizumi rejected demands from the major factions in choosing the cabinet members. However, even Koizumi was often forced to accede to demands from the major party members backed up by the factions in formulating and implementing detailed policies.

Japan's diverse stances on FTAs among the Ministry of Foreign Affairs (MOFA), METI and MAFF, or the lack of the grand design for intellectual property policy stemmed from fragmented administrative operations. The Prime Minister was expected to show a determined leadership in coordinating conflicting interests among the ministries. However, the Prime Minister has often been unwilling to cut into politically sensitive issues, and left responsibility to particular ministers or ministries in handling complicated administrative issues. The decisiveness in political leadership to coordinate various interests and draw up cohesive and persistent policies was still undermined by the immobile nature in Japan's policy-making.

The reactive policies were also produced by regressive political institutions. The regressiveness in political institutions was found in the declining capabilities of the LDP as political mediators to pursue the far-reaching national objectives. This phenomenon was caused by two factors. First, discipline and cohesion within the LDP declined after the mid-1990s. It has been common under the LDP politics that *zoku* members conduct activities for protecting the interests of particular interest groups or particular government agencies. However, the party leaders in the Policy Affairs Research Council often tried to adjust government policies between competing interests (Curtis 1988: 116). Over the agricultural issues, the senior leaders sometimes played a determined role in appeasing agricultural groups and *zoku* members who opposed, and led the policy debates to desirable directions (Taniguchi 1997: 39). However, there were few cases where the senior leaders coordinated the domestic and international interests for the sake of Japan's overall national goals. This was partly because political realignments after 1993 undermined the influence of the senior politicians. When the Takeshita faction that included many senior leaders split into two in July 1993, several influential politicians including Ichiro Ogawa and Tsutomu Hata defected to the opposition. Moreover, there were no distinctive party elders who were called 'kingmakers' after the late 1990s. The elders represented by Noboru Takashita and Shin Kanemaru played a crucial role in leading the policy debates to desirable directions skilfully coordinating political conflicts at the final stage. Their influence often led to less transparent policy-making in Japan, but their presence and role surely provided stabilisation in Japanese politics. The fragmentation of the influential senior politicians and the lack of the party elders led to the loosening of hierarchies within the party, and this enabled individual politicians to act rather freely for the sake of the interest of their own supporters.

Second, both individual politicians and the party as a whole became receptive to demands from their constituencies. In the 1980s, the LDP became a 'catchall party', by expanding its electoral base into the urban and suburban districts (Curtis 1988: 198–212). Moreover, the introduction of the single-member district electoral system in 1994 forced politicians to cultivate a much broader base of support, reducing the relative importance of particular constituencies. However, the LDP seemed to move away from its prior catchall policy towards reliance on the core constituencies after the mid-1990s. The LDP, which experienced the loss of power in summer 1993, became extremely nervous to maintain power at any cost. Nonetheless, the party failed to secure a stable majority at the Diet largely because it has been unable to gain votes from the non-party supporting strata (*mutoha-so*). Accordingly, the party had to depend on its traditional constituencies represented by the agricultural groups and to be highly sensitive to their interests.

In sum, Japan has pursued a more assertive role in East Asia, gradually interweaving strategic policies towards China. These new initiatives reflected the changed preferences of economic bureaucrats and business leaders in response to the evolving industrial and economic conditions in East Asia. However, such initiatives were not transformed into effective policies in some cases. Pursuit for tight linkages with the East Asian economies was undermined when the matter was directly relevant to the interest of the LDP's core supporters. This stemmed from immobile and regressive natures in Japan's political institutions. While fragmented characteristics of the Japanese political system including the weak power of the Prime Minister have remained almost unchanged, discipline and cohesion within the LDP have become loose due to the declining influence of the party's senior politicians.

Issues for future research

This study has sought to exhibit how Japan has formulated its economic policies towards and economic relations with East Asia in the evolving regional environments. However, it did not take into account the influence of the United States on Japan's policies and commitments towards East Asia. Indeed, it referred to the role and influence of the United States as critical factors constraining Sino–Japan co-leadership for regional cooperation. However, the United States has influenced and will influence Japan's regional diplomacy more deeply in various ways. For instance, this study attributed Japan's reactive regional policies to domestic politics. It has also much to do with the US role and preferences as quite a few studies argue (Miyashita 1999; Wimonkan 2000; Maswood 2001). Accordingly, research on Japan's economic diplomacy, which combined regional perspectives such as China's advent and international politics represented by the US influence, will become important. If Japan's pursuit for deeper engagements in East Asian affairs might contradict US regional policy and deteriorate the Japan–US relationship, a real challenge for Japan's East Asian policy is how to balance US interests and its own by carefully calculating costs and benefits from the new initiatives.

The second limitation of the study is that its analysis was confined to economic policy and economic relations. Analyses on security issues have become increasingly important for considering Japan's regional leadership and Sino–Japan relationship. For instance, a critical origin of Japan's activism in regional diplomacy lay in its bitter experiences in the 1991 Gulf War (Er 2001: 121–2). Accordingly, it is important to develop studies of Japan's external policies and relations combining economic and security affairs. Given that Japan's economic resources such as official development assistance are likely to reduce in the future, how to develop a high profile in the political and security domains is a pressing challenge for Japanese policy-makers.

Notes

1 Introduction

1 In this book, 'East Asia' is referred to as the region that covers both Southeast and Northeast Asia. In indicating a particular area, I use the term 'Southeast Asia' or 'Northeast Asia'.

2 The Ministry of International Trade and Industry (MITI) (*Tsusho Sangyo-sho*) changed its organisational name into the Ministry of Economy, Trade and Industry (METI) (*Keizai Sangyo-sho*) in January 2001. In this book, I use the new term METI in order to avoid confusion. The Japanese name of the Ministry of Finance also changed from *Okura-sho* to *Zaimu-sho*, but its English name is the same.

2 Evolving policy preferences in antidumping policy

1 For the overall analysis of antidumping, see Finger (1993) and Miranda *et al.* (1998).

2 In addition to these six antidumping cases, two countervailing suits were petitioned to date.

3 Electronics Industries Association of Japan, *Nihon no denshi kogyo* (The electronics industry in Japan), 1995/96, 1997/98.

4 Administrative guidance is defined as an administrative action that, without any coercive legal effect, 'encourages regulated parties to act in a specific way in order to realize some administrative aim' (Young 1984: 923).

5 *Amakudari* (literally 'descent from heaven') is a custom whereby bureacrats descend into high positions in industrial associations or compaines. Bureacrats, through *amakudari*, exert influence on industries and companies as well as securing beneficial positions in retirement.

6 Major examples are tariff reductions and removals of quotas on various agricultural products including beef, oranges, and citrus juice over the period between 1977 and 1988, the Market Oriented Sector Specific (MOSS) negotiations in 1985–87, and the Structural Impediments Initiative (SII) in 1989–90.

7 After the Uruguay Round was concluded, the law and ordinance were amended in order to bring them into conformance with the Antidumping Agreement.

8 Article XXI, Section 1 of Council Regulation (EC) No.384/96 also provides the administrative authorities with similar discretion. In general, the Japanese antidumping regulation is close to that of the EC than to the United States and Canada in terms of details of legislation and the degree of discretion of the administrative authorities.

9 *Nihon Keizai Shimbun*, 15 February 1983.

10 *Textile Asia*, February 1983: 81.

11 *Nihon Keizai Shimbun*, 8 December 1982.
12 *Nihon Keizai Shimbun*, 17 April 1983.
13 *Nihon Keizai Shimbun*, 19 April 1983.
14 Ferrosilicon and ferrosilicon manganese are used as additive agents to improve quality in the refining process that turns pig iron into steel.
15 *Nikkei Sangyo Shimbun*, 7 March 1984.
16 *Nikkei Sangyo Shimbun*, 2 February 1984.
17 *Nikkei Sangyo Shimbun*, 24 February 1984.
18 *Asahi Shimbun*, 21 October 1988.
19 *Nihon Keizai Shimbun*, 13 September 1988.
20 Interview, FJKIA, Tokyo, March 1998.
21 *Asahi Shimbun*, 22 October 1988.
22 *Toshin*: *Kongo no seni sangyo oyobi sono sesaku no arikata* (Report on the future of the textile industry and its policy measures.), November 1988. METI publishes *Toshin* every five years. *Toshin* is deliberated and drawn up in the joint advisory committee of the Textile Committee of the Industrial Structure Council and the Textile Industry Council.
23 *Asahi Shimbun*, 2 August 1988.
24 *Nihon Keizai Shimbun*, 26 October 1991.
25 *Asahi Shimbun*, 4 February 1989.
26 *Seni Nenkan*, 1989: 56.
27 In January 1988, the US government announced the NIEs would graduate from preferential tariff treatment under the Generalised System of Preferences (GSP). In spring 1989, the government also enforced NIEs to give up special and differential treatment under the GATT (Bayard and Elliot 1994: 171).
28 *Mainichi Shimbun*, 28 November 1991.
29 *Nihon Keizai Shimbun*, 9 December 1992.
30 Interview, JFA, Tokyo, March 1998.
31 *Nikkan Kogyo Shimbun*, 2 May 1992.
32 The cases are as follows: measures on imports of thrown silk yarn complained about by the US in 1977; measures on imports of leather by the US in 1978; measures on imports of leather by Canada in 1979; restraints on imports of manufactured tobacco by the US in 1979; measures on imports of leather by the US in 1983; quantitative restrictions on imports of leather footwear by the US in 1985; restrictions on imports of certain agricultural products by the US in 1986; customs duties, taxes and labelling practices on imported wines and alcoholic beverages by the EC in 1987; trade in semiconductors by the EC in 1987; tariffs on imports of spruce, pine, fir (SPF) dimension lumber by Canada in 1988; restrictions on imports of beef and citrus products by the US in 1988; and restrictions on imports of beef by Australia in 1988. The GATT panel found that Japan's measures were inconsistent with GATT articles in the 1983 leather case, the 1986 agricultural case, the 1987 alcoholic beverage case, and the 1987 semiconductor case.
33 The English title of the report was 'Report on Unfair Trade Policies by Major Trading Partners' until 1994. It was changed into 'Report on the WTO Consistency of Trade Policies by Major Trading Partners' in 1995.
34 *Nikkan Kogyo Shimbun*, 30 January 1993.
35 *The Nikkei Weekly*, 27 December 1993.

36 Interview, JSA, Tokyo, March 1998.
37 *Senken Shimbun*, 18 May 1993.
38 *Toshin*: *Kongo no seni sangyo oyobi sono sesaku no arikata* (Report on the future of the textile industry and its policy measures.), November 1993.
39 *Nihon Keizai Shimbun*, 2 August 1993.
40 *Nikkei Bijinesu*, 24 October 1994: 14.
41 In October 1994, the US government initiated a Section 301 investigation of Japan's automobiles and auto parts largely due to dissatisfaction with market access for auto parts in Japan. The negotiations lasted until June 1995.
42 *Nihon Keizai Shimbun*, 21 April 2001.
43 *Nihon Keizai Shimbun*, 9 July 2002.
44 In November 1999, the Japanese government requested consultation with the United States regarding antidumping measures on hot-rolled steel sheet adopted in the US market. The Japanese government contended that the US Department of Commerce conducted a biased evaluation of the fact, rejecting improperly relevant data from the respondents (METI 2000b).

3 Social demand and state capability in safeguard policy

1 The term of globalisation is an elusive concept with multifaceted uses in political, economic and social dimensions (Cerny 2000: 300–1). I use this term confining the economic process, referring to the growing linkages of national economies through enhanced flows of trade, capital, and foreign direct investment by multinational firms.
2 Japanese firms strengthened their operations in China after the early 1990s. Japanese foreign direct investment into China increased from US$1.69 billion in 1986–90 to US$17.97 billion in 1991–95 then slightly declined from US$17.50 billion in 1996–2000 in contract base.
3 This argument presupposes that I do not support the globalists' contention that the integrated global economy creates the seamless world where the power and role of the states increasingly decline (Ohmae 1990; Horsman and Marshall 1994).
4 The mission was commissioned by the then Prime Minister Keizo Obuchi to conduct a broad evaluation of Japan's aid programs in East Asia. In August–September 1999, the mission, headed by Hiroshi Okuda, President of Toyota Motor Corp. and Chairman of *Nikkeiren* (Japan Federation of Employers' Associations), visited six Asian countries.
5 The new arrangement divides the transition period into three stages – the first stage for three years, the second for four years, and the third for three years – and at the beginning of each stage 16 per cent, 17 per cent, and 18 per cent of the total textile trade will be changed into the general rules.
6 The import restriction is limited for three years after implementation. In the first year, imports are limited to the same level as that of the previous year. In the second and third years of the restriction, this figure is allowed to rise 6 per cent a year.
7 *Senken Shimbun*, 25 February 1995.
8 Interview, JFTIA, Tokyo, December 2001.
9 *Seni Janaru*, 4 August 2000.

10 *Japan Times*, 21 February 2001.
11 Interview, JFKIA, Tokyo, December 2001.
12 Interview, JFKIA, Tokyo, December 2001.
13 *Seni Janaru*, 5 March 2001.
14 Interview, JFKIA, Tokyo, December 2001.
15 *Senken Shimbun*, 1 June 2001.
16 *Senken Shimbun*, 1 June 2001.
17 METI homepage. Available at http://www.meti.go.jp/kohosys/press/0001356/4/010226sfgdemandandsupply.pdf.
18 *Senken Shimbun*, 6 March 2001.
19 *Nihon Keizai Shimbun*, 10 March 2001.
20 *Nihon Keizai Shimbun*, 24 April 2001.
21 METI homepage. Available at http://www.meti.go.jp/kohosys/press/0001969/0/011011towel-sfg.pdf.
22 Interview, METI, Tokyo, December 2001.
23 *China International Trade Statistics*, 1997/98: 399; 2001: 510, 545.
24 *Nihon Nogyo Shimbun*, 22 March 2001.
25 *Nihon Nogyo Shimbun*, 8 April 2001.
26 *Nihon Nogyo Shimbun*, 25 April 2001.
27 *Japan Times*, 7 April 2001.
28 *Nihon Keizai Shimbun*, 12 April 2001.
29 MAFF homepage. Available at http://www.maff.go.jp/sogo_shokuryo/sg_kanren/sg_011024.pdf.
30 *Nihon Nogyo Shimbun*, 22 November, 30 November, 2 December 2001.
31 *Nihon Nogyo Shimbun*, 16 March, 28 March 2001.
32 *Zoku* (tribe, clan) are 'LDP Diet members who exert, formally or informally, a strong influence on specific policy areas mainly at the LDP's Policy Affairs Research Council' (Inoguchi and Iwai 1987: 20).
33 *Nihon Nogyo Shimbun*, 23 November, 25 November 2000.
34 *Asahi Shimbun*, 8 July 2001.
35 *Nihon Nogyo Shimbun*, 27 March 2001; *Nihon Keizai Shimbun*, 19 April 2001.
36 In a nationwide poll for the 126 seats of the 252 member Upper House, the LDP won 36 – down from 69 – while the Japan Socialist Party gained 46 – up from 22.
37 *Asahi Shimbun*, 6 March 2001.
38 Sub-governments are defined as 'small groups of political actors, both governmental and nongovernmental, that specialize in specific issue areas' (Ripley and Franklin 1984: 8).
39 *Nihon Keizai Shimbun*, 14 April 2001.
40 The import value of the three farm products was 23.7 billion yen in 2000, while the export value of the three industrial products was 66.6 billion yen (JMCTI 2001: 75).

4 Japan and the Asian financial crisis: the developmental initiatives

1 Supporting industries are referred to as 'an aggregate of industries that supply raw materials, parts and services needed for the productive activities

of final goods industries, manufacturing machine industries, and machine parts industries' (Mukoyama 1993: 58).

2 Japan and Thailand took the lead in establishing the Working Group on Economic Cooperation in Cambodia, Laos, and Myanmar (CLM-WG). I will explain more about the CLM-WG later.

3 The informal consultative meeting between the ASEAN Economic Ministers and the Ministers of Australia and New Zealand started in 1995, while a similar consultation with the Ministers of Trade of the European Free Trade Association began in 1996.

4 Interview, METI, Tokyo, December 1998.

5 The automobile export group, 'The Interim Report of the Meeting of Automobile Experts from ASEAN, CLM, and Japan', July 1996.

6 *Gyokai* is defined as aggregate entities that fall in the particular sector including firms, trade associations, and leading business leaders (Sone 1993: 300).

7 These were held in Singapore in October 1996, Kuala Lumpur in August 1997, Tokyo and Osaka in April 1998, Singapore in October 1998, Shanghai in November 1999, and Singapore in September 2000.

8 These sectors are food and animal feeds, textile and garments, plastic products, electrical and electronic appliance, auto and auto parts, leather products and footwear, wood products and furniture, rubber and rubber products, ceramics and glass, gems and jewellery, chemicals and pharmaceuticals, iron and steel, and petrochemicals.

9 The original *sathaban* were the Thailand Productivity Institute and the Thai-German Institute, both of which began to work in 1995. Two additional policy-oriented institutes – the Management System Certification Institute and Institute for SME Development – were established later.

10 Interview, Thai Automobile Institute, March 2001.

11 *The Nation*, 2 December 2000.

12 Interview, Thai Automobile Institute, March 2001.

13 *Bangkok Post*, 11 November 1998.

14 In December 1998, the cabinet approved the definition of SMEs that used the net fixed assets as the only classification criterion: small enterprises have maximum fixed assets of 50 million baht in production, services and wholesales and up to 30 million baht in retails; medium enterprises have maximum fixed assets of 200 million baht in production and services, 100 million baht in wholesales, and 60 million baht in retails (Sevilla and Soonthornthada 2000: 4).

15 The SIFC was set up in 1992 through the transformation of the Small Industry Finance Office of the MOI. The SCIGC was established in 1991 by taking over operations of the Small Industry Credit Guarantee Fund.

16 *The Nation*, 11 August 1999.

17 *The Nation*, 11 August 1999.

18 *The Nation*, 6 November 1998.

19 *Bangkok Post*, 25 November 1998.

20 Interview, Japan International Cooperation Agency, Bangkok office, March 2001.

5 Japan and regional industrial transformation: the strategic responses

1 For instance, *Nippon Keidanren* demanded that a certain amount of yen loans be tied to the involvement of Japanese corporations, in its October 2001 position paper entitled *A Proposal for Reform of Japan's ODA*. The Ministry of Economy, Trade and Industry (METI) has sought to expand the scope of tied loans. The special yen loan scheme of a maximum 600 billion yen, which was established in November 1998 for the infrastructure development to stimulate economic recovery in the Asian countries, was tied to Japanese firms.

2 For instance, in March 1994, Malaysian Prime Minister Mahathir Mohamad criticised that Mitsubishi Motors, a partner of its national carmaker Proton, was reluctant to transfer technologies for engines and transmissions, hinting at the possibility that Proton may look to find a more suitable partner. The Indonesian government also announced its national car project in February 1996. The government offered the approval of the project to PT Timor Putra National, which tied up with Kia Motor, a South Korean automaker. The selection of Kia Motor sprang partly from the dissatisfaction of the Indonesian government with slow technology transfer of Japanese automakers.

3 *Business Korea*, February 2002: 42.

4 As of December 2001, China's accumulated outward FDI was US$8.4 billion, while its inward FDI was US$400 billion (Maruya and Abe 2002: 19).

5 The alliance was formed between Toshiba and Hannstar, between Matsushita and Unipac, and between Sharp and Quanta.

6 *Nikkei Sangyo Shimbun*, 30 October 2000.

7 *Nikkei Sangyo Shimbun*, 30 October 2000, 15 November 2001.

8 The West–East Corridor is an area stretching from central Vietnam through central and lower Laos, northeast Thailand to Eastern Myanmar.

9 These projects include the Greater Mekong Subregion Program by the Asian Development Bank, the Forum for the Comprehensive Development of Indochina by the Japanese Ministry of Foreign Affairs, and the ASEAN Mekong Basin Development Cooperation Initiative.

10 Interview, METI, September 2002.

11 The establishment of the group was agreed at an AEM–METI meeting in September 2001.

12 Interview, METI, September 2002.

13 Under the Second Science and Technology Basic Plan (fiscal year 2001–05), the Japanese government planned to spend 24 trillion yen to promote science and technological research aiming at revitalising the country's high-tech industries such as life science, information and communications, environment, and nanotechnology and materials.

14 In March 2002, the council established an Expert Panel on Management of Intellectual Properties.

15 *JAMA Report* 88, May 2001: 3.

16 *Foresight*, April 2002: 66.

17 LDP homepage. Available at http://www.jimin.jp/jimin/discussion/01_12/131207.html.

18 *Nikkei Bijinesu*, 15 October 2001: 46–7.

19 *Shukan Toyo Keizai*, 15 December 2001: 33–5.

6 The liberal democratic party, finance ministry and regional cooperation

1 The hegemonic stability thesis, the representative of this approach, posits that an openness of the international trading system arises when a hegemonic power with a strong free trade preference dominates the world economy (Krasner 1976; Gilpin 1987; Lake 1988).

2 In this regard, there are numerous studies concerning the internationalisation of the yen, see Imamatsu (1997), Murase (2000), and Kwan (2001).

3 These sectors are environmental goods and services, energy-related products and services, fish and fish products, toys, forest products, gems and jewelry, medical equipment and instruments, chemicals, telecommunications, food, rubber, fertiliser, automotive standards, oilseeds and aircraft. The first nine belong to the priority sectors.

4 *Asahi Shimbun*, 23 September 1998; *Yomiuri Shimbun*, 24 September 1998.

5 *Nihon Keizai Shimbun*, 24 October 1998; *Asahi Shimbun*, 29 October 1998.

6 *Nihon Keizai Shimbun*, 23 October 1998; *Asahi Shimbun*, 27 October 1998.

7 *Nihon Nogyo Shimbun*, 29 October 1998.

8 *Nihon Nogyo Shimbun*, 5 November 1998; *Asahi Shimbun*, 5 November 1998.

9 *Nihon Nogyo Shimbun*, 6 November 1998; *Mainichi Shimbun*, 6 November 1998.

10 *Nihon Nogyo Shimbun*, 12 November 1998.

11 *Nihon Nogyo Shimbun*, 14 November 1998.

12 MAFF Minister Nakagawa asserted that Japan and Asia forged tight relationships through the APEC discussion, and Japan could gain understanding from the Asian countries by explaining its stance with concerted efforts and offering economic assistance (*Asahi Shimbun*, 18 November 1998).

13 *Asahi Shimbun*, 26 July 1998.

14 For instance, quite a few Japanese firms called for an early conclusion of an FTA with Mexico. This was because they were apprehensive about a further disadvantage at their operations in Mexico, which concluded FTAs with some 30 countries.

15 MAFF homepage. Available at http://www.maff.go.jp/wto/wto_fta.htm.

16 MAFF homepage. Available at http://www.maff.go.jp/sogo_shokuryo/fta_kanren/seisaku.pdf.

17 *Nihon Keizai Shimbun*, 24 October 2000.

18 *Nikkei Kinyu Shimbun*, 1 October 2001.

19 *Nihon Nogyo Shimbun*, 10 August 2001.

20 *Nihon Nogyo Shimbun*, 4 September 2001.

21 *Japan Times*, 23 November 2001.

22 LDP homepage. Available at http://www.jimin.jp/jimin/senryaku/kougi02.html.

23 LDP homepage. Available at http://www.jimin.jp/jimin/discussion/01_11/131108.html.

24 The Constitution of Japan, Article 73(3).

25 *Nikkei Bijinesu*, 31 October 1994: 35–6.

26 *Nikkei Bijinesu*, 31 October 1994: 36.

27 The result of the research is the World Bank's report, *The East Asian Miracle: Economic Growth and Public Policy*.

28 In July 2001, the office was further strengthened as the Regional Financial Cooperation Division.

29 The Asian financial crisis spread to Russia in summer 1998 and to Brazil in autumn 1998.

30 *Nikkei Kinyu Shimbun*, 12 May 2000; *Asahi Shimbun*, 24 May 2000.

31 'Strengthening the International Financial Architecture: Report from G7 Finance Ministers to the Heads of State and Government', Fukuoka, 8 July 2000. Available at http://www.mof.go.jp/english/if/if019.htm.

32 Ministry of Finance, Policy Research Institute homepage. Available at http://www.mof.go.jp/english/others/ots021.htm. Although the seminar has been organised annually since 1999 by the three research institutes – the Chinese Academy of Social Sciences, Policy Research Institute of Ministry of Finance of Japan, and Korea Institute for International Economic Policy – agreements and common understandings reflect policy preferences of the governments because the heads of the international finance bureaus of the three countries jointly attend the seminar.

33 According to the IMF, surveillance means the process of monitoring and consultation through a dialogue with its member countries on the national and international repercussions of their economic and financial policies. Available at http://www.imf.org/external/np/exr/facts/surv.htm.

34 Between 1998 and 2000, MOF dispatched 22 specialists to Indonesia, eight to Thailand, two to Malaysia and Vietnam CCTFEOT (2002: 36–7).

35 'Exchange rate regimes for emerging market economies', discussion paper jointly prepared by French and Japanese Staff for the 3rd ASEM Finance Ministers' Meeting in Kobe. Available at http://www.mof.go.jp/english/asem/aseme03e.htm.

36 The project consisted of six topics: exchange rate regimes for emerging East Asian and EU accession countries; currency regimes – the European experience and implication for East Asia; strengthening financial cooperation and surveillance; enhancing regional monitoring and integration – instruments, steps, and sequencing; the European and Asian financial systems in Perspective – the Cases of Spain and China; and China in a regional monetary framework. The details of the research are available at http://www.mof.go.jp/jouhou/kokkin/tyousa/kobe_e.htm.

37 'Executive sumamry of research papers and suggestions of the Kobe Research Project'. Available at http://www.mof.go.jp/jouhou/kokkin/frame_2.html.

38 The internationalisation of the yen is defined as 'increasing use of the yen in Japanese cross-border transactions and overseas transactions and increasing yen holdings in non-residents' asset accounts, which is to say, enhancing the yen's role in the international financial system, in ordinary and capital trade and as a reserve currency' (CFEOT 1999: 1–2).

39 The Japanese and US governments established the Yen–Dollar Committee in November 1983 and reached agreement in May 1984 concerning the liberalisation of Japan's financial and capital markets, the internationalisation of the yen, and the lowering of barriers to access for foreign financial institutions participating in Japan's financial and capital markets. The March 1985 report entitled *Internationalisation of the Yen*, proposed financial liberalisation regarding interest rates and short-term capital markets, liberalisation of the euro–yen market, and the establishment of a Tokyo offshore market.

40 Despite Japan's large share of the international economy (14.0 per cent of GDP and 6.8 per cent of world trade in 1997), the yen was used in only 5.0 per cent of world trade in 1992 and comprised 4.9 per cent of world foreign currency reserves in 1997. This made a sharp contrast with the dollar (48.0 per cent of trade and 57.1 per cent of reserves) and various European currencies (31.0 per cent of trade and 22.8 per cent of reserves) (CFEOT 1999: 11).

41 Other industrial associations also issued a study report concerning the internationalisation of the yen. The Japan Foreign Trade Council (*Nihon Boekikai*), an industrial association of trading companies, issued a report entitled *The Internationalisation of the Yen in Trade Transactions: A Survey Report on the Use of the Yen* in October 1998, while the Japanese Bankers Association (*Zenkoku Ginko Kyokai*) released a policy report entitled *For Promoting the Internationalisation of the Yen* in November 1999.

42 The concept of 'leading from behind' was suggested by Alan Rix. According to Rix, Japan seeks to create a regional order 'that accepts Japan as an economic power on its own conditions, but abjures the concept of Japanese leadership through overtly dominant behaviour' (Rix 1993: 65).

7 Japan and China in regional cooperation

1 In addition, the APT meetings of Labour Ministers, Agricultural Ministers and the Heads of Patent Office began in 2001.

2 'Preamble to the Treaty Establishing the European Coal and Steel Community'. Available at http://europa.eu.int/abc/obj/treaties/en/entoc29. htm.

3 For the hegemonic stability theory, see Krasner (1976) and Gilpin (1987).

4 For a similar argument, see Robson and Wooton (1993) and Moravcsik (1998).

5 The Singapore Declaration for the AFTA agreement includes only the dozen or so pages, while the North American Free Trade Agreement (NAFTA) comprises legal documents of more than 1000 pages (Ravenhill 1995: 859).

6 *Financial Times*, 21 March 2002.

7 *Korea Times*, 30 August 2002.

8 Following the recommendations, the first Economic Ministers meeting of Japan, China, and South Korea was held in September 2002.

9 An METI official states that the announcement of China's plan to form an FTA with ASEAN 'effectively accelerated our actions (to conclude more FTAs in Asia). To say the least, we must secure conditions under which companies based in Japan are not put at a disadvantage' (*Japan Times*, 4 May 2002).

10 Interview, METI, September 2002.

11 *Asahi Shimbun*, 9 November 2002.

12 'Press Statement by the Chairman of the seventh ASEAN Summit and the Three ASEAN + 1 Summits'. Available at http://www.aseansec.org/menu_asean +3.htm.

13 This is the main reason why the proposed FTAs between Japan and the ASEAN countries are comprehensive economic partnership agreements that include economic and technical cooperation.

14 While *Bungei Shunju* had special editions of China, 'China, a troublesome neighbour' (*Chugoku, kono yakkaina rinjin*) (October 2001), and 'Distrusting China' (*Chugoku fushin*) (August 2002), *Chuo Koron* had 'The advent of China' (*Chugoku no bokko*) (February 2002) and 'Is China a paradise for the rehabilitation of Japanese firms' (*Chugoku wa nihon kigyo saisei no rakuen ka*) (June 2002).

15 *Asahi Shimbun*, 27 September 2002.

16 *Asahi Shimbun*, 27 September 2002.

17 *Asahi Shimbun*, 27 September 2002.

8 Conclusions

1 The first meeting of the forum was held in Kyoto in 1996. METI has taken the lead in developing the forum, promoting exchanges of data concerning textile products among the member economies.

2 Japan began a bilateral steel dialogue with South Korea in April 1999, with China in April 2001, and Taiwan in November 2001.

3 The growing influence of the China factor on Japan's regional policy might require the realignment of the study of Japan's foreign policy, which has been explained mainly by domestic variables or international politics variables. In analysing Japan's relations and policy in East Asia, consideration to the China factor has become increasingly important.

4 For instance, Yoo Sang-boo, Chairman of Poland Iron and Steel, Korea's leading steel company, proposed that the steel industry would be a centre of market integration in Northeast Asia in the same manner as cooperation at the coal and steel sectors became a basis of the European integration (Yoo 2001). From this viewpoint, it is desirable to develop bilateral steel dialogues among Northeast Asian countries to a regional forum of the steel industry.

Bibliography

Acharya, A. (1997) 'Ideas, identity, and institution-building: from the "ASEAN way" to the "Asia-Pacific way"?', *Pacific Review* 10(3): 319–46.

Alatas, A. (2001) *"ASEAN Plus Three" Equals Peace Plus Prosperity*, Singapore: Institute of Southeast Asian Studies, Working Paper 2 (January).

Alexander, A. J. (1998) 'Japan's mid-life economic crisis: similarities and differences with East Asia's troubles', *Japan Economic Institute Report*, No.1A, 9 January.

Amano, K. (1999) 'Wagakuni handotai sangyo ni okeru kigyo senryaku' [Corporate strategies in the Japanese semiconductor industry], *Nihon Kaihatsu Ginko Chosa* 259: 2–72.

Amsden, A. H. (1989) *Asia's Next Giant: South Korea and Late Industrialization*, New York: Oxford University Press.

Amyx, J. (2002) 'Moving beyond bilateralism in regional financial crisis management? Japan and the Asian Monetary Fund', Paper presented at the Association for Asian Studies Annual Meeting, Washington, D.C., 6 April.

Arase, D. (1995) *Buying Power: The Political Economy of Japan's Foreign Aid*, Boulder, Co.: Lynne Rienner.

Arogyaswamy, B. (1998) *The Asian Miracle, Myth, and Mirage: The Economic Slowdown Is Here to Stay*, Westwood, Co. and London: Quorum Books.

Asami, T. (2002) 'Japan's strong leadership urged to promote regional economic cooperation in East Asia', *IIMA Newsletter* 2, 15 May.

Austin, G. and Harris, S. (2001) *Japan and Greater China: Political Economy and Military Power in the Asian Century*, London: Hurst.

Bayard, T. O. and Elliott, K. A. (1994) *Reciprocity and Retaliation in US Trade Policy*, Washington, D.C.: Institute for International Economics.

Bello, W. (1998) 'East Asia: on the eve of the great transformation?' *Review of International Political Economy* 5(3): 424–44.

Bergsten, F. (2000a) *The New Asian Challenge*, Washington, D.C.: Institute for International Economics, Working Paper 00/4.

—— (2000b) 'Towards a tripartite world', *The Economist*, 15 July: 20–2.

Bergsten, C. F. and Cline, W. R. (1983) 'Trade policy in the 1980s: an overview', in W. R. Cline (ed.) *Trade Policy in the 1980s*, Washington, D.C.: Institute for International Economics.

Bergsten, C. F. and Noland, M. (1993) *Reconcilable Differences?: United States–Japan Economic Conflict*, Washington, D.C.: Institute for International Economics.

Bernard, M. and Ravenhill, J. (1995) 'Beyond product cycles and flying geese: regionalization, hierarchy, and the industrialization of East Asia', *World Politics* 47(2): 171–209.

Bevacqua, R. (1998) 'Whither the Japanese model? the Asian economic crisis and the continuation of Cold War politics in the Pacific Rim', *Review of International Political Economy* 5(3): 410–23.

Blaker, M. (1993) 'Evaluating Japan's diplomatic performance', in G. Curtis (ed.) *Japan's Foreign Policy After the Cold War: Coping with Change*, New York: M. E. Sharpe.

Bowles, P. (2000) 'Regionalism and development after (?) the global financial crises', *New Political Economy* 5(3): 433–55.

—— (2002) 'Asia's post-crisis regionalism: bringing the state back in, keeping the (United) States out', *Review of International Political Economy* 9(2): 230–56.

Calder, K. E. (1988) 'Japanese foreign economic policy formation: explaining the reactive state', *World Politics* 40(4): 517–41.

—— (1993) *Strategic Capitalism: Private Business and Public Purpose in Japanese Industrial Finance*, Princeton, N.J.: Princeton University Press.

—— (1997a) 'Domestic constraints and Japan's emerging international role', in A. Clesse *et al.* (eds) *The Vitality of Japan: Sources of National Strength and Weakness*, Basingstoke: Macmillan.

—— (1997b) 'The institutions of Japanese foreign policy', in R. L. Grant (ed.) *The Process of Japanese Foreign Policy: Focus on Asia*, London: Royal Institute of International Affairs, Asia-Pacific Programme.

—— (1997c) 'Assault on the bankers' kingdom: politics, markets, and the liberalization of Japanese industrial finance', in M. Loriaux *et al.* (eds) *Capital Ungoverned: Liberalizing Finance in Interventionist States*, Ithaca, N.Y.: Cornell University Press.

Castley, R. (1996) *Korea's Economic Miracle: The Crucial Role of Japan*, New York: St. Martin's Press.

CCTFEOT (Council on Customs, Tariff, Foreign Exchange and Other Transactions) (2002) *Responding to the challenges of the Asian economy and financial markets: crisis prevention and realization of stable economic growth, Annex*, mimeo, Tokyo: Okurasho. Available at http://www.mof.go.jp/singikai/kanzegaita/top.htm.

Cerny, P. G. (1990) *The Changing Architecture of Politics: Structure, Agency, and the Future of the State*, London: Sage.

—— (1997) 'Paradoxes of the competition state: the dynamics of political globalization', *Government and Opposition* 32(2): 251–74.

—— (2000) 'Political globalization and the competition state', in R. Stubbs and G. R. D. Underhill (eds) *Political Economy and the Changing Global Order*, 2nd edn, Oxford: Oxford University Press.

CFEOT (Council on Foreign Exchange and Other Transactions) (1998) *Lessons from the Asian Currency Crises: risks related to short-term capital movement and the "21st Century-type" currency crisis*, mimeo, Tokyo: Okurasho. Available at http://www.mof.go.jp/english/tosin/e1a703.htm.

—— (1999) *Internationalisation of the yen for the 21st century: Japan's response to changes in global economic and financial environments*, mimeo, Tokyo: Okurasho. Available at http://www.mof.go.jp/jouhou/kokkin/frame_2.html.

Cheng, J. Y. S. (1999) 'China's ASEAN policy in the 1990s: pushing for regional multipolarity', *Contemporary Southeast Asia* 21(2): 176–204.

Curtis, G. L. (1988) *The Japanese Way of Politics*, New York: Columbia University Press.

—— (1994) 'Meeting the challenge of Japan in Asia', in G. L. Curtis (ed.) *The United States, Japan, and Asia*, New York: W. W. Norton & Company.

Dedrick, J. and Kraemer, K. L. (1998) *Asia's Computer Challenge: Threat or Opportunity for the United States and the World?*, New York: Oxford University Press.

Deng, Y. (1997) *Promoting Asia-Pacific Economic Cooperation: Perspectives from East Asia*, Basingstoke: Macmillan.

Destler, I. M. and Odell, J. S. (1987) *Anti-Protection: Changing Forces in United States Trade Politics*, Washington, D.C.: Institute for International Economics.

Deyo, F. C. (2000) 'The "new developmentalism" in post-crisis Asia: the case of Thailand's SME sector', Paper presented at the conference 'Into the 21st Century: Challenges for Hong Kong and the Asia-Pacific Region', Chinese University of Hong Kong, 13–15 April.

Deyo, F. C. and Doner, R. F. (2001) 'Dynamic flexibility and sectoral governance in the Thai auto industry: the enclave problem', in F. C. Deyo, R. F. Doner and E. Hershberg (eds) *Economic Governance and the Challenge of Flexibility in East Asia*, Lanham, MD: Rowman & Littlefield Publishers.

Dieter, H. (2001) 'East Asia's puzzling regionalism', *Far Eastern Economic Review* 164: 29.

Domon, T. (2002) '"Meido in Chaina" wo maneki iretano wa dareka' [Who invited "made-in-China"?], *Chuo Koron* (June): 156–63.

Doner, R. (1997) 'Japan in East Asia: institutions and regional leadership', in P. J. Katzenstein and T. Shiraishi (eds) *Network Power: Japan and Asia*, Ithaca, N.Y.: Cornell University Press.

Dore, R. (2000) *Stock Market Capitalism, Welfare Capitalism: Japan and Germany versus the Anglo-Saxons*, Oxford: Oxford University Press.

Dornbusch, R. and Frankel, J. A. (1987) 'Macroeconomics and protection', in R. M. Stern (ed.) *US Trade Policies in a Changing World Economy*, Cambridge, MA: MIT Press.

Drysdale, P. and Zhang, D. D. (eds) (2000) *Japan and China: Rivalry or Cooperation in East Asia?*, Canberra: NCDS Asia Pacific Press.

Er, L. F. (2001) 'Japan's diplomatic initiatives in Southeast Asia', in S. J. Maswood (ed.) *Japan and East Asian Regionalism*, London: Routledge.

Ernst, D. (2000) 'Evolutionary aspects: the Asian production networks of Japanese electronics firms', in M. Borrus, D. Ernst and S. Haggard (eds) *International Production Networks in Asia: Rivalry or Riches?*, London: Routledge.

Evans, P. B. (1995) *Embedded Autonomy: States and Industrial Transformation*, Princeton, N.J.: Princeton University Press.

Fallows, J. (1994) *Looking at the Sun: The Rise of the New East Asian Economic and Political System*, New York: Vintage Books.

Finger, J. M. (ed.) (1993) *Antidumping: How It Works and Who Gets Hurt*, Ann Arbor: University of Michigan Press.

Foot, R. (1995) 'Pacific Asia: the development of regional dialogue', in L. Fawcett and A. Hurrell (eds) *Regionalism in World Politics: Regional Organization and International Order*, Oxford: Oxford University Press.

Frieden, J. A. (1990) *Debt, Development, and Democracy: Modern Political Economy and Latin America, 1965–1985*, Princeton, N.J.: Princeton University Press.

Frieden, J. A. and Rogowski, R. (1996) 'The impact of the international economy on national policies: an analytical overview', in R. O. Keohane and H. V. Milner (eds) *Internationalization and Domestic Politics*, Cambridge: Cambridge University Press.

Friman, H. R. (1990) *Patchwork Protectionism: Textile Trade Policy in the United States, Japan, and West Germany*, Ithaca, N.Y.: Cornell University Press.

Funabashi, Y. (1995) *Asia-Pacific Fusion: Japan's Role in APEC*, Washington, D.C.: Institute for International Economics.

Furukawa, E. (2001) 'Tsui ni jitsugen shita higashi ajia kyoryoku tai' [The finally realised East Asian Cooperation Forum], *Boeki to Kanzei* 49(7): 12–18.

Garrett, G. (1998) 'Global markets and national politics: collision course or virtuous circle?', *International Organization* 52(4): 787–824.

Garrett, G. and Lange, P. (1996) 'Internationalization, institutions, and political change', in R. O. Keohane and H. V. Milner (eds) *Internationalization and Domestic Politics*, Cambridge: Cambridge University Press.

Gilpin, R. (1987) *The Political Economy of International Relations*, Princeton, N.J.: Princeton University Press.

Goldstein, J. (1988) 'Ideas, institutions, and American trade policy', *International Organization* 42(1): 179–217.

Grieco, J. M. (1997) 'Systemic sources of variation in regional institutionalization in Western Europe, East Asia, and the Americas', in E. D. Mansfield and H. V. Milner (eds) *The Political Economy of Regionalism*, New York: Columbia University Press.

—— (1999) 'Realism and regionalism: American power and German and Japanese institutional strategies during and after the Cold War', in E. B. Kapstein and M. Mastanduno (eds) *Unipolar Politics: Realism and State Strategies After the Cold War*, New York: Columbia University Press.

Haggard, S. (1997) 'Regionalism in Asia and the Americas', in E. D. Mansfield and H. V. Milner (eds) *The Political Economy of Regionalism*, New York: Columbia University Press.

Hatch, W. and Yamamura, K. (1996) *Asia in Japan's Embrace: Building a Regional Production Alliance*, Cambridge: Cambridge University Press.

Hattori, K. (2001) 'Nicchu boeki masatsu no haikei to taio' [The background of Japan–China trade friction and responses to it], *Toa* 413: 33–48.

Heginbotham, E. and Samuels, R. J. (1999) 'Mercantile realism and Japanese foreign policy', in E. B. Kapstein and M. Mastanduno (eds) *Unipolar Politics: Realism and State Strategies After the Cold War*, New York: Columbia University Press.

Hellmann, D. (1988) 'Japanese politics and foreign policy: elitist democracy within an American green house', in T. Inoguchi and D. I. Okimoto (eds) *The Political Economy of Japan, Volume 2: The Changing International Context*, Stanford, CA: Stanford University Press.

Higashi, S. (2001) 'Tai no seido kaikaku to keizai saikei' [Institutional reform and economic reconstruction in Thailand], in A. Suehiro and S. Yamakage (eds) *Ajia Seiji Keizai Ron: Ajia no Nakano Nihon wo Mezashite* [*The Theory of the Asian Political Economy: Searching for Japan in Asia*], Tokyo: NTT Shuppan.

Higgott, R. (1998) 'The Asian economic crisis: a study in the politics of resentment', *New Political Economy* 3(3): 333–56.

Horsman, M. and Marshall, A. (1994) *After the Nation-State: Citizens, Tribalism and the New World Disorder*, London: HarperCollins.

Hosokawa, H. (1999) *Daikyoso Jidai no Tsusho Senryaku* [*Commercial Policies in the Mega-Competition Era*], Tokyo: NHK Shuppan.

Hosoya, A. (2001) 'Seifu gado hatsudo wo meguru keika to kadai' [The process and problems regarding the safeguard invocation], *Nogyo to Keizai* 67(6): 23–30.

Hughes, C. (2000) 'Japanese policy and the East Asian currency crisis: abject defeat or quiet victory?', *Review of International Political Economy* 7(2): 219–53.

Huntington, S. P. (1993) 'Why international primary matters', *International Security* 17(4): 68–83.

ICSEAD (International Centre for the Study of East Asian Development) (2001) 'Recent trends and prospects for major Asian economies', *East Asian Economic Perspectives* 12.

—— (2002) 'Recent trends and prospects for major Asian economies', *East Asian Economic Perspectives* 13.

Ikenberry, J. G. (2001) 'America no keizai anzenhosho takokukan shugi no anbibaransu' [The ambivalence of US multilateralism in the economy and security], *Higashi Ajia heno Shiten* (September): 71–85.

Ikuta, T. (1996) *Dokyumento Kanryo no Shinso* [*Documentary on the Deep Structure of the Bureaucracy*], Tokyo: Daiyamondosha.

Imamatsu, E. (1997) 'Yen no kokusaika koso no tenkai' [The development of the conception of the internationalisation of the yen], in T. Kamikawa and E. Imamatsu (eds) *Yen no Seiji Keizai gaku* [*The Political Economy of the Yen*], Tokyo: Dobunkan.

Inoguchi, T. (1999) 'Chikyuteki shiya ga hitsuyo ni natta nihon no Ajia gaiko' [Japan's Asian diplomacy that needs global perspective], *Sekai Shuho*, 8 June: 6–10.

Inoguchi, T. (ed.) (2002) *Japan's Asian Policy: Revival and Response*, New York: Palgrave.

Inoguchi, T. and Iwai, T. (1987) *"Zoku Giin" no Kenkyu* [*Research on "Tribal Dietmen"*], Tokyo: Nihon Keizai Shimbunsha.

Iriye, A. (1980) 'Introduction', in A. Iriye (ed.) *The Chinese and the Japanese: Essays in Political and Cultural Interactions*, Princeton, N.J.: Princeton University Press.

Ishiguro, K. (1992) *Bodaresu Ekonomi heno Hoteki Shiza: Bodaresu Shakai heno Hoteki Keisho* [*Legal Perspective on the Borderless Economy and Legal Warning against Borderless Society*], Tokyo: Chuo Keizaisha.

Ishikawa, K. (2002) 'Chokusetsu toshi wo meguru chugoku to ASEAN no kyogo' [Competition between China and ASEAN over direct investment], in F. Kimura, T. Maruya and K. Ishikawa (eds) *Higashi Ajia Kokusai Bungyo to Chugoku* [*International Division of Labour in East Asia and China*], Tokyo: JETRO.

Itani, K. (2001) 'Kyuseicho wo togeru kankoku, taiwan no ekisho gyokai' [The Korean and Taiwanese liquid crystal industry in high growth], *Tokyo Mitsubishi Ginko Chosa Geppo* 62: 1–18.

Japan Patent Office (2002) '2001 nendo moho higai chosa hokokusho' [Survey report on counterfeit injury in 2001], Tokyo: Japan Patent Office. Available at http://www.jpo.go.jp/indexj.htm.

JBIC (Japan Back for International Cooperation) (2001) 'Higashi ajia no jizokuteki hatten heno kadai: tai/mareishia no chusho kigyo shien saku' [Issues of sustainable development in East Asia: focused on SME assistance policy in Thailand and Malaysia], *JBIC Research Paper* 8.

JETRO (2001a) *Sekai to Nihon no Boeki 2001* [*JETRO White Paper on Trade, 2001*], Tokyo: JETRO.

—— (2001b) *2001 Nen no Nicchu Boeki* [*Japan–China trade in 2001*], mimeo, Tokyo: JETRO.

JICA (1988) *The Study on Industries Development in the Kingdom of Thailand*, Tokyo: JICA.

—— (1989) *The Study on Industries Development in the Kingdom of Thailand: The Second Year Report*, Tokyo: JICA.

—— (1990) *The Study on Industries Development in the Kingdom of Thailand: The Third Year Report*, Tokyo: JICA.

JMCTI (Japan Machinery Centre for Trade and Investment) (2001) *Ajia Sangyo no Kyogo Gekika to Masatsu* [*Intensified competition and friction in the Asian industries*], Tokyo: JMCTI.

JODC (2001) 'Total number of experts dispatched'. Available at http://www.jodc.or.jp/e-dispatch/record.html.

Johnson, C. (1982) *MITI and the Japanese Miracle: The Growth of Industrial Policy, 1925–1975*, Stanford: Stanford University Press.

—— (1987) 'Political institutions and economic performance: the government business relationship in Japan, South Korea, and Taiwan', in F. C. Deyo (ed.) *The Political Economy of the New Asian Industrialism*, Ithaca, N.Y.: Cornell University Press.

—— (1995) *Japan, Who Governs?: The Rise of the Developmental State*, New York: Norton.

Kahler, M. (1995) 'Institution-building in the Pacific', in A. Mack and J. Ravenhill (eds) *Pacific Cooperation: Building Economic and Security Regimes in the Asia-Pacific Region*, Boulder Co.: Westview Press.

Katada, S. N. (2001) 'Determining factors in Japan's cooperation and noncooperation with the United States: the case of Asian financial crisis management, 1997–1999', in A. Miyashita and Y. Sato (eds) *Japanese Foreign Policy in Asia and the Pacific: Domestic Interests, American Pressure, and Regional Integration*, New York: Palgrave.

Kato, C. (2001) 'The new matrix of Japan–China ties', *Japan Quarterly* 48(4): 62–71.

Kato, K. (1998) *Tsusho Kokka no Kaihatsu Kyoryoku Seisaku* [*Development Cooperation Policy in Commercial States*], Tokyo: Bokutakusha.

Katzenstein, P. J. (1997) 'Introduction: Asian regionalism in comparative perspective', in P. J. Katzenstein and T. Shiraishi (eds) *Network Power: Japan and Asia*, Ithaca, N.Y.: Cornell University Press.

—— (2000) 'Regionalism in Asia', *New Political Economy* 5(3): 353–68.

Katzenstein, P. J. and Shiraishi, T. (eds) (1997) *Network Power: Japan and Asia*, Ithaca, N.Y.: Cornell University Press.

Katzenstein, P. J. *et al.* (2000) *Asian Regionalism*, Ithaca, N.Y.: East Asia Program, Cornell University.

Keijzer, C. (2001) 'Japan and Asian regional economic integration', *IIMA Research Report* 1.

Kishimoto, S. (2000) 'Ajia keizai saisei misshion hokoku no igi to jinzai shien' [The implication of the mission for revitalization of the Asian economy and assistance to human resources], *Fainansu* (June): 63–83.

Knight, J. (1992) *Institutions and Social Conflict*, New York: Cambridge University Press.

Kodama, K. (1989) 'Hako ni osameta takaramono arui wa nihon no tsushoho' [Japan's commercial laws as jewels in the box], *NBL* 433: 32–9.

Komiya, R., Okuno, M. and Suzumura, K. (eds) (1988) *Industrial Policy of Japan*, Tokyo: Academic Press Japan.

Koryu Kyokai (2000) *Taiwan ni Okeru OEM no Jittai* [*The Current State of OEM in Taiwan*], Tokyo: Koryu Kyokai.

Krasner, S. D. (1976) 'State power and the structure of international trade', *World Politics* 28(3): 317–47.

—— (1978) *Defending the National Interest: Raw Materials Investments and U.S. Foreign Policy*, Princeton, N.J.: Princeton University Press.

Kubota, I. (1999) '"Okurasho no ajia heno torikumi shisei" ni tsuite' [Commitments of the Ministry of Finance to Asia], *Fainansu* (May): 49–51.

Kurimoto, S. (1999) *Jiminto no Kenkyu* [*Research on the Liberal Democratic Party*], Tokyo: Kobunsha.

Kusano, A. (1983) *Nichibei Orenji Kosho* [Japan–US Negotiations on Oranges], Tokyo: Nihon Keizai Shimbunsha.

Kwan, C. (2001) *Yen Bloc: Toward Economic Integration in Asia*, Washington, D.C.: Brookings Institution Press.

Lake, D. A. (1988) *Power, Protection, and Free Trade: International Sources of U.S. Commercial Strategy, 1887–1939*, Ithaca, N.Y.: Cornell University Press.

Laothamatas, A. (1992) *Business Associations and the New Political Economy of Thailand: From Bureaucratic Polity to Liberal Corporatism*, Boulder, Co.: Westview Press.

Lawrence, R. (1996) *Regionalism, Multilateralism, and Deeper Integration*, Washington, D.C.: Brookings Institution.

Liberal Democratic Party Foreign Affairs Division (1997) *Jiyuminshuto Gaiko Seisaku no Shishin I: Nihon no Ajia Taiheiyo Senryaku, Henka heno Chosen* [*Foreign Policy of the Liberal Democratic Party Part I: Japan's Asia Pacific Strategy, the Challenges of Transformation*], Tokyo: Liberal Democratic Party.

Lincoln, E. J. (1997) 'Maybe it's the teacher's fault', *U.S. News & World Report*, 15 December: 54–5.

―――― (1999) *Troubled Times: U.S.–Japan Trade Relations in the 1990s*, Washington, D.C.: Brookings Institution Press.

Manupipatpong, W. (2002) 'The ASEAN surveillance process and the East Asian Monetary Fund', *ASEAN Economic Bulletin* 19(1): 111–22.

Maruya, T. and Abe, H. (2002) 'Chugoku no sangyo hatten to kaigai chokusetsu toshi' [Industrial development in China and foreign direct investment], in F. Kimura, T. Maruya and K. Ishikawa (eds) *Higashi Ajia Kokusai Bungyo to Chugoku* [*International Division of Labour in East Asia and China*], Tokyo: JETRO.

Maruya, T. and Ishikawa, K. (2001) 'Soron' [Introduction], in T. Maruya and K. Ishikawa (eds) *Meido in Chaina no Shogeki* [*The Impact of Made-in-China*], Tokyo: JETRO.

Mason, M. (1992) *American Multinationals and Japan: The Political Economy of Japanese Capital Control, 1899–1980*, Cambridge, MA: Council on East Asian Studies, Harvard University.

Mastanduno, M. (1999) 'A realist view: three images of the coming international order', in T. V. Paul and J. A. Hall (eds) *International Order and the Future of World Politics*, Cambridge: Cambridge University Press.

Maswood, S. J. (2001) 'Conclusion', in S. J. Maswood (ed.) *Japan and East Asian Regionalism*, London: Routledge.

Mattli, W. (1999) *The Logic of Regional Integration: Europe and Beyond*, Cambridge: Cambridge University Press.

Mendl, W. (1995) *Japan's Asia Policy: Regional Security and Global Interests*, London: Routledge.

METI (1989) *Dai 3 Kai Kaigai Toshi Tokei Soran* [*The 3rd Statistical Report on Foreign Investment*], Tokyo: Okurasho Insatsukyoku.

―――― (1992) *Keizai Kyoryoku no Genjo to Mondaiten, Soron* [*Economic Cooperation and its Problems: General Description*], Tokyo: Tsusho Sangyo Chosakai Shuppanbu.

—— (1994a) *Prospects and Challenges for the Upgrading of Industries in the ASEAN Region*, Tokyo: Tsusho Sangyo Chosakai Shuppanbu.

—— (1994b) *Dai 5 Kai Kaigai Toshi Tokei Soran* [*The 5th Statistical Report on Foreign Investment*], Tokyo: Okurasho Insatsukyoku.

—— (1998) *Dai 26 Kai Wagakuni Kigyo no Kaigai Jigyo Katsudo* [*The 26th Survey on Overseas Activities of Japanese Firms*], Tokyo: Okurasho Insatsukyoku.

—— (1999a), *1999 Nen Tsusho Hakusho* [*White Paper on International Trade 1999*], Tokyo: Okurasho Insatsukyoku.

—— (1999b) *Heisei 12 nendo tsusho sangyo seisaku no juten* [*The priorities in commercial and industrial policy in 2000*], mimeo, Tokyo: METI.

—— (2000a) *Fukosei Boeki Hakusho 2000* [*Report on the WTO Consistency of Trade Policies by Major Trading Partners 2000*], Tokyo: Okurasho Insatsukyoku.

—— (2000b) 'United States: Anti-dumping Measures on Certain Hot-rolled Steel Products from Japan, First Submission of the Government of Japan'. Available at http://www.meti.go.jp/english/information/data/cAntiSt1e.html.

—— (2001a) *2001 Nen Tsusho Hakusho* [*White Paper on International Trade 2001*], Tokyo: Okurasho Insatsukyoku.

—— (2001b) 'Ajia wo chushin to shita kokusai bungyo no genjo to kadai' [The current state and issues of an international division of labour centred on Asia]. Available at http://www.meti.go.jp/report/downloadfiles/g10920ej.pdf.

—— (2001c) 'Sangyo kozo shingikai shin seicho seisaku bukai chukan tori-matome' [Interim summary report of the New Growth Policy Committee of the Industrial Structure Council], mimeo, Tokyo: METI.

—— (2002) *Dai 30 Kai Wagakuni Kigyo no Kaigai Jigyo Katsudo* [*The 30th Survey on Overseas Activities of Japanese Firms*], Tokyo: Okurasho Insatsukyoku.

MEXT (Ministry of Education, Culture, Sports, Science and Technology) (2002) *Heisei 14 Nenban Kagaku Gijutsu Hakusho* [*White Paper on Science and Technology 2002*], Tokyo: Okurasho Insatsukyoku.

Mikamo, T. (2001) '"Chukan ninniku senso" ga motarasu imi' [Implications of garlic war between China and South Korea], *Norin Tokei Chosa* (September): 27–33.

Mikanagi, Y. (1996) *Japan's Trade Policy: Action or Reaction?*, London: Routledge.

Milner, H. V. (1988) *Resisting Protectionism: Global Industries and the Politics of International Trade*, Princeton, N.J.: Princeton University Press.

Miranda, J., Torres, R. A. and Ruiz, M. (1998) 'The international use of antidumping: 1987–1997', *Journal of World Trade* 32(5): 5–71.

Miyashita, A. (1999) 'Gaiatsu and Japan's foreign aid: rethinking the reactive–proactive debate', *International Studies Quarterly* 43(4): 695–731.

Miyashita, A. and Sato, Y. (eds) (2001) *Japanese Foreign Policy in Asia and the Pacific: Domestic Interests, American Pressure, and Regional Integration*, New York: Palgrave.

Miyazaki, C. (1998) *Futo renbai seido no gaiyo to genjo ni tsuite* [*Overview and the current state of the antidumping system*], mimeo.

Mizuno, J. (2001) 'Kankoku no kanagata seizo no gijutsu kakushin to yushutsu no zoka' [Technological innovation and export expansion in the Korean die mould industry], *Ajiken Waarudo Torendo* 69: 4–7.

Mizutani, S. (1999) 'Tai koku ni okeru sangyo kozo chosei to keizai saiken' [Industrial structuring adjustment and economic reform in Thailand], speech at the Japan/Thailand economic cooperation seminar. Available at http://www.jtecs.or.jp/S-99-4.html.

MOFA (2000) 'Asian Economic Crisis and Japan's contribution'. Available at http://www.mofa.go.jp/policy/economy/asia/crisis0010.html.

Moon, C. (1999) 'Political economy of East Asian development and Pacific economic cooperation', *Pacific Review* 12(2): 199–224.

Moon, C. and Prasad, R. (1998) 'Networks, politics and institutions', in S. Chan, C. Clark and D. Lam (eds) *Beyond the Developmental State: East Asia's Political Economies Reconsidered*, Basingstoke: Macmillan.

Moon, C. and Rhyu, S. (2000) 'The state, structural rigidity, and the end of Asian capitalism: a comparative study of Japan and South Korea', in R. Robison *et al.* (eds) *Politics and Markets in the Wake of the Asian Crisis*, London: Routledge.

Moravcsik, A. (1998) *The Choice for Europe: Social Purpose and State Power from Messina to Maastricht*, Ithaca, N.Y.: Cornell University Press.

Mukoyama, H. (1993) 'Development of supporting industries in ASEAN: a case study of Thailand', *RIM Pacific Business and Industries* 4: 58–72.

Mulgan, A. G. (2000a) *The Politics of Agriculture in Japan*, London: Routledge.

——— (2000b) 'Japan's political leadership deficit', *Australian Journal of Political Science* 35(2): 183–202.

Munakata, N. (2001) 'Nihon no chiiki keizai togo seisaku no keisei' [The formation of Japan's regional economic integration policy], in N. Munakata (ed.) *Nicchu Kankei no Tenki* [*A Turning Point of Japan–China Relations*], Tokyo: Toyo Keizai Shinposha.

Murase, T. (2000) 'The internationalisation of the yen: essential issues overlooked', *Pacific Economic Papers* 307.

Muscat, R. J. (1994) *The Fifth Tiger: A Study of Thai Development Policy*, Armonk, N.Y.: M.E. Sharpe.

Nakajima, T. (1999) 'Nihon no gaiko seisaku kettei katei ni okeru jiyu minshu to seimu chosa kai no yakuwari' [The role of the LDP's Policy Affairs Research Council in the Japanese foreign policymaking process], in Gaiko Seisaku Kettei Yoin Kenkyukai (ed.) *Nihon no Gaiko Seisaku Kettei Yoin* [*Domestic Determinants of Japanese Foreign Policy*], Tokyo: PHP Kenkyujo.

Nakakita, T. (2002) 'FTA to nihon keizai no saihensei' [FTA and the restructuring of the Japanese economy], in S. Urata and Japan Centre for Economic Research (eds) *Nihon no FTA Senryaku* [*Japan's FTA Strategy*], Tokyo: Nihon Keizai Shinbunsha.

Nester, W. R. (1991) *Japanese Industrial Targeting: The Neomercantilist Path to Economic Superpower*, New York: St. Martin's Press.

Nihon Keizai Shimbunsha (ed.) (1995) *Dokyumento Nichibei Jidosha Kyogi* [*Documentary on Japan–US Auto Negotiations*], Tokyo Nihon Keizai Shimbunsha.

NIRA (National Institute for Research Advancement) (1989) *Nichi Bei O no Keizai Masatsu wo Meguru Seiji Katei* [*Political Processes Surrounding Economic Friction among Japan, the United States and Europe*], Tokyo: NIRA.

Niwano, H. (2002) 'Wagakuni seizogyo no henyo to chugoku shinshutsu no jittai' [The transformation of the Japanese manufacturing industry and the advancement into China], *Kogin Chosa* 308: 2–57.

Nordlinger, E. (1981) *On the Autonomy of the Democratic State*, Cambridge, MA: Harvard University Press.

North, D. (1990) *Institutions, Institutional Changes, and Economic Performance*, New York: Cambridge University Press.

Ohmae, K. (1990) *The Borderless World*, New York: Collions.

Orr, R. M. (1990) *The Emergence of Japan's Foreign Aid Power*, New York: Columbia University Press.

Ota, H. (1998) 'Tai no keizai kiki to nihon' [Japan and the economic crisis in Thailand], *Bankoku Nihonjin Shoko Kaigisho Shoho* (September): 1–9.

Otsuji, Y. (2001) 'Ajia tsusho senryaku no shinka' [The deepening of commercial strategies toward Asia], in A. Suehiro and S. Yamakage (eds) *Ajia Seiji Keizai Ron: Ajia no Nakano Nihon wo Mezashite* [*The Theory of Asian Political Economy: Searching for Japan in Asia*], Tokyo: NTT Shuppan.

Otsuji, Y. and Shiraishi, T. (2002) 'Building closer ties with ASEAN', *Japan Echo* 29(2): 8–12.

Oyama, K. (1996) *Gyosei Shido no Seiji Keizai Gaku: Sangyo Seisaku no Keisei to Jisshi* [*Political Economy of Administrative Guidance: The Formation and Implementation of Industrial Policy*], Tokyo: Yuhikaku.

Pang, E. (2000) 'The financial crisis of 1997–98 and the end of the Asian developmental state', *Contemporary Southeast Asia* 22(3): 570–93.

Pekkanen, S. M. (2001) 'International law, the WTO, and the Japanese state: assessment and implications of the new legalized trade politics', *Journal of Japanese Studies* 27(1): 41–79.

Pempel, T. J. (1982) *Policy and Politics in Japan: Creative Conservatism*, Philadelphia: Temple University Press.

—— (1998) *Regime Shift: Comparative Dynamics of the Japanese Political Economy*, Ithaca, N.Y.: Cornell University Press.

—— (1999) 'Structural gaiatsu: international finance and political change in Japan', *Comparative Political Studies* 32(8): 907–32.

Rana, P. B. (2002) 'Monetary and financial cooperation in East Asia: the Chiang Mai Initiative and beyond', *Asian Development Bank*, ERD Working Paper Series 6.

Rapkin, D. P. (2001) 'The United States, Japan, and the power to block: the APEC and AMF cases', *Pacific Review* 14(3): 373–410.

Ravenhill, J. (1995) 'Economic cooperation in Southeast Asia: changing incentives', *Asian Survey* 35(9): 850–66.

—— (2002) 'A three bloc world? The new East Asian regionalism', *International Relations of the Asia-Pacific* 2(2): 167–95.

Ray, E. (1981) 'Determinants of tariff and nontariff trade restrictions in the U.S.', *Journal of Political Economy* 89(1): 105–21.

Regnier, P. (2000) *Small and Medium Enterprises in Distress: Thailand, the East Asian Crisis and Beyond*, Aldershot: Gower.

Ripley, R. B. and Franklin, G. A. (1984) *Congress, the Bureaucracy, and Public Policy*, 3rd edn, Homewood, Ill.: The Dorsey Press.

Rix, A. (1993) 'Japan and the region: leading from behind', in R. Higgott, R. Leaver and J. Ravenhill (eds) *Pacific Economic Relations in the 1990s: Cooperation or Conflict?*, St Leonards, NSW: Allen & Unwin.

Robson, P. and Wooton, I. (1993) 'The transnational enterprise and regional economic integration', *Journal of Common Market Studies* 31(1): 71–90.

Rogowski, R. (1989) *Commerce and Coalitions: How Trade Affects Domestic Political Alignments*, Princeton, N.J.: Princeton University Press.

Rosenbluth, F. M. (1989) *Financial Politics in Contemporary Japan*, Ithaca, N.Y.: Cornell University Press.

—— (1996) 'Internationalization and electoral politics in Japan', in R. O. Keohane and H. V. Milner (eds) *Internationalization and Domestic Politics*, Cambridge: Cambridge University Press.

Ruan, W. (2001) 'Chugoku no yasai nosei to yasai yushutsu' [Policies for and exports of vegetables in China], *Norin Kinyu* (June): 27–43.

Rüland, J. (2000) 'ASEAN and the Asian crisis: theoretical implications and practical consequences for Southeast Asian regionalism', *Pacific Review* 13(3): 421–51.

Ryo, S. (2000) 'Tainichi kanjo ga akka suru chugoku no chishikijin so' [China's intellectuals with growing ill feelings against Japan], *Ronza* (December): 154–65.

Saito, E. (2001) 'Kiro ni tatsu taiwan kanagata sangyo' [The Taiwanese die mould industry at the crossroads], *Ajiken Waarudo Torendo* 69: 8–11.

Sakakibara, E. (1999) 'Mister yen's message on the financial crisis', *Japan Echo* 26(5): 45–9.

—— (2000) *Nihon to Sekai ga Furueta Hi: Saiba Shihon Shugi no Seiritsu* [*The Day Japan and the World Shivered: The Birth of Cyber-Capitalism*], Tokyo: Chuo Koron Shinsha.

Sandholtz, W. and Zysman, J. (1989) '1992: recasting the European bargain', *World Politics* 42(1): 95–128.

Schoppa, L. J. (1997) *Bargaining with Japan: What American Pressure Can and Cannot Do*, New York: Columbia University Press.

—— (1999) 'The social context in coercive international bargaining', *International Organization* 53(2): 307–42.

Seki, M. (1993) *Furusetto Gata Sangyo Kozo wo Koete* [*Beyond the Full-Set Industrial Structure*], Tokyo: Chuo Koronsha.

Sevilla, R. C. and Soonthornthada, K. (2000) *SME Policy in Thailand: Vision and Challenges*, Nakhon Pathom: Institute for Population and Social Research, Mahidol University.

Shindo, M. (1992) *Gyosei Shido: Kankai to Gyokai no Aida* [*Administrative Guidance: Between Administrative Agency and Industrial Circles*], Tokyo: Iwanami Shoten.

Shiraishi, M. (1998) 'Posuto reisenki indoshina ken no chiiki kyoryoku' [Regional cooperation in Indochina after the Cold War], in K. Isobe (ed.) *Betonamu to Tai: Keizai Hatten to Chiiki Kyoryoku* [*Vietnam and Thailand: Economic Development and Regional Cooperation*], Tokyo: Daimeido.

Shiraishi, T. (1997) 'Japan and Southeast Asia', in P. J. Katzenstein and T. Shiraishi (eds) *Network Power: Japan and Asia*, Ithaca, N.Y.: Cornell University Press.

Skocpol, T. (1985) 'Bringing the state back in: strategies of analysis in current research', in P. B. Evans, D. Rueschemeyer and T. Skocpol (eds) *Bringing the State Back In*, New York: Cambridge University Press.

Sone, Y. (1993) 'Conclusion: structuring political bargains: government, *gyokai*, and markets', in G. D. Allinson and Y. Sone (eds) *Political Dynamics in Contemporary Japan*, Ithaca, N.Y.: Cornell University Press.

Stone Sweet, A. and Sandholtz, W. (1998) 'Integration, supranational governance, and the institutionalisation of the European polity', in W. Sandholtz and A. Stone Sweet (eds) *European Integration and Supranational Governance*, Oxford: Oxford University Press.

Sudo, S. (2002) *The International Relations of Japan and South East Asia: Forging a New Regionalism*, London: Routledge.

Suehiro, A. (2000) 'Tai no keizai kaikaku' [Economic reform in Thailand], *Shakai Kagaku Kenkyu* 51(4): 25–65.

—— (2001) 'Nihon no aratana ajia kanyo' [Japan's new commitments to Asia], in A. Suehiro and S. Yamakage (eds) *Ajia Seiji Keizai Ron: Ajia no Nakano Nihon wo Mezashite* [*The Theory of the Asian Political Economy: Searching for Japan in Asia*], Tokyo: NTT Shuppan.

Tadokoro, M. (2000) 'Ajia ni okeru chiiki tsuka kyoryoku no kosatsu' [Regional monetary cooperation in Asia], *Revaiasan* 26: 45–69.

Takacs, W. E. (1981) 'Pressures for protectionism: an empirical analysis', *Economic Inquiry* 19(4): 687–93.

Takahashi, M. (1998) 'Nihon no tai kohatsu kaihatsu tojokoku muke enjo no saikento' [Re-examination of Japan's aid to less developing countries], in H. Imaoka (ed.) *Enjo no Hyoka to Kokateki Jisshi* [*The Evaluation and Effective Implementation of Aid*], Tokyo: Ajia Keizai Kenkyujo.

Takayasu, K., Toyama, J. and Mori, M. (1997) 'ASEAN no sangyo kozo' [Industrial structure of ASEAN], *Kan Taiheiyo Bijinesu Joho RIM* 4(39): 12–39.

Takii, H. (2001) 'Korekara dosuru seifu gado' [How do we deal with safeguards], *Ronza* (October): 100–9.

Taniguchi, M. (1997) *Nihon no Taibei Boeki Kosho* [*Japan's Trade Negotiations with the United States*], Tokyo: Tokyo Daigaku Shuppankai.

Taylor, M. Z. (1995) 'Dominance through technology', *Foreign Affairs* 74(6): 14–20.

Taylor, R. (1996) *Greater China and Japan: Prospects for an Economic Partnership in East Asia*, London: Routledge.

Terada, T. (2001) 'ASEAN + 3 no kanosei wo saguru' [Searching for the possibility of ASEAN + 3], *Gaiko Foramu* 156: 62–7.

Terry, E. (1996) 'An East Asian paradigm?', *Atlantic Economic Journal* 23(3): 183–200.

Tilton, M. (1996) *Restrained Trade: Cartels in Japan's Basic Materials Industries*, Ithaca, N.Y.: Cornell University Press.

Trebilcock, M. J. and Howse, R. (1995) *The Regulation of International Trade*, London: Routledge.

Uchiyama, Y. (1999) 'WTO to wagakuni tsusho seisaku no tenkan' [WTO and changes in commercial policy in Japan], *Boeki to Kansei* 47(1): 32–47.

Unico International Corporation (1995) *The Study on Supporting Industries Development in the Kingdom of Thailand*, Tokyo: JICA.

Unico International Corporation (1999) *The Follow-up Study on Supporting Industries Development in the Kingdom of Thailand*, Tokyo: JICA.

Uriu, R. M. (1996) *Troubled Industries: Confronting Economic Change in Japan*, Ithaca, N.Y.: Cornell University Press.

van Wolferen, K. (1989) *The Enigma of Japanese Power: People and Politics in a Stateless Nation*, London: Macmillan.

Vogel, S. K. (2001) 'The crisis of German and Japanese capitalism: stalled on the road to the liberal market model?', *Comparative Political Studies* 34(10): 1103–33.

Wade, R. (1990) *Governing the Market: Economic Theory and the Role of Government in East Asian Industrialization*, Princeton, N.J.: Princeton University Press.

—— (1996) 'Japan, the World Bank, and the art of paradigm maintenance: the East Asian miracle in political perspective', *New Left Review* 217: 3–36.

Wakamatsu, I. (2001) 'Tai' [Thailand], in T. Maruya and K. Ishikawa (eds) *Meido in Chaina no Shogeki* [*The Impact of Made-in-China*], Tokyo: JETRO.

Wan, M. (1995) 'Spending strategies in world politics: how Japan has used its economic power in the past decade', *International Studies Quarterly* 39(1): 85–108.

———— (2001) *Japan between Asia and the West: Economic Power and Strategic Balance*, Armonk, N.Y.: M.E. Sharpe.

Wang, J. (2002) 'Adjusting to a "strong–strong relationship": China's calculus of Japan's Asia policy', in T. Inoguchi (ed.) *Japan's Asian Policy: Revival and Response*, New York: Palgrave.

Watanabe, K. (2001) 'Ranhansha suru nihon imeiji' [Japanese image with diffusing reflection], *Sekai* (March): 122–6.

Webber, D. (1999) 'Introduction', in D. Webber (ed.) *The Franco–German Relationship in the European Union*, London: Routledge.

———— (2001) 'Two funerals and a wedding? the ups and downs of regionalism in East Asia and Asia-Pacific after the Asian crisis', *Pacific Review* 14(3): 339–72.

Weiss, L. (1998) *The Myth of the Powerless State: Governing the Economy in a Global Era*, Cambridge: Polity Press.

Weiss, L. and Hobson, J. M. (1995) *States and Economic Development: A Comparative Historical Analysis*, Cambridge: Polity Press.

Wesley, M. (2001) 'APEC's mid-life crisis? the rise and fall of early voluntary sectoral liberalization', *Pacific Affairs* 74(2): 185–204.

Wimonkan, K. (2000) *Half a Hegemon: Japan's Leadership in Southeast Asia*, Ann Arbor, MI.: University Microfilms International.

Wolf, C. (1998) 'What caused Asia's crash? too much government control', *Wall Street Journal*, 4 February: A22.

World Bank (1993) *The East Asian Miracle: Economic Growth and Public Policy*, New York: Oxford University Press.

Xide, J. (2002) 'The background and trend of the partnership', in M. Soderberg (ed.) *Chinese–Japanese Relations in the Twenty-First Century: Complementarity and Conflict*, London: Routledge.

Yamada, Y. (2002) 'Higashi ajia chiiki keizai togo to chugoku' [Regional economic integration in East Asia and China], *Chugoku Keizai* 438: 16–32.

Yamakage, S. (2001) 'Nihon no tai ASEAN seisaku no henyo' [The evolution of Japan's ASEAN policy], *Kokusai Mondai* 490: 57–81.

Yamazawa, I. (1994) 'Promotion of SMEs for industrial upgrading in ASEAN: a Japanese proposal for industrial co-operation', *ASEAN Economic Bulletin* 11(1): 16–24.

Yoo, S. (2001) 'Tekkogyo wo chiiki sangyo togo no moderu kesu ni' [Proposal for making the steel industry as the model case for regional industrial integration], in Nihon Keizai Shimbunsha (ed.) *Ajia: Chiiki Togo heno Mosaku [Asia in Search for Regional Integration]*, Tokyo: Nihon Keizai Shimbunsha.

Yoshimatsu, H. (1998) 'Japan's Keidanren and political influence on market liberalization', *Asian Survey* 38(3): 328–45.

———— (1999) 'Japanese government-business collaboration and the operations of Japanese corporations in Asia: a telecommunications case', *Pacific Economic Papers* 296.

———— (2000) 'State-market relations in East Asia and institution-building in the Asia-Pacific', *East Asia: An International Quarterly* 18(1): 5–33.

———— (2002) 'Preferences, interests, and regional integration: the development of the ASEAN Industrial Cooperation Arrangement', *Review of International Political Economy* 9(1): 123–49.

Young, M. K. (1984) 'Judicial review of administrative guidance: governmentally encouraged consensus dispute resolution in Japan', *Columbia Law Review* 84(4): 923–83.

Index